The New Economics of Income Distribution

The New Economics of Income Distribution

Introducing Equilibrium Concepts into a Contested Field

Friedrich L. Sell

*Professor of Macroeconomics and Economic Policy,
Universität der Bundeswehr München, Germany*

 Edward Elgar
PUBLISHING

Cheltenham, UK • Northampton, MA, USA

Published by
Edward Elgar Publishing Limited
The Lypiatts
15 Lansdown Road
Cheltenham
Glos GL50 2JA
UK

Edward Elgar Publishing, Inc.
William Pratt House
9 Dewey Court
Northampton
Massachusetts 01060
USA

A catalogue record for this book
is available from the British Library

Library of Congress Control Number: 2015933347

This book is available electronically in the **Elgar**online
Economics subject collection
DOI 10.4337/9781783472376

MIX
Paper from
responsible sources
FSC
www.fsc.org   FSC® C013056

ISBN 978 1 78347 236 9 (cased)
ISBN 978 1 78347 237 6 (eBook)

Typeset by Servis Filmsetting Ltd, Stockport, Cheshire
Printed and bound in Great Britain by T.J. International Ltd, Padstow

Contents

Preface

When I studied economics in the late 1970s at Freiburg University (famous, among other things, for Martin Heidegger's contribution to philosophy in the 1930s and for the few years Friedrich A. Von Hayek held a chair at the economics faculty during the 1960s), the field of distribution economics was well established. Gerold Blümle, who later supervised my PhD thesis, was then a young professor specialized in this area. He gave courses about personal and functional income distribution and he was not afraid to mention Karl Marx and the project of socialism. All of this was well received by students, a considerable part of them still very close to the left-wing students' revolution led in 1968 by Rudi Dutschke. Years passed and when I left Freiburg in 1987, the economics of distribution apparently had lost some of its earlier attractiveness. The neoclassical school of rational expectations had conquered textbooks and classrooms. Income distribution, of course, was still there, but it was no longer a subject of significance. Both inequality and equality were not an issue anymore.

Things changed in the new millennium when globalization was finally considered by many experts as a worldwide phenomenon with huge effects on factor and goods' prices, output and employment. But it was only in recent years that famous economists such as Anthony Atkinson, Joseph Stiglitz and Thomas Piketty, among others, raised the subject of income and wealth distribution in the era of globalization. It was obvious to everybody that globalization had a tremendous impact on income distribution. My impression was and still is that the economics of income distribution – beyond measuring these effects – was not well prepared to address this new challenge. There was almost no understanding of the existence of equilibria in income and wealth distribution that were explicitly chosen by economic agents, unions, firms and in the end by the whole society. Globalization destroyed these earlier equilibria. But we have to understand the mechanics and the dynamics of these equilibria. Only then are we able to assess which new equilibria will most likely and hopefully evolve. This is what this book is primarily about.

This is the right place to thank a number of people who made this book possible. Laura Mann, Chloe Mitchell, Elaine Ross and Harry Fabian from Edward Elgar gave generous help and assistance. I also thank three anonymous referees chosen by the publisher, who provided useful comments from which I benefited considerably.

Dr Beate Sauer and Martina Meidenbauer (Universität der Bundeswehr München, Neubiberg) helped in designing and depicting numerous diagrams and tables and were successful in their attempt to fight the formatting pitfalls of Word. Dr Markus Grabka (Deutsches Institut für Wirtschaftsforschung, Berlin) generously put at my disposal a number of illustrative data and graphs. I also appreciated the help of my student assistants Florian Pfaff and Sebastian Nabers. Together, we collected and systematically evaluated data on income distribution; we checked the mathematical formulas and the bibliography. I also thank my university (Universität der Bundeswehr, München) and its institutions who gave me the opportunity of six months sabbatical in the winter and spring of 2014. I remember with gratitude the discussions and exchange of ideas I had with Gerold Blümle over the last 25 years. Some of the equilibrium concepts presented in this book go back to some remarkable earlier papers penned by him.

Last but not least, I thank my wife, Heidi, and my daughters, Marie Jeanne and Caroline. They were always patient with me and allowed me to spend many extra hours working on this book.

I hope that readers of this book may feel some of the enthusiasm I felt when working on this subject. If not, then it will be my fault because the cause deserves all our attention.

Abbreviations

ABCT	(New) Austrian Business Cycle Theory
CES	Center for Economic Studies
CIS	capital income share
DB	Deutsche Bundesbank
DESTATIS	Deutsches Statistisches Bundesamt
DIW	Deutsches Institut für Wirtschaftsforschung
ECB	European Central Bank
ECU	European currency unit
ED	excess (export) demand
EMU	European Monetary Union
ES	excess (export) supply
EU	European Union
EUROSTAT	European Statistical System
FDI	foreign direct investment
FOOC	first order optimality condition
GANL	Germany, Austria, Netherlands, Luxembourg
GDP	gross domestic product
GIIPS(C)	Greece, Italy, Ireland, Portugal, Spain, (Cyprus)
GLNF	Germany, Luxembourg, Netherlands, Finland
GNI	gross national income
GNP	gross national product
HOS(S)	Heckscher-Ohlin-Stolper(-Samuelson)
IFO	Leibniz-Institut für Wirtschaftsforschung an der Universität München
IMF	International Monetary Fund
ISCED	International Standard Classification of Education
IUT	inequality unemployment trade-off
LIS	labour income share
MC	marginal cost
MCH	marginal costs of hiring labour
MCR	marginal cost reduction of providing public services
MM(T)	Modigliani-Miller (theorem)
MNFB	marginal net fiscal benefit
MNFC	marginal net fiscal costs

MPC	marginal productivity of capital
MPC	Monetary Policy Committee
MPL	marginal productivity of labour
MRP	marginal revenue product
MRS	marginal rate of substitution
MVL	marginal value of labour
OECD	Organisation for Economic Co-operation and Development
PIT	personal income tax
PPF	production possibility frontier
PPP	purchasing power parity
PTC	political transformation curve
RL	Rybczynski line
ROW	rest of the world
RPT	rational partisan theory
SOEP	Soziöokonomisches Panel
SW	social welfare
TARGET2	Trans-European Automated Real-Time Gross Settlement Express Transfer System (Second Generation)
TFP	total factor productivity
TOT	terms of trade
USA	United States of America

Symbols

α	capital share in income
α_i	a constant with $i = 1, 2, \ldots, n$
α_s, β_s	weighting factors in the utility function of small share-holders
b	capital/income ratio
α_l, β_l	weighting factors in the utility function of large share-holders
γ	size of demand for fairness; a constant
δ	discount factor
$\varepsilon, \varepsilon_t$	time (in)variant stochastic shock
η	price elasticity of labour supply
θ	preference for price stability
ω	degree of fairness
$\hat{\omega}_i$	idiosyncratic fairness parameter for individual i
λ	Lagrange operator; a constant
μ_L	mean logarithm of incomes
υ	factor of production associated with voters
ℓ	factor of production associated with lobbying industries
π	actual rate of devaluation/inflation; institutional bias
π^e	expected rate of devaluation/inflation
π_M	profit of the monopsonistic firm
π_C	profit of the competitive firm
v	discount factor
ρ_t	rate of decay of voters' memories
σ (σ^e)	(expected) standard deviation
σ^2	variance
σ_L^2	variance of the logarithm of incomes
σ_{Lt}^e	expected standard deviation of the logarithm of incomes
σ^*_{Lit}	natural standard deviation of the logarithm of incomes
σ_{gw}	standard deviation of the growth rate of wages
g_w	growth rate of wages
τ	representative import tax
Ω	degree of fairness
Π	total profit income

A	a constant
A	economically active persons; physical and psychological work environment
B	a constant
C	marginal propensity to consume
C	consumption
$C[\ldots]$	consumption function
D	real rate of return from dividends
D	demand
e	autonomous consumption, effort
E	expectations operator
$E[\ldots]$	expected value of . . .
ED	export demand, excess demand
ES	export supply, excess supply
EX	export
$f(\ldots)$	function of . . .
F	foreign countries
g	percentage increase in the value of capital; per capita real growth rate
g_w	growth rate of wages
G	Gini coefficient
$\hat{G}$	perceived squewness of income distribution
$\tilde{G}$	equilibrium distribution of personal incomes
H	home countries
I	indifference curve
IQ	investment quota
K	capital intensity
K	total capital
$\overline{K}$	rate of return from investing in shares
L	labour
L^D	labour demand function
L_M	monopsonistic labour input
L_C	competitive labour input
L_s	skilled employment
L_u	unskilled employment
LF	total labour force
LIS	labour income share
M	money supply
MC	marginal cost
$MNFB$	marginal net fiscal benefit
MPL	marginal productivity of labour
MRS	marginal rate of substitution

MVL	marginal value of labour
N	stock of innovations
N	population growth rate
P	price
P	population size
PC	perceived costs
PU	perceived utility
r	real rate of return on capital
r_a	effective yield for savers
r_b	effective costs for investors
rwl	relative wage line
R	revenue of a firm
S	representative export subsidy
S	Savings, Supply
$SW[\dots]$	social welfare function
T	time period, tax rate
T	Tax income
TFP	total factor productivity growth
U_t	control variable
$U(\dots)$	utility of . . .
U^f	utility function of firms
U^u	utility function of unions
U_I	private utility
u	benefit
V_t	voting function
V_{Mt}	voting function in a monetary union
V_{iMt}	voting function of member i in a monetary union
V	profit dispersion
W	wage
$W[\dots]$	social welfare function
w	wage rate
w^a	wage rate under autarky
w^g	wage rate under globalization
w_{ar}	average wage rate
w_c	average competitive wage rate
w_m	monopsonistic wage rate
w_s	skilled wages
w_u	unskilled wages
$X[\dots], X$	output
X	traded quantity
Y	income
Y^s	total supply

Y^D	total demand
y	income
y_{mo}	modus of incomes
y_{me}	median of incomes
y_{ar}	arithmetic mean of incomes

1. Introduction

1.1 WHAT IS NEW IN THE NEW ECONOMICS OF INCOME DISTRIBUTION?

> The study of income inequality is of fundamental importance to economics. The most obvious reason is that if economics is at all concerned with understanding the development of the economy over time, we must understand not only changes in means, but also changes in distributions.
> (Gordon and Dew-Becker 2008, p. 46)

The inequality of income (and wealth) distribution is a subject neglected for a long time in the discipline of economics. The new and rising interest has to do with a number of quite different phenomena. A selection of them could be the following. One is undoubtedly the obvious exaggeration to be observed in the remuneration of managers in general and of investment bankers in particular. Another is linked to recent trends in personal income distribution of OECD countries, where significant increases of the Gini coefficient (after taxation) have been detected in the two past decades. A third quite visible aspect raised by such prominent fellows as Nobel Prize winner Joseph Stiglitz is related to the distribution of income and wealth within emerging economies, but also between this (rather heterogeneous) group of countries on the one side and representatives of the northern hemisphere on the other.

If one looks at the set of (more or less) accepted goals of economic policy, a more or less equitable income and wealth distribution is a part of them, but it has never been defined in a sound way. By contrast, 'full employment', 'acceptable rates of economic growth', 'balance of payments equilibrium' and 'price stability' seem to be in comparison easy to capture and well understood. The science of economics, surprisingly, has used with some success in the past the notion of 'equilibrium' in so many areas, as in the analysis of markets (for labour, among others) and competition, of growth processes, inflation trends and balance of payments situations (recently, for example, in conjunction with the Target imbalances within the Euro system). The main purpose of this book is to develop – on different levels and in various fields – a concept of equilibrium in the area of income distribution. This is what we label the 'new economics of income distribution'.

The last one and a half decades have been dominated by the literature on social preferences such as fairness and reciprocity (Fehr and Schmidt 1999; Bolton and Ockenfels 2000). In both concepts, which are quite similar to each other, empirical and game theory-based experiments reveal that economic agents have an aversion against 'taking it all'. This is quite helpful in explaining why a Gini coefficient in the neighbourhood of 1 is not sustainable, neither on a social nor individual level. But then the question remains, why some countries have Gini coefficients of almost 0.5 while others seem to live well with coefficients below 0.25. Furthermore, one finds that in many cases these coefficients tend to be quite stable and robust over time. Why is this? A hypothesis followed in this book suspects that the fairness and reciprocity literature has based its arguments too much on the attitude of 'inequity aversion', neglecting the somewhat opposite, but (at least) as plausible preference of 'equity aversion' (see Sell and Stratmann 2009): people don't want to take it all, but they don't want to leave too much to the others either. Every Sunday's cake division at the heart of the family meal may serve as proof. In economics, the concept of 'equilibrium' still retains much intellectual attractiveness and theoretical appeal though the Lehman Brothers case showed to all of us in 2008 how fragile presumed equilibria (in the financial markets) can be – if the financial market it is an equilibrium phenomenon at all.

What then are the new equilibrium aspects introduced by this book? Firstly, we offer some sort of a methodological innovation as we discuss income distribution on all three levels of equilibrium concepts in economics: market equilibrium, bargaining equilibrium and political economy equilibrium. In doing so, we are interested in the dynamics of these equilibria in the vein of Schumpeter: when and why are these equilibria destroyed, what happens during phases of disequilibrium and which forces may push income distribution back again into a (new) equilibrium? Second, we address the question of how main factor markets (labour, capital) are related to income distribution. We investigate not only – as traditional economics of income distribution do – global income quotas, the aggregate distribution of income between labour and capital and so on, but also the distribution of incomes within the group of labour income and the group of profit income earners. Third, we offer some new models – for instance, rooted in the field of fauna evolution science – to explain the dynamics of income distribution during business cycles and as a companion to long-term economic growth. Fourth, we identify – via the channels of trade flows, of capital and of labour mobility – the way globalization affects income distribution. Fifth, in all of these chapters, we look at income distribution as a result of the struggle within society between different social preferences such as inequity aversion, on the one hand, and (the much less popular though important) equity aversion, on the other hand. Sixth, we ask for future research to adopt a more comprehensive theory of income distribution. Seventh, we close by concluding our findings.

1.2 WHY THIS BOOK AFTER PIKETTY'S *CAPITALISM IN THE TWENTY-FIRST CENTURY*?

Thomas Piketty (2014) has written a comprehensive, eloquent and brilliant book about the historical trends and the future prospects in the distribution of income and wealth. Is there a need for additional contributions in the same field of economics? We believe so and in order to substantiate our argument we shall briefly describe the main hypothesis put forward by Piketty. The model he uses has the following components/(in)equations:

$$r > g \qquad (1.1)$$

$$\alpha = r \cdot \beta \qquad (1.2)$$

$$\beta = s/g \qquad (1.3)$$

The first, and according to Piketty, essential inequation says that the real rate of return on capital, r, is substantially higher than the overall real growth rate of the economy, g. Piketty calls it the 'fundamental force for divergence' (Piketty 2014, p.25). If this is the case, 'then it logically follows that inherited wealth grows faster than output and income . . . and the concentration of capital will attain extremely high levels' (p. 26). The second equation, following Piketty, is the 'first fundamental law of capitalism' (p. 52), which argues that the share of income from capital, α, is given by the product of the real rate of return, r, and the capital/income ratio, β. The third equation, according to Piketty, the 'second fundamental law of capitalism' (p. 166), states that the capital income ratio of each economy is given by the ratio between the savings rate, s, and the overall real growth rate, g. Notice that the third equation can be rearranged so that Solow's famous equilibrium growth rate appears:

$$g = s/\beta \qquad (1.4)$$

According to Solow, β is nothing but the capital coefficient. So if Piketty shows for the world and for single countries (pp. 196, 461) that this coefficient grows – unless large parts of the active capital stock are being destroyed, as happened during the years 1914–45 (p. 25) – he does not prove more or less that in the course of the increased capital intensity of production, the capital coefficient *must* move upwards. But Solow also shows that a growing capital intensity of production, whenever the production function is linear homogeneous, is *always* accompanied by a declining marginal productivity of capital. The latter, in turn, will reduce the real rate of return, *ceteris paribus* (Engelkamp and Sell 2013, pp. 308–12). In steady state, r and g may converge fully, a phenomenon that Phelps has given the attribute of a 'golden rule of accumulation' (Piketty 2014, p. 563).[1]

If one solves the second equation for the rate of return, r, and combines it with the first inequation and the third equation, we achieve (see also Piketty 2014, p. 652):

$$\alpha/\beta > s/\beta \text{ or } \alpha > s \tag{1.5}$$

As a, say, modified condition for the concentration of wealth, this new inequation, however, can be shown to be not so much a 'fundamental force for divergence', but the mere consequence of some appropriate definitions in the vein of Nicholas Kaldor's theory of income distribution (Kaldor 1955):

$$S/Y = s = \alpha s_\alpha + (1 - \alpha)s_{(1-\alpha)} \tag{1.6}$$

This (not more than a) definition explains the domestic savings rate as a weighted average (the weights being capital income share (CIS), the share of income from capital, α, and $(1 - \alpha)$, the labour income share (LIS), or likewise human capital) of the (distinct) savings rates of the two main income groups in society: owners of physical and owners of human capital. Rearranging this definition yields:

$$\alpha = \frac{s - s_{(1-\alpha)}}{s_\alpha - s_{(1-\alpha)}} = \frac{s}{s_\alpha - s_{(1-\alpha)}} - \frac{s_{(1-\alpha)}}{s_\alpha - s_{(1-\alpha)}} \tag{1.7}$$

Whenever

$$s_\alpha, s_{(1-\alpha)} > 0; 0 < s_\alpha, s_{(1-\alpha)} < 1 \text{ and } s_\alpha > s_{(1-\alpha)} \tag{1.8}$$

we can be quite (but not totally) sure that $\alpha > s$. Let us make two numerical examples. Assume $s_\alpha = 0.6$; $s_{(1-\alpha)} = 0.2$. Then, we achieve for $\alpha = 0.3$, $s = 11/50 < 3/10 = 15/50 < \alpha$! Also, if $s_\alpha = 0.9$; $s_{(1-\alpha)} = 0.2$, $\alpha = 0.3$ yields: $s = 21/100 < 30/100 < \alpha$! To be totally sure, however, we have to make some calculations:

$$\alpha\,(s_\alpha - s_{(1-\alpha)}) = s - s_{(1-\alpha)} \Rightarrow s = \alpha\,(s_\alpha - s_{(1-\alpha)}) + s_{(1-\alpha)} \quad (1.9)$$

Then the 'Piketty condition' $\alpha > s$ from above is satisfied if and only if:

$$\alpha > \alpha\,(s_\alpha - s_{(1-\alpha)}) + s_{(1-\alpha)} \text{ or} \quad (1.10)$$

$$\alpha > \frac{s_{(1-\alpha)}}{(1 + s_\alpha - s_{(1-\alpha)})}^2 \quad (1.11)$$

A second observation emerges from the combination of his equations two and three:

$$g/s = r/\alpha \text{ or } \alpha = \frac{s \cdot r}{g} \text{ and } (1 - \alpha) = \frac{g - s \cdot r}{g} \quad (1.12)$$

This formula can also be 'vitalized' by a simple numerical example. Suppose the overall growth rate to reach 0.02 and the measured LIS to equal 0.7 (CIS = 0.3). Then we have $s \cdot r = 0.02 - 0.02 \times 0.7 = 0.015$. Assume $s = 0.1$, then we achieve: $r = 0.06$!

From the above result, we may easily derive what is (not) in the interest of labour because it affects positively (negatively) the LIS:

$$\frac{\partial \text{LIS}}{\partial g} = \frac{\partial\left[\dfrac{g - s \cdot r}{g}\right]}{\partial g} = \frac{s \cdot r}{g^2} > 0 \quad (1.13)$$

$$\frac{\partial \text{LIS}}{\partial r} = \frac{\partial\left[\dfrac{g - s \cdot r}{g}\right]}{\partial r} = -\frac{s}{g} < 0 \quad (1.14)$$

These two results are interesting insofar as they match exactly the hypotheses of the so-called 'partisan theory' of monetary policy, which has proved to be very relevant for US policy and elections: the electorate of the Democratic Party in the USA – owners of low, medium and (less so of) high skills – favours an expansionary monetary policy, that is, low real interest rates and high economic growth (Sell 2007, pp. 116–20).

A third observation concerns Piketty's third basic equation, his 'second fundamental law of capitalism': if we realize that the growth rate of national income equals the population growth rate, n, plus the per capita real growth rate, G (see also Piketty 2014, p. 593):

$$g = (G + n); G = g - n \qquad (1.15)$$

Then, we achieve:

$$\beta = s/(G + n) \qquad (1.16)$$

The problem with the first formula and, hence, indirectly with the denominator of the second formula is that g and n are not independent from each other or, put another way, there is an endogeneity problem affecting g. As Siebert (2000a, p. 103) explains, a low population growth leads to ageing societies; the latter, in turn, tend to achieve much lower growth rates. That is, when n comes down, g is also negatively affected:

$$G = g(n) - n; \frac{\partial g(n)}{\partial n} > 0 \qquad (1.17)$$

$$\frac{\partial G}{\partial(-n)} = -\frac{\partial G}{\partial n} = -\frac{\partial g(n)}{\partial n} + 1 \qquad (1.18)$$

This repercussion from ageing societies on the growth rate g and hence on the 'second fundamental law of capitalism' was not considered by Piketty.

A fourth observation applies to the impact of ageing societies on the rate of return to capital, r: following Siebert (2000a), ageing and low population growth societies exhibit a greater abundance of capital and a greater scarcity of labour. As a consequence, real wages should increase and real rates of return should decline. The relative abundance of capital will moreover be strengthened by the increasing need of the working labour force to substitute (or at least to complement) the fading resources of the pay-as-you-go system by private pension schemes. A higher supply of savings on the capital market will, in turn, lower the real rate of return.

A fifth observation concerns the time horizon of Piketty's analysis. It is doubtful whether we can look at the phenomenon of income and wealth distribution the way Piketty does: do those long time spans he is looking at really exist any longer in a globalized world, where the distinct phases of economic development are becoming shorter and shorter (Von Bechtolsheim 2014, p. 48)? By the way, we have serious doubts whether the 'second globalization' 'has been under way since the 1970s' (Piketty 2014, p. 28). Many indicators show that this second wave of globalization did not start before the late 1980s or early 1990s.

A sixth observation is related to Piketty's severe critique against the use of specific economic or statistical tools. This applies in the economic sphere to the principle of marginal productivity and in the sphere of statistics to the Gini coefficient. Piketty's point against the principle of marginal productivity (see Piketty 2014, pp. 330–3), which is seemingly unable to explain the remuneration of the 'super-managers', is in our view flawed. If the latter is a phenomenon of globalization, the enormous increase in worldwide mergers and acquisitions coupled with growing firm sizes and 'the growing diversity of functions within the firm' (p. 334) are good examples too. In this area, we clearly have discontinuities and large shifts in the production function. To make or not to make a big deal has significant consequences for the firms' productivity and does not in principle contradict the marginal analysis of factor rewards.

Piketty also has a clear predilection for the deciles, centiles and so on as a means to measure inequality: 'the statistical measure of income inequality that one finds in the writings of economists as well as in public debate are all too often synthetic indices, such as the Gini coefficient, which mix very different things, such as inequality with respect to labour and capital, so that it is impossible to distinguish clearly among the multiple dimensions of inequality and the various mechanisms at work' (p. 243; see also pp. 266–7). The limitations of the Gini as well as the Theil index are well known and it is true that they mix measurement of inequity of capital and of labour income. However, they meet another, highly relevant target as they reflect inequality to be an ubiquitous, integral and overwhelming phenomenon of economies/societies.

A seventh observation affects Thomas Piketty's policy suggestions. In the vast majority of cases, we can fully support his views: 'the best way to increase wages and reduce wage inequalities in the long run is to invest in education and skills' (p. 313). Or: 'if a small group of employers occupies a monopsony position in a local labour market . . . imposing a minimum wage may be not only just but also efficient' (p. 312; see also Werner et al. 2013). If labour income falls short of the dynamics of capital income, why not follow the many proposals put forward in the 1970s to let the factor labour participate in the profits of the firm rather than install national (and necessarily) global taxes on capital? If labour wins a share of profits, a part of former fixed costs turns into variable costs, which can be adjusted downwards easier in the case of a recession (Von Bechtolsheim 2014, p. 48). Piketty sees two possibilities to correct the distribution of wealth: a well-defined, progressive one-time tax on private capital 'or, failing that, by inflation' (2014, p. 567). Here, it is quite difficult to follow the author because the regressive effects of medium and high inflation rates are well documented, both theoretically and empirically.

Last but not least, what is Piketty's position towards the idea of equilibrium in the distribution of incomes and wealth? 'Inequality is not necessarily bad in itself: the key question is to decide whether it is justified, whether there are reasons for it' (p. 19). The first argument is normative, the second rather positive. But the latter is not very convincing: one can enumerate many reasons for multifarious effects and causes, what is important are whether social preferences endorse either these results or the corrections of these results by economic policy. In contrast, Piketty is right when he finds that 'how this history plays out depends on how societies view inequalities' (p. 35).

Furthermore, 'inegalitarian consequences [of globalization over the course of the next two centuries] would be considerable and would probably not be tolerated indefinitely' (p. 358). This said, one gets the impression that Piketty also has some sort of equilibrium in the distribution of income and wealth in mind. The longer this equilibrium is disturbed, the greater the likelihood for a severe correction of the lasting disequilibrium by economic policy or by the people itself (revolution). On page 361 of Piketty's book, we do find the headline 'Is there an equilibrium distribution?', but his answer (pp. 361–4) is more of a short journey through history than a clear affirmation or rejection. Later on, he finds, 'If the difference $r - g$ surpasses a certain threshold, there is no equilibrium distribution: inequality of wealth will increase without limit . . .' (p. 366). This statement, however, does play with the idea of a mathematical extreme value of income distribution rather than accept the idea of a social consensus on distribution. In his thoughtful discussion of 'Pareto's law' (pp. 366–8), he seems to doubt much more the stability of personal income distribution than the existence of equilibria (p. 368).

Make no mistake, Piketty is quite critical when he blames American TV series 'offering a hymn to a just inequality' (p. 419). But equilibrium in wealth and income distribution is not necessarily a question of justice or of religio-moral judgements. It can be just the outcome of a social consensus achieved by bargaining and/or electoral processes (see the next chapter). And equilibrium is, in the end, a question of taxes: 'all the rich countries, without exception, went in the twentieth century from an equilibrium in which less than a tenth of their national income was consumed by taxes to a new equilibrium in which the figure rose to between a third and a half' (p. 476).

1.3   A STARTING POINT FOR THIS BOOK

The main hypothesis that shall take the reader through this monograph is the idea of equilibrium in income distribution. This idea of equilibrium in income distribution is not new at all: Blümle (1992), following already famous Vilfredo Pareto (1895), held the view that social distribution of incomes was situated in a stable over time equilibrium. He based his statement on the observation that the dispersion of incomes did not fluctuate, either internationally or inter-temporally. Ramser (1987), in turn, detected stationarity in his empirical research in the secondary (that is, net of government intervention with taxes and transfers) distribution of incomes, but not so in the primary (that is, out of the market process) distribution of incomes. The time span covered by his research was 1927–87 and the countries investigated were mostly developed.

The possible existence of equilibrium in income distribution has quite interesting implications: on the one hand, it would mean that the preservation of a specific degree of income inequality is not accidental, but intentional: the existing skewness of income distribution could be interpreted as a display of overall social preferences (Blümle 1992, p. 224). In a democracy, such an outcome can only endure if it is backed by corresponding majorities in the parliament. On the other hand, this result would in principle contradict the assumption made by Anthony Downs (1968), according to which democracies tend to achieve in the long run an equitable distribution of incomes, provided this process is not interrupted by external problems/shocks of the society in question. Also, equilibrium in income distribution would raise doubt as to whether some degree of inequality in income distribution has to be taken always as something that reduces welfare (Blümle 1992, p. 212). Distributional justice continues to be an economic goal for economic policy, but not in the strict sense of a perfect equitable income distribution. Now, also in the long run, some degree of inequality is accepted, if not warranted (see Blümle 1992, p. 225).

Let us become a little more specific: if one looks at the distribution of incomes, no matter what definition of income is supposed, no matter which economy is regarded and no matter what time period is under consideration, it is surprising to see that distribution of incomes is skewed to the right and left-steep. This has important consequences for the parameters of the density function. The maximum of this function – which is called modus (y_{mo}) and is the most frequent event – will usually be located to the left of the median (y_{me}) and the latter, in turn, is located to the left of the arithmetic mean (y_{ar}). The characteristics of this sort of density function are depicted in Figure 1.1.

In order to verify and, at the same time, support this view, we look at some time-stable figures for Germany. In 1969 (the year in which the first coalition of the social democrats with the liberals was established), 64.8 per cent of total households received a (net) income lower than the arithmetic mean (y_{ar}). At the same time, the modus of incomes (y_{mo}) stood at around 65 per cent and the median (y_{me}) at, by and large, 85 per cent of the average of incomes. This result is extremely stable over time and it strongly points to the stability of income distribution (Blümle 2005, pp. 2ff.).

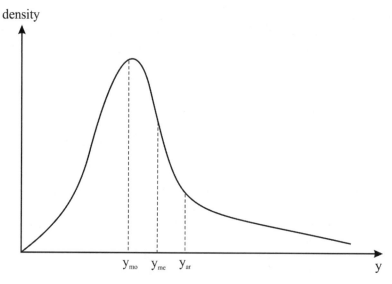

density

y_{mo} y_{me} y_{ar}

y

Source: Blümle (2005).

Figure 1.1   The time-invariant distribution pattern of personal incomes

What is the explanation for these findings? When economic agents perceive their general circumstances of life, it is very likely that the most frequent event – in our case the modus of incomes, (y_{mo}) – will be taken as typical and representative. In other words, the average of incomes (y_{ar}) will not achieve the same degree of relevance as the modus. The consequence of this is far-reaching: according to Blümle (2005), a majority of economic agents will receive an income above the modus. Based on this observation, agents will have the impression of being well posed. Therefore, their attitude towards a redistribution of incomes should be quite critical. When the same agents were asked about their degree of satisfaction with their economic situation during the polls conducted both in 1990–95 and 1996–2000, 66 per cent of those polled answered that they were content. This figure corresponds almost exactly to the percentage of income receivers who earn an income above the modus. One may suppose that this outcome is a major reason for the political stability of income distribution in Germany (at least until the beginning of the new millennium) and it was a strong argument against tendencies to level the inequality of incomes, particularly as the income distribution pattern found for the overall economy also applied to the different groups of income recipients (Blümle 2005, pp. 2ff.).

Looking at the individual level, we find a synonymous effect: the modus of incomes of one's own peer group is decisive for our judgements, not the modus of total incomes in society. Closely watched, however, this difference is not as relevant. Why? The distribution of income in the respective subgroups of incomes follows the same pattern as the density function in Figure 1.1. Even for the lowest income groups, we can say that their income is not too far away from the overall modus, given the left-steep and skewed to the right distribution of incomes. As a consequence, feelings of unfairness among the members of such low income groups are (at least were, see above) not widespread. Whenever the modus is lower than the median and the arithmetic mean, one can expect a majority of the population to be satisfied, by and large, with their own status, given their group of reference (see Blümle 2005, p. 5).

There is an additional effect that tends to establish a sort of status theory of income distribution: when low income receivers compare their own income with the modus, they can be more or less satisfied the lower the modus is, *ceteris paribus*. In this case, the likelihood increases to be neighbouring the modus income. In a sense, individuals are prepared to reduce their pretensions regarding their own income and thereby be 'happy' with a status of a rather low income. Status is perceived here as one's own relative income (in the sense of Duesenberry 1967), in this case relative to the modus income. Gains in status can be achieved the higher the relative income grows with respect to the reference income, the modus. At the same time, such a status theory of income distribution argues implicitly with 'bounded rationality': individuals do confuse the arithmetic mean with the modus of incomes.

A major advantage of Blümle's approach is in its simplicity, plausibility and vividness. The limitations of his theory, though, are obvious. The equilibrium may not be unambiguous. According to Blümle (2005), the equilibrium in income distribution is reached when an overwhelming majority of individuals is pleased with its own household income. The share of satisfied agents did in fact correlate almost perfectly in the past with the share of income receivers that gained an income above the modus of incomes. As a consequence, one may say that this equilibrium is as stable as the modus of the underlying distribution of incomes. Over time, however, an increasing share of individuals whose income exceeds the modus will increase satisfaction in society and will make redistribution policies of the government less likely. But what if the opposite occurs? By how much must the degree of satisfaction decrease to make redistribution not only likely but inevitable? In a sense, Blümle's concept of equilibrium is still quite provisional: the model is not yet 'closed' appropriately. We shall show in the following section as well as in Chapters 3 and 4 how this deficiency can be healed.

Even if these theoretical weaknesses were not there, it is a fact that the concentration of incomes (measured by the net Gini coefficient) has increased in Germany, but also in many other developed countries since the beginning of the new millennium (Sell and Stratmann 2013). We shall give evidence for this statement in later chapters. As Table 1.1 reveals, German society has changed its evaluation of the distribution of personal incomes since 1995 dramatically: while in 2000, the last (!) year of the old millennium, the approval rate was 35 per cent and the rate of rejection stood at 47 per cent, the same sample of interviewed persons accepted the concentration of incomes in 2010 with a rate of only 21 per cent, while 58 per cent denied the fairness of income distribution.

Contrary to Thomas Piketty, we believe that it is primarily the process of globalization that has destroyed earlier equilibria in income distribution. Globalization has created a new dilemma: on the one side, it has contributed to make income distribution more unequal. This applies not only to inter-income comparisons, that is, to labour and capital shares in GDP, but also to intra-income comparisons, that is, to the shares of skilled and unskilled labour, to the distribution of profits and so on. On the other hand, globalization has weakened the traditional welfare state and its scope and ability to correct the income distribution out of the market according to the goals of the electorate/median voter. This is due to tax competition and to new institutional settings like the EU/Eurozone, where the member states and their governments give away a part of their autonomy and sovereignty. Also, unemployment plays an important role: rigid real wages were and are the wrong answer to afford the challenges of the integration of large, emerging economies like China and India into the world economy. This integration has not only changed the relative scarcity of capital vis-à-vis labour on a world scale but has put under severe pressure wages for the low and medium qualified labour force in the North of the world economy.

It is not very likely that Western societies can live for a long time with huge disequilibria in the distribution of incomes and wealth. It is in the self-interest of each society to search for a new equilibrium and not necessarily to restore the old equilibrium. What are the policy options? Thomas Piketty has made several proposals (see above), figuring prominently the international coordinated taxation of wealth. We believe this could be erroneous. International coordination of tax policy is a must if the erosion of the tax base is to be stopped. But is the introduction of a new tax for the owners of wealth the right measure? If capital is the big winner of globalization and (more or less) unqualified labour is the loser, there are other alternatives, which, by the way, do follow much more the suggestions of modern psychology: you will achieve a better result if you do not punish for 'bad action' but instead reward for 'good action'. Incentives for 'good action' should consist in helping the (more or less) unqualified labour force to

*Table 1.1   How Germans evaluate fairness of personal income distribution
            between 1995 and 2010*

Year	Distribution is considered as fair (%)	Distribution is considered as not fair (%)
1995	39	43
1998	23	60
1999	30	57
2000	35	47
2001	31	47
2002	29	56
2004	21	63
2005	27	52
2006	28	56
2007	15	56
2010	21	58

Source: Sell and Stratmann (2012).

better participate in the gains of capital: either by working on the accumulation of their human capital, or by enabling the workforce to share part of the firm's profits or, finally, by creating more attractive offers for the labour force to realize savings in the financial sector of the economy. Notice that these three options cannot be taken as substitutes but as close complements.

1.4   A FLAVOUR OF THE NEW CONCEPT

F.A. Von Hayek (1977) put forward the type of reasoning in the late 1970s that will pass through this book: according to him, the traditional viewpoint of the unions and many associated experts which asserts that income in an economy can be distributed once it has been generated is definitely wrong. It is rather the expected distribution of the pie that will determine its actual size![3] Assume we proxy the expected distribution of income by its standard deviation σ^e and model its impact on total supply Y^s in the following, simple manner:

$$Y^S = Y^S(\overset{+/-}{\sigma^e}) \tag{1.19}$$

The first derivative of Y^S with respective to σ^e is ambiguous: the more equal the distribution of incomes, the less efficient the allocation and productivity of labour, given the existing differences in skills and talents. Once

σ^e surpasses a critical level, a further increase in the expected inequality of income will depress income: a too high concentration of expected incomes will hamper competition and will give rise to envy, jealousy and so on, which necessarily dampens productivity.

To close the model, we go beyond Von Hayek, and specify (this simplification will be abolished later on in this book), in the vein of Nicholas Kaldor, demand to be negatively correlated with the standard deviation of incomes: the more (un)equal the distribution, the (lower) higher total demand.

$$Y^D = Y^D(\overline{\sigma}) \qquad (1.20)$$

Finally, we assume rational expectations vis-à-vis the distribution of incomes:

$$\sigma_t^e = \sigma_t + \varepsilon_t \text{ with } E[\varepsilon_t] = 0 \qquad (1.21)$$

As a result, we may be confronted with more than one possible equilibrium, as depicted in Figure 1.2. On the y axis we have total (linear falling) demand and total (backward bending) supply, on the x axis we

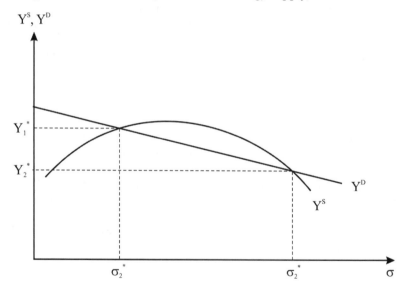

Source: Author.

Figure 1.2   Determining simultaneously income level and income concentration

find the standard deviation of incomes, σ. We disregard the difference between expected and realized values of total supply. At the first intersection point between total demand and total supply, we find a high income/intermediate concentration equilibrium. At the second intersection point between total demand and total supply, we achieve an intermediate income/high concentration equilibrium. Shifts in the supply and/or the demand schedules will necessarily lead to new intersection points or likewise equilibria.

A major insight of this enhanced Von Hayek approach is that income and income distribution are both endogenous variables and that only their simultaneous equilibrium can provide us with an almost accurate description of economic reality.

1.5 SKETCHING THE NEW FACTS OF INCOME DISTRIBUTION IN THE WORLD

It is fair to say that reports on income distribution from the IMF, the OECD and major national research institutes of the developed world have raised enormous interest in present times. In the following, we present our own statistical basis. It will focus on the world in total, on the one hand, and on Germany, in particular, on the other hand. Germany is a special and interesting case for many reasons. It is one of the very few countries that managed to leave the world economic crisis of 2009 even stronger than it was before. It is one, if not *the*, reference for the Continental European welfare state. Germany, as one of the world's leading exporters, is exposed to the forces of globalization to a larger extent than the majority of OECD countries. An equitable income distribution, furthermore, has always belonged to the set of macroeconomic goals of economic policy in Germany. Last, but not least, it is the country best known by the author over a career of almost 35 years as an economist.

Looking at the concentration of incomes over the world is an almost unresolvable issue. Even so, there are attempts to assess such a concentration (Berthold and Brunner 2010). Our own procedure is closely linked to the way data of income distribution are collected and presented by the World Bank (2013, 2014). In the first place, we follow the World Bank's classification of low income (LI), lower medium income (LMI), higher medium income (HMI) and high income (HI) countries. Because of the severe missing observations problem (see also Berthold and Brunner 2010, p. 5) and our special interest in the impact of globalization (see above and subsequent chapters), we secondly start our analysis only in 1990. Thirdly, we have computed, for each year of observation, unweighted average Gini coefficients for each income group. Why unweighted? In our context, it is not meaningful to give a special weight to small or large economies, either measured by population or GDP figures. On the contrary, we want so see whether the (rising, falling or stable) development of the Gini coefficient is a ubiquitous phenomenon for all kinds of economies, provided, however, they belong to the same World Bank classification. The Gini coefficient, as is well known, measures the concentration of personal incomes, stemming from both labour and/or capital. As we saw above, when commenting on Thomas Piketty's extensive monograph, it somewhat mixes up the concentration of capital income and labour income. Even so, the Gini coefficient is a useful tool of analysis. Figure 1.3 reveals an interesting result: there is an obvious tendency for convergence of the country group-specific (net, after taxation and transfers) Gini coefficients since 1990. While high income (HI) countries seem to converge from below, low income (LI) and middle income countries (LMI, HMI) tend to converge from above. The latter result is in harmony with the predictions of the Kuznets-curve (see Chapter 6), the former points at the possibility that the Kuznets-curve may not end as an inverted U, but may have a 'third' knot.

Note that the main message of Figure 1.3 is highly interesting: globalization and possibly other forces linked to the revolution in communication and information technologies have contributed to an almost worldwide convergence in the distribution of personal incomes.

More precisely, one can say that developing (developed) countries have become more equal (unequal). What does this imply? In the first place, it somehow confirms the popular (but often not really substantiated) view that globalization works as a dynamic equalizer. So far, theory and empirical research has shown this effect only to be significant for goods' prices, for factor prices, adopted technologies and so on. Secondly, it is obvious that countries that leave their earlier position in income distribution tend to destroy old equilibria, but this process may be productive, as in Schumpeter's creative destruction concept. As a consequence, it is thirdly all the more important to understand the determinants for an equilibrium in income distribution.

Looking at the special case of Germany, it is worthwhile to plot both the Gini coefficient out of the market and the net Gini coefficient (Figure 1.4). It seems as if redistribution policy (see also Chapter 4, which presents some econometric evidence) was able to stabilize, by and large, the ups and downs of the market-induced variations in income distribution during the 1990s. Since the beginning of the new millennium, however, concentration of incomes after redistribution policies of the government shows a clear upward trend that fiscal policy was unable to correct according to the preferences of the electorate. The other possibility – a change of preferences

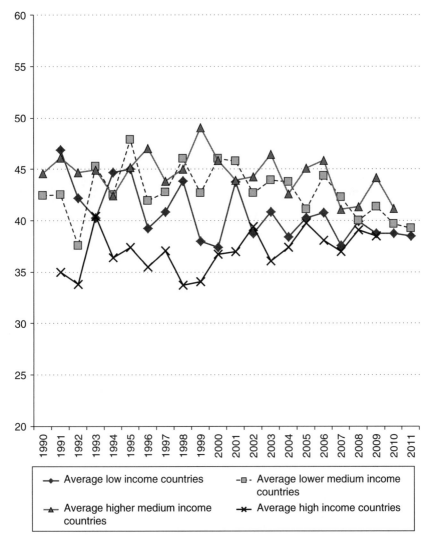

Source: World Bank, US Census Bureau and author's calculations.

Figure 1.3 *The development of Gini coefficients for different income groups according to the World Bank classification (1990–2011)*

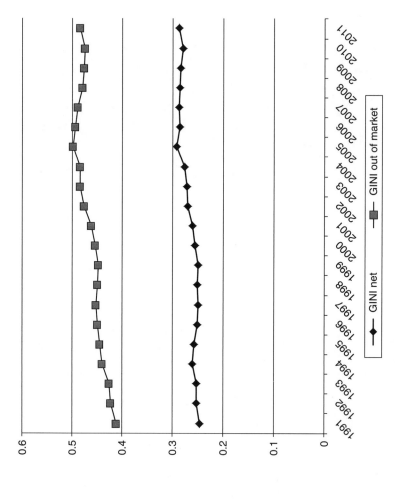

Source: Courtesy of Markus Grabka (DIW, SOEP) and author's calculations.

Figure 1.4 *The development of market-determined and government-corrected Gini coefficients in Germany (1991–2011)*

18

towards more inequality – is rather unlikely. Various polls conducted by different institutions show, on the contrary, that the German electorate shifted its preferences in the respective period towards more equality.

Does this finding match circumstances in other OECD countries? Why don't we have a look across the Atlantic Ocean? In an earlier, very often cited study on the USA, Gordon and Dew-Becker (2008, pp. 6–10) diagnose, when analysing the 90th, 50th and 10th percentiles, 'a distinct increase of the 90–10 ratio between 1980 and 1988, followed by a plateau between 20 and 25 per cent above its 1979 level' (p. 7). Looking closely, one discerns even a slight upward trend from the end of the 1990s onwards. The same applies to the 50/10 and 90/50 ratios. A recent publication of Standard & Poor's Capital IQ (2014) confirms this suspicion and finds that 'the US Gini coefficient, after taxes, has increased by more than 20% from 1979 – to 0.434 in 2010' (p. 2). Furthermore, 'all sources of income were less evenly distributed in 2007 than in 1979' (p. 3).

The evaluation of the US government's policies is similar to our own given above with regard to Germany's: 'government policies on taxation and government transfers, such as Social Security and Medicare, have done little to reduce income inequality – and may have contributed to a further widening of the gap' (Standard & Poor's Capital IQ 2014, p. 4). Standard & Poor's finds that 'the current level of inequality in the U.S. is dampening GDP growth' (p. 1). In a way, this fits nicely with our view that a number of developed countries have in the meantime moved quite a bit away from early equilibria in the distribution of incomes and wealth.

Another debated and sometimes even disputed field in the empirical analysis of income concentration is the area of macroeconomic income shares (profit share versus wage share). Ellis and Smith (2007) have made a thorough analysis of the presumed upward (downward) trend in the profit (wage) share, covering major industrialized countries, including the USA and Germany.

In Figure 1.5, we have two highly correlated curves: one plots the development of the uncorrected wage share/quota (W/Y), the other the course of the corrected wage share/quota $(W/Y)^c$. 'Correction' means in this context to take account of the changing ratio between the economically active persons (A) and the total labour force (LF) during time:

$$\left(\frac{W}{Y}\right)^c_t = \frac{W_t \dfrac{LF_0}{LF_1}}{Y_t \dfrac{A_0}{A_t}} = \left(\frac{W}{Y}\right)_t \frac{\dfrac{LF_0}{A_0}}{\dfrac{LF_t}{A_t}} \qquad (1.22)$$

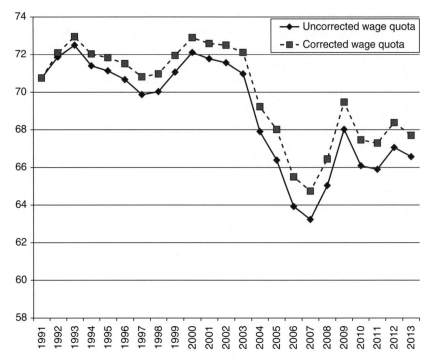

Source: German Federal Bureau of Statistics and author's calculations.

*Figure 1.5   The development of the uncorrected and corrected wage share
in Germany (1991–2013)*

It is obvious that in the recent past the wage share has had two tendencies.
There continue to be observed up- and downswings related to the business
cycle (see Chapter 5 for a more detailed analysis). At the same time, there
seems to be a downward trend in the underlying time series.

1.6   AN OVERVIEW OF FORTHCOMING CHAPTERS

The main body of the book consists of Chapters 2 to 8; this first chapter
serves as an introduction and Chapter 9 gives some final remarks including a view on redistribution policies, the scope of future research as well
as a summary of findings. In this section we present not quite an overview of the forthcoming chapters but a selection of topics that will be
dealt with.

Chapter 2

In economics, there exist a number of different concepts of equilibrium. This is not a disadvantage for our own approach, quite the contrary: in microeconomic theory and in the theory of optimal allocation, equilibrium is associated with a vector of (goods, factors of production) prices that clears the respective markets and maximizes utilities/revenues. In public choice theory/political economy of business cycles, equilibrium stands likewise for the maximization of voting functions, given some 'economic laws' that have to be respected, such as, for example, the Phillips curve. In modern welfare economics, we minimize social loss functions, given again some sort of economic constraints that have to be taken into account. In both of the latter cases, expectations and expectation changes play significant roles. In this monograph, we will present, according to the diversity shown above, various equilibrium concepts for income distribution, both for the distribution of personal incomes as well as the distribution of real income between labour and capital (income quotas). Given the above distinctions, one can investigate at least the existence of either 'market', 'social' or 'political economy' equilibria in the distribution of incomes. If the 'market solution' goes along with (positive or negative) external effects, it is indispensable to consider also an internalization strategy, which is the social planners' view (which is not being confounded with the 'social equilibrium' from above).

Chapter 3

The policy of introducing a minimum wage pursues manifold goals; one is without doubt to change, that is, to 'improve' income distribution in favour of labour and to the detriment of capital. Whether this can happen or not and under what conditions can be analysed in simple market diagrams both for the extreme case of full competition and the other extreme of a monopsony. Why then is this not (or very seldom) done? The minimum wage is a good case for showing how income distribution would look in equilibrium and what changes are introduced once the market itself is turned into disequilibrium, or a new but different equilibrium. The resulting income distribution after the implementation of a minimum wage hinges to a considerable extent on the assumed production function and the involved elasticities of substitution. This analysis, in turn, is less graphical and more formal.

Chapter 4

The integration and globalization of financial markets has increased both the volume and the mobility of capital flows. Abundant capital in the North shows decreasing returns and tends to flow into the comparatively capital scarce South of the world economy where the real rate of interest and the marginal productivity of capital is higher. These flows change the capital intensity of production both in the South and in the North of the world economy and, hence, go along with important changes in the income distribution between labour and capital. If there was an 'old equilibrium' in the distribution of incomes, this has been necessarily destroyed. The question arises as to how economic policy faces these facts: with more/less regulation and/or protectionism? Is there room for compensation policies, and if so, in which areas?

Chapter 5

Status and consumption theory of income distribution, which goes back to contributions of Duesenberry (1967) and Johnson (1951, 1952a), is nearly forgotten, but it remains so important for the matter. The authors leave the traditional 'two persons/two classes' framework of Nicholas Kaldor behind and decide in favour of a setting with three income groups, where the 'middle class' figures prominently. This is highly relevant to the background of the recent discussion about a shrinking middle class accompanied by significant real income losses facing globalization. Furthermore, this school, so to say, incorporates two visible patterns of behaviour in consumption. One is the 'keep ahead of the Smiths' attitude, which has a lot to do with the social preference of 'equity aversion' mentioned above. The other has been labelled 'keep up with the Joneses' and represents quite well the opposite social preference of 'inequity aversion'. As has been shown recently by Sell and Stratmann (2013), the Duesenberry-Johnson framework helps to understand why during the business cycle a 'keep up with the Joneses' behaviour tends to strengthen the upswing of the economy while a 'keep ahead of the Smiths' attitude helps to stabilize the course of the cycle.

Chapter 6

In the context of a Schumpeterian economic growth theory, the twin notions to 'keep ahead'/'keep up' are innovation and imitation (see Blümle 1989b). The relationship to the income distribution issue is straightforward: innovators, especially in their role of temporary monopolists, tend to create a high inequality in the distribution of profits; the latter, in turn, attracts imitators into the market/sector. Their investment behaviour has a threefold effect: it organizes the diffusion of new knowledge throughout the economy, it perpetuates the initial growth stimulus produced by innovators and it also has a levelling effect on the distribution of profits. The next growth cycle begins when new innovators come up again with technological progress located in the production process, in the organization of the enterprise or in the design of products.

Chapter 7

A further stylized fact of the globalization phenomenon is factor mobility in general and migration in particular. There are at least two types of emigrants: one group stands for a more or less skilled part of the domestic labour force that expects to achieve higher market wages in the country of destination. By leaving the country, it reduces the domestic amount of human capital and tends to lower the average productivity of labour. A second group of emigrants has quite different expectations: its main aim is to leave poverty behind and to achieve the benefits of social programmes offered by the welfare state in the country of destination. When leaving their country of origin, they won't affect the stock of existing human capital and their decision to emigrate will by tendency increase the average productivity of labour. In the immigration country, these two totally different groups of the labour force will produce contradictory effects on (at least the relative) abundance of human capital and the level and dispersion of wages.

Chapter 8

Globalization has increased trade flows between the North and the South of the world economy. This fact applies to the exchange of goods and services ('horizontal globalization') as well as to the trade with fragments ('vertical globalization'). At the same time, large emerging economies such as China and India integrated into the world economy with their huge reserves of low and medium qualified labour force and, in comparison, rather small stock of physical capital. This process of integration via trade and factors of production has significant impacts on the world's (both absolute and relative) endowment with capital and labour. Hence, income distribution between these two factors of production is affected, both in the North and in the South of the world economy.

NOTES

1. Piketty found a U-shaped curve for β between 1870 and the present (2014, p. 461). This is no surprise given the vast destruction of physical capital between 1914 and 1945, which is also suitable to the Solow model!
2. Notice that if one finds the Kaldorian split into labour income and capital or likewise profit income too strict, the reader is referred to Luigi Pasinetti who considers in addition labour income of capitalists and capital income of workers. This differentiation, however, does not alter the essence of our results (see Külp 1974, pp. 33–7).
3. Von Hayek (1977, pp. 27, 29, 33–5).

2. Various concepts of equilibrium in economics

2.1 INTRODUCTION

The discipline of economics distinguishes between at least three different concepts of equilibrium: the market equilibrium, some sort of contractual equilibrium and the political economy equilibrium. This corresponds to the conviction that in a decentralized economy the plans of the involved agents can be coordinated either by the market process – that is, by adjustable prices and the flexible response of demand and supply – or by the contract seeking forces driven by bargaining agents or, last but not least, by the voting power of the electorate.[1]

It is the aim and scope of this chapter to demonstrate that in all of the three mentioned cases it is the distributional contest between the involved parties that motivates the interests, goals and actions of the participating agents. Market, contractual and political economy outcomes are not 'accidentally' responsible for income distribution effects as a sort or by-product of the respective coordination schemes. This view has been shared for a long time by many defenders of the capitalist market order/system. Their argument was simple: it is fair to expect unequal results of the market process given that so many differently enabled agents come into play on the demand side and on the supply side. And, if a more or less unequal distribution of incomes is a sort of 'natural' companion of market equilibrium incomes, there is no special need to discuss the unequal distribution of theses incomes, let alone the normative aspects of whether we can accept or not accept as a society a far too uneven distribution of incomes (or wealth for the matter).

We believe that the opposite is true: market, contractual and political economy outcomes are rather a by-product of the distributional contest, which is in the background of all economic actions. This is, as we show in more detail below, by no means an argument that contradicts the efficiency gains associated with the capitalist market order/system. On the contrary, decentralized, liberal and democratic societies are best suited to channelize and to absorb the distributional contest in a highly productive and hence efficient way.

2.2   THE DISTRIBUTIONAL CONTEST CHANNELLED THROUGH MARKETS

2.2.1   Supply Side Effects

Consider for a moment a quite simple market diagram (Figure 2.1): assume for simplicity reasons that the item of concern is a durable consumption good and that x stands for the quantity traded, p for the price. D represents the (falling) demand schedule, S the upward sloped supply curve. At the intersection of both curves, we achieve the equilibrium price p*. At prices below p*, demand exceeds supply.

Competition between (potential) buyers leads to price increases. Conversely, at prices above p*, supply exceeds demand. Competition between (potential) sellers leads to price decreases.

The market equilibrium explained so far may, however, not be sustainable. As is well known, there is at least indirect competition between different branches of an economy. This linkage is due to the fact that entrepreneurs observe differences in the profitability of markets. This point has been explained by Israel M. Kirzner in his 'classic' of 1973, *Competition and Entrepreneurship*. If, for example, the profit rate that is associated with the price p* lies significantly above the average profit rate of the economy

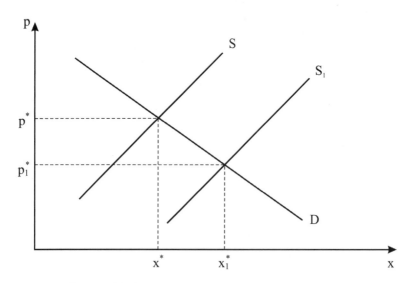

Source: Engelkamp and Sell (2013, p. 28).

Figure 2.1   Equilibrium on the simple goods market

(achievable on comparable markets for durable goods), further potential suppliers will be attracted to enter the new market and to leave their actual field of activity. Hereby, the supply will be enhanced – the supply curve shifts from its old position S to its new position S_1 – with the consequence that the amount of traded goods on this market will increase (x_1^*) and the price will fall (p_1^*). As the level of profits in principle follows the development of prices, the profit rate will go down and will tend to adjust to the level achieved in other branches. The opposite will occur in the latter, a fact that explains a strong reduction in the inequality of profit rates economy-wide. Notice that the observed market mechanism runs from greater disparity in the earnings of firms to a greater cohesion (convergence) of profit rates via the mobility of entrepreneurs between different branches/markets. Of course, such a process hinges upon the condition of free market entry and exit in all of the relevant markets. This condition prevents the economy from having markets with excessive high profit rates for a longer time.

Obviously, the observed changes in volumes (from x^* to x_1^*) and prices (from p^* to p_1^*) are a 'by-product' of the distributional contest among the entrepreneurs in the economy. The equilibrium in the distribution of profits explains the (new) market equilibrium and not the other way around!

Notice that so far we have neglected any sort of (positive or negative) external effects. If, for example, negative external effects on the production side occur, any internalization strategy (such as the Pigou tax) necessarily would cause a leftward shift in the supply curve and a higher market price, *ceteris paribus*. The higher price, however, would be interpreted correctly by other entrepreneurs not to be the consequence of a higher profitability in the respective market. For the rest of the book we shall in general, if not stated explicitly, disregard external effects and also the activity of a social planner.

An objection to the above arguments could read as follows: what has been shown for the supply side of the economy has no relevance for the demand side. Put in different words: firms and markets follow the needs and wishes of consumers and distributional aspects will have no impact/ relevance on/for the demand of consumers on (at least) single markets. But this argument is erroneous too. As we shall put forward in the following, well-known patterns of individual consumption behaviour, such as the bandwagon and the snob effects, emerge from (at least felt) disequilibria in the distribution of incomes. These effects have significant impacts on traded volumes and charged prices in markets for consumption goods and tend to restore the equilibrium in the distribution of incomes.

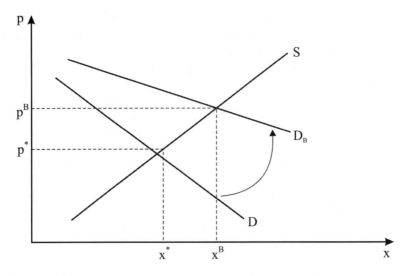

Source: Author.

Figure 2.2   Market equilibrium in the presence of bandwagon effects

2.2.2   Demand Side Effects

Assume we start in a situation where income distribution is in equilibrium. Now consider the case of a redistribution of incomes from profit earners to wage earners, no matter for what reason (market or policy induced). This will boost consumption demand of workers. One of the most popular mechanisms that can be observed now is the 'bandwagon effect': this positive network externality (Blanchard and Illing 2003, pp. 192–4) makes individual consumers demand more, the higher their estimate of total demand of the other consumers is. This attitude is typical for medium and lower income groups, hence for the majority of the workforce. As a consequence, the total demand schedule itself becomes more elastic, *ceteris paribus*. The demand curve D turns counterclockwise into its new position D_B. As depicted in Figure 2.2, the volume traded (x^* changes into x^B) and the price charged (p^* changes into to p^B) in the new equilibrium are both higher than before. Profits rise, real wages fall, so income distribution tends to move again towards the old equilibrium.

What happens in the opposite case, that is, when we consider a redistribution of incomes from wage earners to profit earners? We expect that the consumption pattern of profit earners is relatively more important now. Most likely, the 'snob effect' will become (more) relevant (than before): this negative

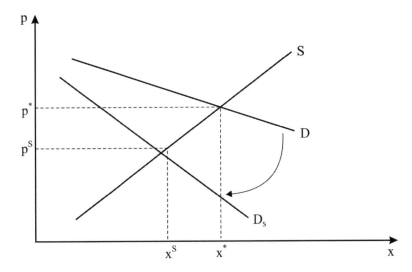

Source: Author.

Figure 2.3   Market equilibrium in the presence of snob effects

network externality (Blanchard and Illing 2003, pp. 194–7) makes individual consumers less willing to buy a certain good, the more this good is demanded by the other consumers. This attitude is typical for high and highest income groups. As a consequence, the total demand schedule itself becomes more inelastic, *ceteris paribus*. As depicted in Figure 2.3, the demand curve D turns clockwise into its new position D_S. The volume traded (x^* changes into x^S) and the price charged (p^* changes into to p^S) are both lower in the new equilibrium than in the old equilibrium. Profits fall, real wages rise, so income distribution tends to move again towards the old equilibrium.

2.3   THE DISTRIBUTIONAL CONTEST CHANNELLED THROUGH BARGAINING PROCESSES: EFFICIENT CONTRACTS

In the following, we replicate briefly a well-known result from welfare economics: what are the conditions for efficient contracts between two individuals in a barter economy? We assume that there are only two goods given in fixed quantities: $(\bar{x}_1)$ and $(\bar{x}_2)$ that are distributed totally and exclusively between household 1 and household 2. The overall quantity of each good is given by:

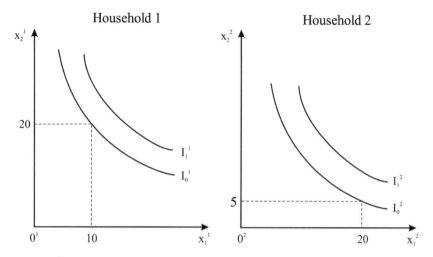

Source: Engelkamp and Sell (2013, p. 434).

Figure 2.4   Map of indifference curves in the two households case

$$\bar{x}_1 = x_1^1 + x_1^2 \tag{2.1}$$

$$\bar{x}_2 = x_2^1 + x_2^2 \tag{2.2}$$

We assume the existence of well-behaved utility functions for each of the two individuals. So there is an indifference curve map for each of the two agents. O^1 (O^2) is the origin for the indifference curve map of individual 1 (2). As depicted in Figure 2.4, we have 30 units of good 1 and 25 units of good 2 distributed initially in such a way so that household 1 (household 2) possesses 10 (20) units of good 1 and 20 (5) units of good 2. This presumably is not an equilibrium in the allocation of goods among individuals 1 and 2!

Each of the two individuals has an interest to reach higher utility levels with the help of an exchange of goods. Both are looking for beneficial trades (Nicholson 1992, p. 222). The contest for a better relative position is conducted here as a struggle (via mutual trade) to reach higher utility levels than each one had in the initial situation. The search for an exchange/ trade equilibrium and of a concomitant vector of equilibrium prices is an outcome of a bargaining process. The latter, in turn, reflects the distributional contest between the involved economic agents.

Any efficient contract found represents an equilibrium distribution of goods between the individuals. A graphical analysis of this bargaining

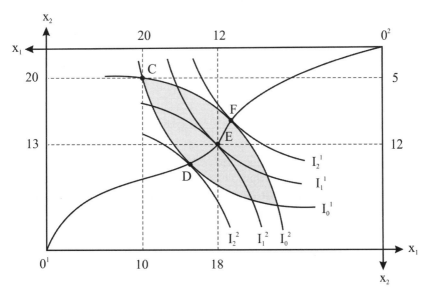

Source: Engelkamp and Sell (2013, p. 434).

Figure 2.5 *Efficient contracts as a result of bargaining between two households*

process is given in the box diagram – also called Edgeworth box diagram – shown in Figure 2.5.

Let C represent the initial distribution of goods between the households already known from Figure 2.4. This point lies on the point of intersection of indifference curves I_0^1 and I_0^2. They represent the initial utility levels reached by agents 1 and 2 respectively. Obviously, this allocation is 'inefficient' in 'that these goods can be reallocated in a better way' (Nicholson 1992, p. 222). The oval-shape shaded area or lens defines and contains the field of possible contracts that fulfil the Pareto criterion. Possible equilibrium contracts are points D (F), where household 2 (1) improves his utility with regard to C, without an associated loss of utility for household 1 (2). This could be explained by a higher (hence unequal) bargaining power of household 2 vis-à-vis household 1. A much more likely result is symbolized by point E: here, the two households sign a contract for the exchange/trade of goods, which renders both of them in a better utility performance than in C: the solution E is mutually beneficial (Nicholson 1992, p. 223).

In the framework of game theory we have what is called a 'win-win situation'. A common feature of all of the efficient contracts F, E, D is that we have tangential solutions. 'The set of all efficient allocations in an

Edgeworth box diagram is called the *contract curve*' (p. 225). In other words, it holds for all equilibria along the contract curve that the marginal rate of substitution (MRS) between good 2 and good 1 are identical for both individuals. In this case, we have a unique implicit price ratio (p_1/p_2) for the goods involved in the exchange/trade contract. In E, for example, we have:

$$MRS^1_{x_1,x_2} = -\frac{p_1}{p_2} = MRS^2_{x_1,x_2} \qquad (2.3)$$

Notice that the implicit price ratio (p_1/p_2) in the trade/exchange equilibrium is *not* an outcome of a market process – to which demand and supply factors would have to contribute – but the result of bargaining between two individuals/economic agents.

2.4   THE DISTRIBUTIONAL CONTEST CHANNELLED THROUGH ELECTIONS: THE RATIONAL PARTISAN POLITICAL BUSINESS CYCLE

Both the traditional (Hibbs 1977) and the modern, likewise rational partisan theory (Alesina 1987) maintain that left-wing or at least liberal administrations (and their supporting parties) tend to favour a lax monetary policy that helps to boost employment and output while more conservative governments (and their supporting parties) prefer a rather restrictive monetary policy stance, strictly oriented towards the goal of price stability. This model – though criticized when tested empirically by some authors (see Heckelman 2006) – has been developed further (see Sieg 1997) and continues to be a robust part of modern political economy approaches.

The number of fields and countries where modern rational partisan theory (RPT) has been applied meanwhile is considerable. Berlemann and Markwardt (2006) found that 'in line with most previous studies, our empirical analysis supports the hypothesis of partisan differences in the inflation rate under left-wing and right-wing governments, as they should occur according to variable rational partisan theory' (p. 876). 'Variable', by the way, means that RPT is applied to countries with variable electoral terms (p. 877). The sample included countries such as Australia, France, Germany, Sweden, UK and USA (pp. 884–5).

Bhattacharjee and Holly (2010) have analysed the voting behaviour of the Bank of England's Monetary Policy Committee (MPC) and found that RPT can explain voting behaviour under forecast uncertainty about the output gap. Even when preference heterogeneity is absent, MPC members may have differing views of the world, such as different judgements on the importance of the supply side, the relevance of asset markets or the transmission channel of monetary policy (Bhattacharjee and Holly 2010, p. 4). According to the authors, RPT is able to explain those differences that result in varying views on the magnitude of the output gap. The holders of these views could be classified as 'hawks' or 'doves' (p. 12).

Clark and Arel-Bundock (2012) have conducted a somewhat similar investigation on the Federal Reserve's policy over half a century in the USA. In contrast to Bhattacharjee and Holly (2010), their results seem to contradict the RPT:

> We find that the Fed raises interest rates as elections approach when Democrats control the White House, but lowers interest rates as elections approach under Republican administrations. Furthermore, when Democrats control the White House, the Fed increases interest rates in response to increased inflationary expectations, especially as elections approach, but is insensitive to the gap between actual and potential output. The pattern is reversed under Republicans: the Fed lowers interest rates in response to declining growth – especially as elections approach – but is insensitive to inflationary expectations. (Bhattacharjee and Holly 2010, p. 5)

Well understood, these findings do not contradict RPT at all, but just deliver another mutant version. Obviously, central bankers of the Fed seem to have conservative, 'Republican' preferences. This can be explained, for example, with 'Thomas Becket effects' (Sell 2007) among independent central banks. This effect postulates that once central bankers are appointed to their new job, they tend to cut earlier ties to politics/administration and concentrate merely on their task to guarantee long-term price stability. In order to guarantee such long-term price stability, central bankers have to make sure that the conservative/Republican party gains or retains power and that the progressive/Democratic party loses elections. For this, it can be even viable to boost growth/employment in the short run to the detriment of price stability, given that the US median voter is more interested in employment than in price stability!

The RPT has been tested also for the case of developing economies (see Köksal and Caliskan 2012): in the case of Turkey, the authors found that 'the stock market returns temporarily decrease (increase) at the beginning of a right-wing (left-wing) government, providing supporting evidence for RPT' (p. 185). The reasoning for this conclusion has to do with agents' perceptions of the economy. When a right-wing government takes over, growth and employment perspectives are less optimistic than when a left-wing government comes into power.

Authors like Bullock et al. (2013) have extended the RPT model with the purpose of better understanding the outcome of survey responses: 'surveys give citizens an opportunity to cheer for their partisan team' (pp. 4–5). Therefore, one may suspect that 'large differences between Democrats and Republicans in stated attitudes about factual matters' (p. 3) do not reflect 'sincere differences in beliefs about the truth' (p. 4). It could rather be that 'deep down . . . individuals understand the true merits of different teams and players' (p. 5), but is their intention to produce a specific partisan effect via the expressive answers given by them in survey responses. 'Differences in survey responses arise because surveys offer partisans low-cost opportunities to express their partisan affinities' (p. 29).

The original modern RPT uses a specific type of classification. The underlying reason for that has a lot to do with the associated clientele of the different governments and their supporting parties: the electorate of 'left-wing administrations' tends to hold their wealth primarily in the form of human capital. Owners of human capital hence profit from an expansionary monetary policy via a reduction of the unemployment rate. However, such a policy will usually bring about a higher inflation rate, which taxes the owners of financial capital.

Opposite to this, the electorate of conservative, 'right-wing governments' basically holds its wealth in the form of financial capital. As a consequence, the conservative government has a high interest to protect the real value of this financial capital by a rather restrictive monetary policy. A high degree of price stability can be achieved, however, in many instances only at the cost of a higher unemployment rate. This is what we have learned recently from the still relevant Phillips curve (Sell and Reinisch 2013). A higher and persistent unemployment rate, in turn, taxes the owners of human capital given the experience that the depreciation of human capital increases with the extent and duration of unemployment.

The connection to our main issue of income distribution is clear: 'left-wing governments' ('right-wing-governments') have a strong incentive to change the income distribution in favour of their favourite electorate: the lower medium and the lower income groups (the upper medium and the higher income groups).

The rationale of the partisan business cycle theory can be modelled easily when drawing on the Barro-Gordon (1983) framework. In the following, we minimize a typical macroeconomic loss function subject to an expectations augmented Phillips curve (see Berlemann and Markwardt 2006; Shelton 2007, 2012). Let L_t be the actual welfare loss for the economy of concern, u_t the actual inflation rate, $\bar{u}$ the politically desired unemployment rate, θ the parameter that symbolizes the intensity of preferences for the inflation goal, π_t the actual inflation rate, $\bar{\pi}$ the politically desired inflation rate and π_t^e actual inflationary expectations:

$$L_t = (u_t - \widehat{u})^2 + \theta(\pi_t - \widehat{\pi})^2; \theta > 0 \tag{2.4}$$

$$u_t = -(\pi_t - \pi_t^e) + \varepsilon_t; \varepsilon_t = \text{stochastic demand shock} \tag{2.5}$$

The resulting equilibrium levels (variables denoted by an asterisk) of inflation, inflation expectations and unemployment rate are:

$$\pi_t^* = \widehat{\pi} - \frac{1}{\theta}\widehat{u} + \frac{1}{1 + \theta}\varepsilon_t \tag{2.6}$$

$$\pi_t^{e*} = \widehat{\pi} - \frac{1}{\theta}\widehat{u} \tag{2.7}$$

$$u^* = \frac{\theta}{1 + \theta}\varepsilon_t \tag{2.8}$$

The crucial assumption now is that 'liberal governments tend to have lower θ and or lower $\widehat{u}$ and higher $\widehat{\pi}$ than conservative governments' (Shelton 2007, p. 9). Let us explore this aspect in more detail. Firstly, we take a total differential of the above loss function. This helps us, in the second step, to determine the marginal rate of substitution between the inflation and the unemployment rate along an iso-loss function:

$$dL_t = 2(u_t - \widehat{u})du + 2\theta(\pi_t - \widehat{\pi})d\pi \overset{!}{=} 0 \tag{2.9}$$

$$\frac{d\pi}{du} = -\frac{1}{\theta}\frac{(u_t - \widehat{u})}{(\pi_t - \widehat{\pi})} < 0 \text{ for } u_t > \widehat{u} \text{ and } \pi_t > \widehat{\pi} \tag{2.10}$$

In the case of a liberal (conservative) government, hence, the iso-loss curves (I_i) will be comparatively steep (flat). Consider the different curvatures in Figure 2.6.

In the left (right) diagram, we have the case of a conservative (liberal) government. The logic in the map of iso-loss curves implies that the higher the distance to the respective origin of the diagram, the higher the perceived loss in the macro economy. Comparing, for example, I_3 in the left and I_3 in the right part of Figure 2.6 reveals that a conservative (liberal) government can afford a higher unemployment (inflation) rate as long as the latter is associated with a low inflation (unemployment) rate (see also De Grauwe 1992, pp. 46–8).[2]

Let us now consider two different governments, one liberal, one conservative. Both are shown in Figure 2.7.

Point A in the left diagram stands for a stable, rational partisan business

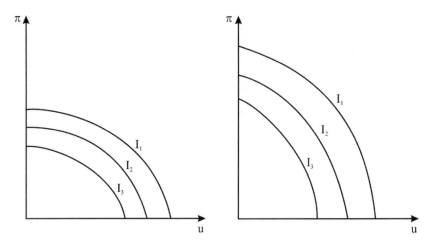

Source: De Grauwe (1992, p. 48).

Figure 2.6   Wet and hard-nosed governments and their respective map of Phillips curves

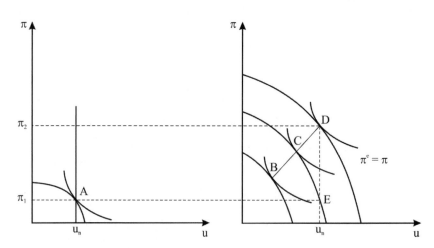

Source: De Grauwe (1992, p. 52).

Figure 2.7   Conservative and liberal administrations and their respective business cycle equilibria

cycle equilibrium of a conservative administration. The point of departure E in the right diagram is, however, not an equilibrium for the ruling liberal administration. As Shelton (2007, 2012) puts it, the respective government is tempted to cause a political surprise by an unanticipated expansionary shift in monetary policy. The economy will first move upwards along the given short-run Phillips curve towards point B. B, however, is not a stable equilibrium. Rising inflation expectations will now let the short-run Phillips curve shift rightwards, so that the concerned economy moves further to C and finally to D. As a result, monetary policy has raised inflation from its old level π_1 to its new level π_2 and has brought unemployment back 'to the natural rate' (Shelton 2007, p. 9).

It should be clear that any conservative (liberal) government is prepared to tax the owners of human (financial) capital by allowing for a substantial unemployment (inflation) rate. In both cases, the respective administration acts in favour of its preferred electorate and tends to change income distribution to the detriment of the less preferred clientele. As in the previous cases of market and of bargaining equilibria it is again the distributional contest or likewise conflict that is at the core of political economy decision processes. The rational partisan political business cycle theory provides a sound framework for the explanation of the possible equilibria that can emerge.

NOTES

1. Also Piketty (2014, p. 654) recognizes that the idea that voting is another efficient way of aggregating information (and more generally ideas, reelections and so on) is also very old. It goes back to Condorcet.
2. A slightly more sophisticated model is provided by Helland (2011).

3. Income distribution and the labour market

3.1 INTRODUCTION

In this chapter, we apply the order of analysis proposed earlier and explained in detail in Chapter 2. We stick to our premise that the outcomes of markets, of negotiations and of elections (or of any results of voting) in democratic and pluralistic societies are driven by the distributional contest. Now that the labour market is in focus, our main interest is in the distribution of wages.

The chapter is organized as follows. In Section 3.2, we deal with 'simple market solutions' with a special emphasis on wage structures, market imperfections and the impact of minimum wages and efficiency wages. In a special 'excursion', we inspect the interesting case of the monopsony.[1]

Section 3.3 looks at the bargaining solutions in the labour market, illustrated by the theory of efficient contracts. Here, some algebra is needed to formulate explicitly the interests of unions and employers and to finally identify the scope for the distributional contest. Under certain, not too abstract conditions, the conflict between both sides is just about wages, not about employment.

Section 3.4 treats political economy aspects of income distribution in the labour market. Unlike many other contributions, our main subject here is the relationship between unions, on the one side, and their clientele, that is, unionized and potentially unionized workers, on the other. Given the interest of employees in high, but not too widely spread wages, unions have to offer an optimal mix of return and variance, respecting the log-normal distribution capabilities of the workforce.

In Sections 3.5 and 3.6, we first discuss some misleading indicators related to the distribution of incomes between labour and capital. It is shown that the wage share is by no means a reasonable indicator for the competitiveness of firms/economies. Finally, in Section 3.7, we offer some recent facts and figures on income distribution in the labour market of Germany.

3.2 SIMPLE MARKET SOLUTIONS

3.2.1 Overview

In the second chapter, competition and entrepreneurship helped us to understand why existing differentials in prices and profit rates on different but comparable goods markets tend to be reduced if they are significantly divergent beforehand. The structure of profits in an economy is a highly dynamic economic variable. There is a continuous tendency to divergence and an opposing trend towards convergence. What is the analogy to the labour market(s)?

On labour markets, we observe differentials in wages on different, but comparable markets. The resulting picture in an economy is the wage/salary structure. In broad terms, this 'structure' emerges from the fact that labour itself is an inhomogeneous factor of production: there are at least two groups, one of skilled, another of unskilled workers.

A second, rather complicating aspect can come into play: the markets for skilled and for unskilled workers may differ significantly with regard to the degree of competition. In other words, if one wants to explain the level of nominal/real wages on their specific markets, at least the following four different scenarios must be distinguished: (1) perfect competition on the goods and on the labour market; (2) monopoly on the goods market/perfect competition on the labour market; (3) perfect competition on the goods market/monopsony on the labour market; (4) monopoly on the goods market/monopsony on the labour market (Blümle 1975, pp. 115–18).

A third aspect is when employers don't pay equilibrium wages, but either minimum or efficiency wages. What are the distributional aspects of general interest here that should be addressed in this chapter?

Suppose to begin that we have perfect competition in each of the two pairs of (labour/goods) markets.

3.2.2 Determinants of the Wage Structure

Lane (2011) and Borjas (2005) have designed a short-run and a long-run version respectively of the labour market in the presence of different skills. The short-run version is depicted in Figure 3.1.

The relative supply (demand) of skilled labour (L_s) is assumed to be a positive (negative) function of the relative wage of skilled workers (w_s / w_u). The higher the relative wage of skilled workers, the more pronounced is wage dispersion and hence the skewness of wage earnings distribution. The majority of experts associate the (absolute and relative) demand for skilled labour with the expansion of 'high-technology sectors'

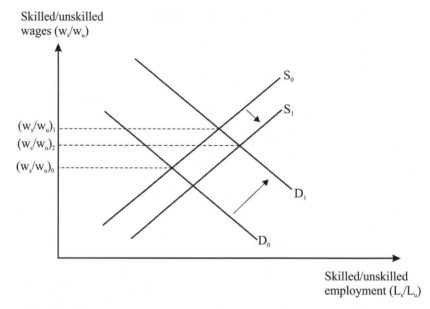

Skilled/unskilled
wages (w_s/w_u)

Source: Lane (2011, p. 207).

*Figure 3.1   Comparative statics in the markets for skilled and unskilled
labour (short run)*

in the economy. Unskilled labour (L_u), in turn, is a factor of production
mostly needed in 'low-technology sectors'.

The initial equilibrium in Figure 3.1 may be disturbed both by supply (S)
and by demand (D) factors. On the demand side, the expansion (shrinkage)
of the high-tech sector (low-tech sector) can be responsible for a higher
relative demand for skilled workers. This expansion (shrinkage) may have
domestic (change of preferences with rising GDP per capita) and/or international reasons (globalization enforces a stronger specialization in goods/
services of comparative advantage). A further reason for an increased relative demand for skilled workers could be skill-biased technological change
(Lane 2011, p. 206; Borjas 2005, p. 297). As a result, the demand schedule
shifts to the right and the relative wage of skilled workers (w_s / w_u) goes
upwards.

Also on the supply side, several reasons can be responsible for a rightward (but also for a leftward) shift: both immigration and emigration are
most likely driven by earnings differences between the domestic economy
and economies abroad. If immigration is biased in favour of skilled
(unskilled) workers, the relative supply curve of skilled workers will shift

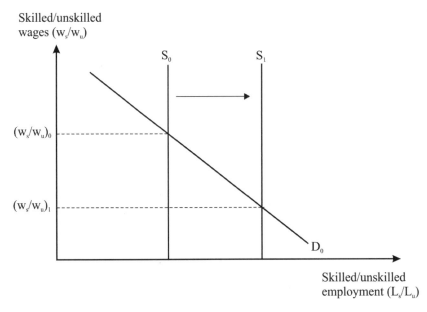

Skilled/unskilled
wages (w$_s$/w$_u$)

S_0　　　S_1

$(w_s/w_u)_0$

$(w_s/w_u)_1$

D_0

Skilled/unskilled
employment (L$_s$/L$_u$)

Source:　Borjas (2005, p. 294).

Figure 3.2　Comparative statics in the markets for skilled and unskilled labour (long run)

to the right (left). If emigration is biased in favour of skilled workers, the relative supply curve of skilled workers will shift to the left (right).

If the factors responsible for the relative supply change of skilled labour are of a long-term nature, the supply curve will become inelastic: variations in the relative wage of skilled workers will have no or little impact on the relative scarcity of skilled workers. See Figure 3.2 for the long-run perspective:

Biased higher population growth (like the occurrence of baby boomers in the 1960s and 1970s), which accompanies a change in the composition of abilities/capabilities in the workforce, will lead to a shift in the long-run supply schedule. The same applies, at a constant rate of population growth, to changes in the educational composition of the workforce as a consequence of policies directed at increasing the share of college education for a given cohort.

Notice that a high share of university trained young adults can become, under certain conditions, a pathological characteristic of an economy. For example, in Spain, two sectors were responsible for the high economic growth between 1986 and 2008: tourism and the housing and construction sector. Young graduates used to fill positions in these branches – which usually are in need of other skills – for which they were obviously over-qualified. After the Lehman Brothers case, the bubble burst in the Spanish housing sector and in the following world economic crisis, many of these academics lost their job. Nowadays, as bizarre as it sounds, young university trained adults are Spain's 'best export variety': they are the 'goods' for which Spain seems to possess comparative advantage in the classical Ricardian meaning of the word (García-Montalvo 2013, p. 15).

3.2.3   The Effects of Market Imperfections

The degree of competition on both the goods and the concomitant labour market has a crucial impact on the extent of wage dispersion. As well known from marginal productivity analysis, the following four scenarios are possible for every good/factor of production (see Blümle 1975, pp. 115–20): (i) perfect competition on the goods and on the labour market; (ii) monopoly on the goods market/perfect competition on the labour market; (iii) perfect competition on the goods market/monopsony on the labour market; (iv) monopoly on the goods market/monopsony on the labour market. More precisely, the following real wages can emerge.[2] Suppose w is the nominal wage rate, p is the price of the respective good, X stands for production/output:

$$\left(\frac{w}{p}\right)_i = \left\{\frac{\partial X}{\partial L} \cdot 1\right\}_i; \ i = s,u \text{ and } s = \text{skilled}; u = \text{unskilled} \quad (3.1)$$

$$\left(\frac{w}{p}\right)_i = \left\{\frac{\partial X}{\partial L} \cdot \left(1 - \frac{1}{\varepsilon}\right)\right\}_i; \ i = s, u \text{ with} \quad (3.2)$$

$$\varepsilon = -\frac{dX}{X} : \frac{dp}{p} \text{ (price elasticity of labour demand)} \quad (3.3)$$

$$\left(\frac{w}{p}\right)_i = \left\{\frac{\partial X}{\partial L} \cdot \frac{1}{(1 + \psi)}\right\}_i; \ i = s,u \text{ with } \psi = \frac{1}{\eta} = \text{rate of exploitation and} \quad (3.4)$$

$$\eta = \frac{dL^s}{L^s} : \frac{dw}{w} \text{ (price elasticity of labour supply)} \quad (3.5)$$

$$\left(\frac{w}{p}\right)_i = \left\{\frac{\partial X}{\partial L} \cdot \frac{\left(1 - \frac{1}{\varepsilon}\right)}{(1 + \psi)}\right\}_i; \ i = s, u \quad (3.6)$$

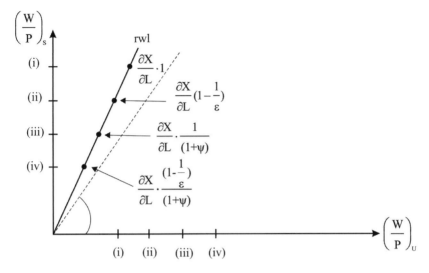

Source: Author.

Figure 3.3 *The structure of real wages in the skilled and in the unskilled sector*

In principle, each of these market imperfections can affect any branch/sector. In Figure 3.3, we have ordered real wages from low (bottom) to high (top) according to cases (i) through (iv) for the relatively skilled part of the labour force on the y axis and for the relatively unskilled part of the labour force on the x axis. Notice that ranking (ii) before (iii) contains the assumption that monopsonistic structures in the labour market dampen real wages more than monopolistic structures on the goods market.

The metric on both axes is different, as marginal labour productivity in the (skill-intensive) high-tech sectors will be structurally higher than in the (unskilled-intensive) low-tech sectors. The steep relative wage line (rwl) from the origin of the diagram combines all pairwise identical market forms in both sectors and discloses the respective real wages. Its angle stands for the ratio of real wages paid to skilled workers to the real wages paid to unskilled workers. The steeper the line is, the higher the wage dispersion averaged over all possible market forms.

Suppose we neglect for a moment the problem of different metrics on the axes and start initially from a situation where all relevant markets are perfect in each sector. This moment is depicted in Figure 3.4 by point D on the above identified relative wage line (rwl). This is rather unrealistic. If labour markets have oligopsonistic or even monopsonistic structures in

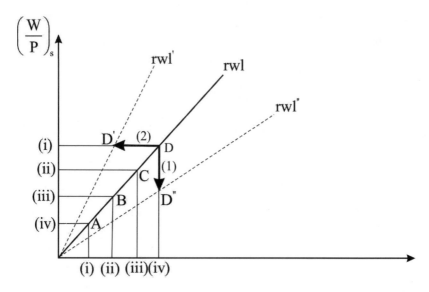

Source: Author.

*Figure 3.4   The structure of real wages in the skilled and in the unskilled
                sector in the presence of market imperfections*

the low-tech sector, we will move leftwards from D to D′ (arrow 2). The
latter point lies on the steeper rwl′! In this framework, the skewness in the
distribution of wages has increased, *ceteris paribus*. If monopolistic competition plays a major role in the high-tech sector, we will move downwards
from point D to point D″ (arrow 1), which lies on the less steep rwl″. Now,
the degree of wage dispersion decreases, *ceteris paribus*.

3.2.4   Minimum Wages

How do minimum wages affect wages and employment? Consider again
the (full employed) labour market in the presence of different skills under
perfect competition in both segments. Figure 3.5 distinguishes explicitly between the market for skilled labour and the market for unskilled
labour. All demand (D) and supply (S) schedules depend on the relative
wage (w_s / w_u). Assume we have an initial equilibrium in point A (right
part) and in point G (left part) of Figure 3.5. Now let the government
introduce a minimum wage for unskilled labour ($\overline{w}_u$). The ratio of skilled
to unskilled wages will then come down and create an excess demand
(ED) for skilled labour (right part) and an excess supply (ES) for unskilled

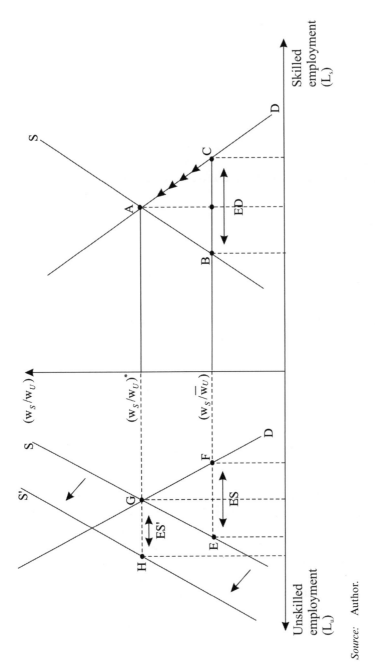

Source: Author.

Figure 3.5   The impact of a minimum wage for unskilled labour when labour markets are interlinked

labour (left part). The resulting excess demand for skilled labour can in principle be eliminated by rising (absolute and relative) wages for skilled workers until we reach the old equilibrium in A: 'as long as the two types of labour are substitutes, employers will substitute towards skilled labour, putting upward pressure on demand' (Neumark and Wascher 2008, p. 108). The new relative price for labour, however, is not associated with a new equilibrium on the market for unskilled labour:

As can be seen in the left part of Figure 3.5, one may expect an outward shift in the supply curve (from S to S'). This effect is due to the well-known pull forces that are active after the instalment of a minimum wage: part of the so far 'passive' workforce now decides to enter the market for unskilled labour while it was reluctant to do so before. As a result, there will remain an excess supply (ES') on the market for unskilled labour, corresponding to the distance HG. Notice, therefore, that minimum wages have induced unemployment among unskilled workers (Barr 2005, p. 589).

Hence, in this setting, minimum wages for unskilled labour are an inappropriate policy instrument to change income distribution in favour of unskilled workers. We may call this result of the analysis conducted with the help of Figure 3.5 the 'irrelevance theorem of minimum wages'.

There is the need for an additional qualification, however. Does the induced higher demand for high-skilled workers always increase their employment? This is not certain, because, as Neumark and Wascher (2008) put it, 'the implication for employment of skilled labour [after introducing a minimum wage for unskilled labour]) is ambiguous' (p. 108). In reality, we observe both substitution effects in favour of a 'higher wage and higher employment of skilled labour' (p. 108) as well as a negative scale effect that reduces employment incentives for all types of labour.

What are the effects of minimum wages on the wage distribution if we look beyond the above neoclassical model? 'Workers whose wages are bound by the minimum, and who retain their jobs, no doubt experience a wage increase' (p. 116). The minimum wage has in fact raised in many cases the 'wages of the lowest-skilled workers and creates a spike in the wage distribution at the minimum' (p. 115). But how far does this distribution effect affect the total distribution of wages? It is well known that minimum wages tend to boost, at the same time, wages of workers who previously earned somewhat more than the minimum wage (p. 138). Experts call this phenomenon 'spillover effects' on the wage distribution (p. 123). As a result, the introduction of minimum wages can contribute in making the wage distribution more dispersed than it was before. Moreover, 'the evidence suggests that higher minimum wages tend, on average, to reduce the economic well-being of affected workers' (p. 139).

Bosch and Manacorda (2010) have analysed the contribution of the minimum wage to the well-documented rise in earnings inequality in Mexico between the late 1980s and the early 2000s: 'the data show a clear fanning out of the distribution, with earnings inequality rising markedly both at the top and at the bottom of the distribution' (p. 5). However, there are different interpretations for this finding. The authors themselves attribute this result to be potentially linked to the 'erosion of the real value of the minimum wage' (p. 21). This finding is somewhat backed by the conclusion that the observed increase in the inequality of the wage distribution in the USA 'from 1979 to 1988 was largely due to the decline in the real value of the minimum wage' (Neumark and Wascher 2008, p. 128). There are at least two more interpretations. One links the deterioration of personal income distribution to the potential displacement effects of the minimum wage in the vein of Neumark and Wascher (2008, p. 127). A second interpretation asks for control of the impact of globalization on the observed change in income distribution. As discussed later in much more detail, major economic channels of globalization tend to increase wage dispersion, *ceteris paribus*.

Manning (2011) has conducted empirical research on the effects of minimum wages in the UK: 'A regression shows the relationship [between increases in the minimum wage and changes in the 50/10 ratio[3]] is negative but the coefficient . . . is not statistically different from zero at conventional levels' (p. 138).

Summing up after a large number of empirical studies, Machin (2011, p. 165) states: 'It seems sensible to conclude that union decline and [an erosion of the real value of] minimum wages may help to explain some part of the changes in wage inequality, but their effect is probably fairly modest.'

3.2.5 Efficiency Wages

A second possible reason – beyond minimum wages – that the remuneration of labour wages exceeds the full employment equilibrium level is efficiency wages (see Barr 2005, pp. 595–600). Let us assume that firms are prepared to pay efficiency wages to their employees. If this is optimal for many if not for all of the implied firms, unemployment will result. Moreover, if there is a recession, efficiency wages will not be affected (as firms have no incentive to deviate from their efficiency maximizing Solow condition) and unemployment will increase, *ceteris paribus*.

Two aspects of inequality come into play here. One applies to the heterogeneity of the labour force (economic) situation. If there was full employment before, inequality increases necessarily if a part of the labour force is unemployed after the introduction of efficiency wages. This can be shown

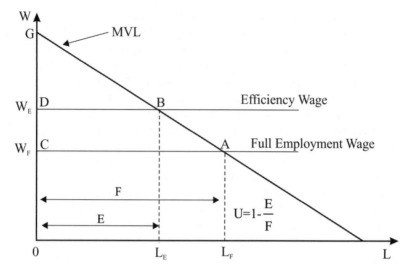

Source: Author.

Figure 3.6   The impact of efficiency wages on employment and income distribution

easily with the help of Figure 3.6. Let labour demand be represented by the marginal value of labour (MVL) schedule. Initially, there exists a full employment wage rate W_F. Thereafter, a higher efficiency wage rate W_E is installed. If unemployment was nil before, now a positive rate of unemployment $u = 1 - E/F$ emerges.

The second aspect deals with the distribution of income between capital and labour. Initially, capital income amounted to the area GCA at the full employment wage. Thereafter, capital income equals the area GDB. But has the capital share of income changed? And if so, in what direction? It is easy to assess the impact of efficiency wages on the distribution of income between labour and capital with the help of a very traditional, but effective concept, the elasticity of substitution:

$$\sigma = \left(\frac{d\frac{K}{L}}{\frac{K}{L}} \right) : \left(\frac{d\frac{w}{r}}{\frac{w}{r}} \right) \tag{3.7}$$

The answer is: it depends. If σ equals 1, there will be no change in the income distribution between capital and labour, if σ exceeds (falls short of)

1, the capital share will increase (decrease). Empirical estimates (see Sell 2012, p. 8) of the elasticity of substitution (between capital or energy and labour) range between 0.2 (in the short run) and 0.6 (in the long run). This would point to a tendency for the capital share to shrink (expand) with rising (decreasing) wage-rental ratios. As globalization (see later chapters) has tended to lower the wage-rental ratios – at least in the northern hemisphere – the observed gain for capital and the corresponding loss for labour in the struggle for the distribution of incomes receives some sort of a confirmation, when the concept of σ is used.

Meeussen and Stravrevska (2013) have summarized brilliantly the two major impacts of efficiency wages on income distribution: 'They firstly move a proportion of the population into joblessness. These are paid an unemployment compensation lower than the efficiency wage. This generates inequality within working population between the employed and the non-employed. Secondly, efficiency wages result in an increase in the wage rate that is higher than that of the return to capital, thereby decreasing inequality between wage earners and capital owners' (p. 201). The first of these effects may be exacerbated if there is an 'increase in working population or an adverse supply shock', which would 'produce an increase in unemployment as a result of a widening wage gap [between the market-clearing wage rate and the efficiency wage rate]' (p. 208). An additional impact is the consequence of an inter-group effect: 'It is obvious that if the efficiency wage mechanism would be stronger for skilled than for unskilled workers then this would widen the wage gap separating both groups' (p. 213).

3.2.6 Unemployment and Wage Inequality

That said, it is important to address the relationship between unemployment, on the one hand, and wage inequality, on the other hand. A quite popular argument – called by Michel Dumont (2013) the 'inequality-unemployment trade-off' (p. 147) or IUT – says that 'both the US and Europe have experienced an increase in the demand for high-skilled workers (relative to low-skilled workers), e.g., due to globalization [this aspect will be discussed extensively in Chapter 8] and/or technological change. In the US, where labour markets are competitive, the rise in the demand has resulted in higher inequality (skill premium). On the other hand, more egalitarian institutions in the EU that prevented wage adjustment have prompted increasing unemployment of the low-skilled' (p. 147). The empirical evidence, however, is not totally conclusive and it seems worthwhile to inspect country by country: 'In line with the IUT assumption, continental Europe (Belgium, France and

Germany, but also Finland) is characterized by high unemployment and low inequality and Anglo-Saxon countries (Australia, Canada, Ireland, New Zealand, the UK and the US) by high inequality and low unemployment' (p. 150).

Furthermore, 'interactions between different labour market institutions and technological change are yet not well understood and undoubtedly complicate the empirical verification of a possible trade-off' (p. 168).

3.3   EFFICIENT CONTRACTS IN THE LABOUR MARKET

Consider the following utility function of a union in a specific sector of the economy. It depends on the (nominal and) real wage rate w (given that the price is normalized at 1), on the employment (L) of the union members in the respective sector (which equals labour demand L^D) and on the real wage rate that the rest of the union members, M-L, can earn outside this sector, w_A. The latter is often called 'outside option':

$$U(w, L) = \underbrace{L \cdot w}_{\substack{\text{income of the union} \\ \text{members when} \\ \text{employed in the sector}}} + \underbrace{(M - L) \cdot w_A}_{\substack{\text{income of the union} \\ \text{members when not} \\ \text{employed in the sector}}} \tag{3.8}$$

We hence take into account total income of the union members. Total differentiation of the utility function leads to:

$$L \cdot dw + w \cdot dL - w_A \cdot dL = 0 \tag{3.9}$$

Rearranging terms results in:

$$L \cdot dw = -dL \cdot (w - w_A) \tag{3.10}$$

Obviously, there is a trade-off relationship between the level of wages, on the one side, and the size of employment, on the other. Any income gain via a wage increase (left side of the above equation) must be matched by an income loss due to less employment (right side of the equation) so that the level of utility remains unchanged. Solving for the slope of the indifference curve gives:

$$\frac{dw}{dL} = -\frac{w - w_A}{L} \tag{3.11}$$

$$\frac{dw}{dL} = -\frac{w - w_A}{L} = 0 \text{ if } w = w_A \qquad (3.12)$$

$$\frac{dw}{dL} = -\frac{w - w_A}{L} < 0 \text{ if } w > w_A \qquad (3.13)$$

$$\frac{dw}{dL} = -\frac{w - w_A}{L} > 0 \text{ if } w < w_A \qquad (3.14)$$

In the model of efficient contracts, the two sides of industry bargain over both the level of the wage and the level of employment. Optimal solutions can be found where iso-profit curves of the firms have joint tangential points with indifference curves of the union. Only then, the slopes of the respective curves are identical. The profit of the firms is given by:

$$\pi = y(L) - w \cdot L \qquad (3.15)$$

The total differential of this equation is given by:

$$d\pi = Y_L \cdot dL - w \cdot dL - L \cdot dw \qquad (3.16)$$

Along iso-profit curves we find $d\pi = 0$. The slope of the iso-profit curve is hence defined by:

$$\frac{dw}{dL} = \frac{Y_L - w}{L} \} \begin{matrix} > 0 \to Y_L > w \\ = 0 \to Y_L = w \\ < 0 \to Y_L < w \end{matrix} \qquad (3.17)$$

In any optimal solution, the slope of the iso-profit curve has to equal the slope of the union's indifference curve:

$$-\frac{(w - w_A)}{L} = \frac{Y_L - w}{L} \qquad (3.18)$$

Let U_i represent a troop of indifference curves, Π_i a band of iso-profit curves. If there is a union in a comfortable monopoly situation (facing a great number of firms), it can choose point D on the labour demand function L^D. L_M will then result as employment and w_M as the corresponding wage rate. But D is also an intersection point between indifference curve U_1 and iso-profit curve Π_0. These two curves create a shaded lens or likewise a 'room' for contract solutions. Starting from D (w_M, L_M), one realizes that any solution on or within the shaded lens can provide Pareto superior contracts between unions and firms (Figure 3.7).

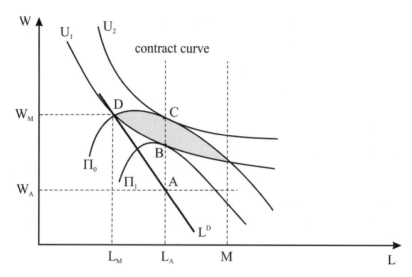

Source: Author.

Figure 3.7   Efficient contract solutions between unions and firms

As one can easily see, solution B would improve the profit situation of the firms, leaving unions at their utility level already reached in D. The opposite would occur in C, where the unions do better than in D and the firms retain their former level of profits already attained in D. Point A represents a lower bound solution, as efficient as C and B, but this time unions are worse off compared to D. Employed union members in the corresponding sector only receive the outside option wage rate w_A, employment here amounts to L_A. This wage rate is equivalent to the 'competitive wage rate' within the sector and it is located on the firms' demand curve. A peculiarity of this efficient contract frontier is that it is a vertical line. This implies that all efficient solutions – besides A – are located to the right of the labour demand curve L^D. Which of the possible efficient solutions results in the end of course depends on the bargaining power of either side. The case of a vertical contract curve is labelled in the literature as a 'strongly efficient contracts' line (Borjas 2005, pp. 416–22). As Goerke and Holler (1997) emphasize, the contract curve is vertical under the condition that the utility function of the employees signals risk neutrality.

Cahuc and Zylberberg (2004) make the same point by showing that a vertical contract line emerges if bargaining is not only over wages but also unemployment benefits: 'it has the effect of making the level of employment equal to its competitive value' (p. 400). In the case of risk love (aversion), the contract curve would be a downwards falling (upwards rising) curve (p. 190). Notice that in the case of risk love, the falling contract curve must lie to the right of the labour demand curve and hence is steeper than the latter: employers have no incentive to accept bargaining solutions that, for example, would lead to higher employment at the same wage rate (Cahuc and Zylbelberg 2004).

If unions are, so to say, powerless, then point A is a likely bargaining solution. Here, firms reach a (at least relative) 'maximum maximorum' of their profits. If, on the contrary, unions are quite powerful, point C is a probable outcome. However, no matter where we find contracts signed between both sides, employment stays constant (on the vertical line) at level L_A. The latter is identical with the competitive level of employment. The struggle is hence between profits and wages, at a given employment rate. The choice of a point on the vertical contract line 'is equivalent to a particular way of slicing the *same* pie' (p. 420, emphasis added): at a given employment level, output is a constant, *ceteris paribus*. Hence we have a case of a 'pure' distribution conflict between labour and capital. Notice that the employment level reached at L_A is not necessarily a full employment level, if we think of M being the capacity (dotted) line of labour supply.

A striking feature of the vertical contract curve is that the analysis 'suggests that both firms and unions want to move off the (labour) demand curve' (p. 421). This statement needs clarification, however: firms would be happy to stay and remain in A, provided the low bargaining power of the union allows it! For income distribution economics, the special interest of the vertical contract line lies in the involved 'pure income redistribution mechanism'. If empirically relevant – that one should find, by and large, no significant correlation between the size of employment and wages that exceed the competitive wage rate – it would indirectly strongly confirm that bargaining processes in the labour market (like in any other market) are just a reflex of the ongoing distributional conflict/contest.

3.4 THE POLITICAL ECONOMY OF THE LABOUR MARKET

In principle, under this heading, a considerable number of different approaches are feasible. The political economy of the labour market may be addressed, for example, as Saint-Paul (1993) did, from the viewpoint of political reforms. The likelihood of labour market reforms depends crucially on the 'political support to fight unemployment' (Saint-Paul 1993, p. 154). If labour market policy is able to 'generate a consensus between the employed and the unemployed over greater flexibility' (p. 154), two targets could be achieved simultaneously: firstly, incumbent parties can win a majority of the electorate and secondly (a precondition to pursue reforms), 'a better economic functioning of the labour market will generate stronger *political* support for measures against unemployment' (p. 179, emphasis added).

The 'majority of the voters' problem is at the heart of Tapio Palokangas's paper (2002). In his contribution, the power of unions is no longer a given or likewise fixed variable; on the one hand, the government can control the bargaining power of the labour unions in many ways (Palokangas 2002, p. 2). Interest groups (employers, unions), on the other hand, can influence the government on the types of policy being carried out (Palokangas 2002). In this setting, the bargaining process between unions and employers is to a large extent endogenous. The political economy constraint of the model consists is that each (new) labour market legislation is in need of a majority of voters.

The political economy of labour market legislation – with an application to the European case of qualified majority voting – is at the centre of interest in Roland Vaubel's 2008 journal article (p. 440): 'market integration prevents the workers from raising their rents by obtaining labour regulations from the government. This raises their interest in international labour market regulation, and the politicians, wanting to be re-elected, may be willing to supply it. By colluding with the governments of other countries, they try to prevent the demand and MRP [marginal revenue product] curves from becoming more elastic[4] and, if possible, to render them more inelastic [only then, the regulation renders positive/higher rents].'

A further possibility to model the political economy of the labour market emerges from the analysis on how governments and unions (being an active interest group) interact when deciding both on wages and product market distortions (Rama 1997). A typology of three different policy regimes can be observed: the regime where 'organized labour strikes and the government does not redistribute income (called Latin American, for short) has higher product market distortions and sectorial wage differentials than the regime with income redistribution and no strikes (Scandinavian). The regimes with strikes and no income redistribution (East Asian) occupy an intermediate position' (Rama 1997, pp. 329–30). Policy regimes, however, can only be changed when both sides cooperate. A change in the policy regime, in turn, is a precondition for a successful economic reform (p. 330).

We, as Rama, are also interested in the wage differential issue. But our focus is slightly different. A stylized fact in the labour market organization is the following: 'Very frequently, workers with different skill levels are represented by the same union' (Cahuc and Zylberberg 2004, p. 401).

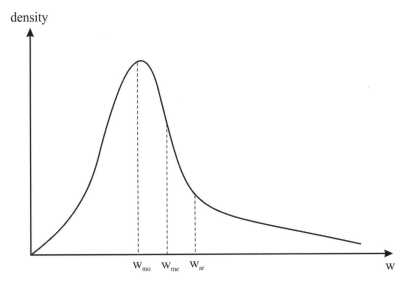

density

w_{mo} w_{me} w_{ar} w

Source: Author.

Figure 3.8   The stylized distribution pattern of wages

Unions, however, when seeking a higher level of union membership, have a tendency to reduce the spread of wages during the negotiations with the employers in comparison to a situation where each employee is paid according to their marginal productivity. Why this is often the case will be explained in this section. In principle, unions can offer 'in extremis' to their members either a contract with unified, identical wages or a contract with a great variety of different wages, by and large according to the existing differences in skills. In the first case, wage dispersion is necessarily low, while in the second case it is high.

Assume the initial distribution of wages is already left-steep and skewed to the right as given by the density function shown in Figure 3.8

This density function can be approximated rather accurately by a log-normal distribution of wages:

$$w = \exp(X) \text{ with } X = N(\mu, \sigma^2) \tag{3.19}$$

The expected or likewise average wage rate is then given by (see Beichelt and Montgomery 2003, pp. 46–8):

$$E(w) = w_{ar} = \exp\left(\mu + \frac{1}{2}\sigma^2\right) \tag{3.20}$$

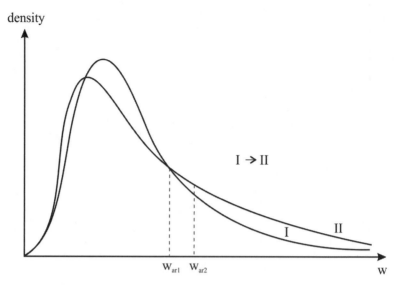

Source: Author.

Figure 3.9   Increasing the standard deviation in the distribution of wages

Taking the full differential of this expression from left to right leads to:

$$dE(w) = dw_{ar} = (d\mu + \sigma d\sigma) \exp\left(\mu + \frac{1}{2}\sigma^2\right) \qquad (3.21)$$

Proposition 1: With rising σ, the expected (or average) wage rate will increase, ceteris paribus.

If unions succeed in adjusting the original distribution of wages (I) more to the even stronger skewed distribution of skills, this will, for example, result in the distribution labelled II in Figure 3.9. As one can easily see, the average wage rate will 'walk to the right', so to speak.

One important conclusion is raised here: if the average wage rate increases in line with a higher variance (or likewise standard deviation) in the distribution of wages, the total wage sum will also increase. This statement hinges upon the condition of constant employment. However, when wage distribution fits better the distribution of abilities and skills, one can expect not only constant but even a higher rate of employment. It is hence important to have a considerable skewness in the distribution of wages if the goals pursued by the unions consist in raising the average wage rate and the total wage sum.

But unions, as we said above, also have a tendency to satisfy another strong demand of their members: a low spread in the distribution of wages (σ) signals 'solidarity', 'communitarism', in one word: 'equity'. Assume for simplicity that unions compete for potential members with the regularity of political elections and are confronted with the following voting function:

$$V_t = \lambda - \alpha(1/w_t^{ar}) - \beta\sigma_t; \text{ with } \alpha, \beta > 0 \qquad (3.22)$$

Fixing $V_t = V_t^*$ and defining $\tilde{w}_t = 1/w_t^{ar}$ gives us combinations of $(\tilde{w}_t; \sigma_t)$, which lead to the same share of votes:

$$V_t^* = \lambda - \alpha\tilde{w}_t - \beta\sigma_t; \qquad (3.23)$$

$$V_t^* + \beta\sigma_t - \lambda = \alpha\tilde{w}_t \qquad (3.24)$$

$$(1/\alpha)(V_t^* + \beta\sigma_t - \lambda) = \tilde{w}_t \qquad (3.25)$$

Total differentiation of the voting function allows us to inspect the marginal rate of substitution (MRS) between $\tilde{w}_t$ and σ_t (omitting for a moment the time index):

$$dV = d\tilde{w}\frac{\partial V}{\partial \tilde{w}} + d\sigma\frac{\partial V}{\partial \sigma} \qquad (3.26)$$

$$dV = -\alpha\, d\tilde{w} - \beta\, d\sigma = 0 \qquad (3.27)$$

$$\frac{d\tilde{w}}{d\sigma} = (-\beta/\alpha) < 0; \quad \frac{d^2\tilde{w}}{d\sigma^2} = 0 \qquad (3.28)$$

Hence, any iso-voting schedule is a linear falling curve. As the MRS demonstrates, this line will be the steeper (flatter), the stronger the preference for 'equality' β (for a given α) is.

We have depicted three different iso-voting (I_0, I_1, I_2) lines in Figure 3.10: DD stands for the log-normal distribution of wages and recalls proposition 1, where we found a positive (negative) relationship between the expected or average wage rate (inverse wage rate), on the one hand, and the standard deviation of wages, on the other hand. As can be seen in Figure 3.10, the closer the respective iso-voting lines are located vis-à-vis the origin, the higher the voting share a single union can expect. In P we have an equilibrium in the sense that the 'distribution constraint' DD is tangential to the iso-voting line I_1. Here, the union chooses the optimal combination of the average wage rate and the dispersion of wages over all

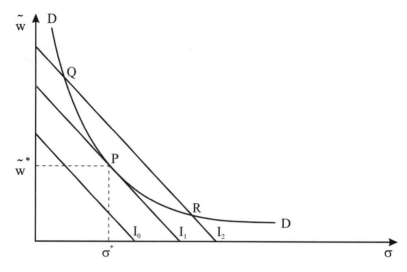

Source: Author.

Figure 3.10   *The political economy model of unions*

relevant jobs/skills. Points on I_2, such as, for example, Q and R fulfil the
'distribution constraint' DD, but they are associated with a much lower
share of the electorate corresponding to I_2.

Notice that if the voting function is slightly modified in the vein of portfolio theory, our results change only to a minor extent. If now the variance
of wages – instead of the standard deviation of wages – enters the voting
function,

$$V_t = \lambda - \alpha(1/w_t^{ar}) - \frac{1}{2}\beta\sigma_t^2; \text{ with } \alpha, \beta > 0 \qquad (3.29)$$

Fixing $V_t = V_t^*$ and defining $\tilde{w}_t = 1/w_t^{ar}$ gives us combinations of
$(\tilde{w}_t; \sigma_t^2)$, which lead to the same share of votes:

$$V_t^* = \lambda - \alpha\tilde{w}_t - \frac{1}{2}\beta\sigma_t^2; \qquad (3.30)$$

$$V_t^* + \frac{1}{2}\beta\sigma_t^2 - \lambda = \alpha\tilde{w}_t \qquad (3.31)$$

$$(1/\alpha)\left(V_t^* + \frac{1}{2}\beta\sigma_t^2 - \lambda\right) = \tilde{w}_t \qquad (3.32)$$

Total differentiation of the voting function allows us to inspect the MRS
between $\tilde{w}_t$ and σ_t (omitting for a moment the time index):

$$dV = d\widetilde{w}\frac{\partial V}{\partial \widetilde{w}} + d\sigma \frac{\partial V}{\partial \sigma} \tag{3.33}$$

$$dV = -\alpha d\widetilde{w} - \beta\sigma d\sigma = 0 \tag{3.34}$$

$$\frac{d\widetilde{w}}{d\sigma} = (-\beta\sigma/\alpha) < 0 \text{ as } \sigma > 0; \quad \frac{d^2\widetilde{w}}{d\sigma^2} = (-\beta/\alpha) < 0 \tag{3.35}$$

In this case, any iso-voting curve is concave to the origin of the diagram. As the MRS demonstrates, this curve will be steeper (flatter), the stronger the preference for 'equality' β (for a given α) is. Also, it holds that

$$\lim_{\sigma \to 0} \frac{d\widetilde{w}}{d\sigma} = (-\beta\sigma/\alpha) = 0 \tag{3.36}$$

Again, an equilibrium is feasible whenever the 'distribution constraint' DD is tangential to any of the concave iso-voting lines. Also in this case, the union may choose an optimal solution, because it maximizes the votes of the employees. This solution is a combination of the optimal average wage rate and the optimal dispersion of wages over all relevant jobs/skills.

What is the insight gained by these findings? In the political economy approach, wage dispersion is not an outcome of relative demand for and supply of the skilled/unskilled workforce (see above), but a direct consequence of the vote maximizing behaviour of unions.

There is ample empirical evidence for our approach. In a recent paper, Rios and Hirsch (2012) evaluated the impact of unions and unionization on wage dispersion in the USA, Chile and Bolivia. Their findings are not surprising: 'although sizeable wage premiums [in our model this is the size of the average wage] attract a large queue of workers wanting union job, they (the unions) retard the creation and sustainability [this follows in our model from the trade-off between the 'organic' dispersion of wages and the unions' intent to reduce wage inequality] of such jobs' (Rios and Hirsch 2012, p. 22). How do they do it? The authors explain: 'In addition to increasing (average) wages, unions typically reduce wage inequality among their members by reducing wage returns with respect to measured and unmeasured worker attributes and by "compressing" or "standardizing" wages among workers with similarly measured attributes' (p. 16). These effects are similar in all of the above mentioned countries notwithstanding the obvious differences in these nations' legal and economic backgrounds: 'Unions are found to have similar and substantial effects in reducing wage inequality in the three countries, much of this the result of reducing right-tail wage dispersion' (p. 21).

3.5   SOME MISLEADING INDICATORS

Change in the so-called 'labour share' – defined as the ratio of the total wage sum over GDP – is a prominent indicator to measure a gain or loss of labour in the distribution of income between wages and profits. As the following formula demonstrates, the 'labour share' is identical with the concept of real wage costs per unit of production:[5]

$$\Lambda = \frac{wL}{Y} = \frac{wL}{py} = \frac{(w/p)L}{y} = (w/p):(y/L) = \frac{\partial y}{\partial L} \cdot \frac{y}{L} \qquad (3.37)$$

However, it is totally misleading to use real wage costs per unit of production or likewise the labour share as an indicator of competitiveness (see below). This insight solves the so-called 'Blanchard-Puzzle' from the 1990s: Olivier Blanchard (1998, 2000) had detected for the period between 1970 and 1995 that many European countries that experienced a lowering in their labour share (hence lower real wage costs per unit of production) were also confronted with higher unemployment. The reasoning for this effect is quite simple: a lower labour share (and hence lower real wage costs per unit of production) can go along with constant, decreasing or even with increasing employment. This can be shown quite easily with the help of Figure 3.11.

Suppose, for example, that our economy in question is hit by either a

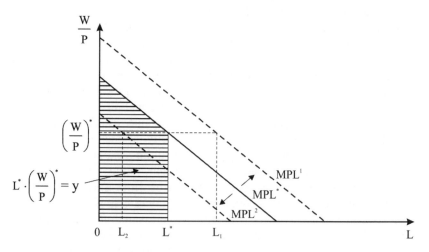

Source: Author.

Figure 3.11   The impact of productivity shocks on employment and the labour share

positive or a negative productivity shock. Assume that unions accept a constant real wage rate in the case of a positive productivity shock following the concept of wage moderation that had been so successful, for the most part, in Germany between 1995 and 2010. In the case of a negative productivity shock, unions, however, are often reluctant to lower the real wage rate. The positive (negative) productivity shock would hence increase (lower) the respective competitiveness. In that case, the original MPL*-curve shifts either to the right (at MPL^1 employment is increased to L^1, *ceteris paribus*) or to the left (at MPL^2 employment is decreased to L^2, *ceteris paribus*).[6] However, in both cases, the effect on income distribution is ambiguous:

$$\Lambda = \frac{\partial y}{\partial L} : \frac{y}{L} \qquad (3.38)$$

If the average productivity of labour increases (decreases) as much as the marginal productivity of labour, the labour share remains constant. The latter happens, for instance, in the case of a Cobb-Douglas production function, where the labour share is a 'technological variable' denoted by the symbol α. If the average productivity of labour increases (decreases) more (less) than the marginal productivity, the quota of labour will come down (go up).

Recent empirical studies on the capital and the labour share, such as in Buch (2013), provide some interesting results:

1. 'descriptive statistics show a decline in the unconditional volatility of labour and capital income growth' (p. 425)
2. 'on average, the relative volatility of labour income has not changed much between the 1980's and the 1990's' (p. 426)
3. 'a higher labour share quite consistently lowers the relative volatility of labour income' (p. 426)
4. 'although greater import openness tends to increase labour income volatility, greater openness lowers volatility' (p. 426).

Especially this last outcome will be addressed in more detail in forthcoming chapters.

3.6   EXCURSION: THE SPECIAL CASE OF THE MONOPSONY

In the market form of a monopsony, there are plenty of agents on the supply side, but there is only one on the demand side. The case is interesting especially for the labour market: firstly, because this specific market form has been shown to be relevant for a number of branches (as in the sector of services) and secondly, because a monopsony that is regulated by minimum wages can produce the opposite results that minimum wages used to trigger in perfect labour markets (Card and Krueger 1997; Manning 2003). In this excursion we shall put forward the model of a non-discriminatory monopsony on the labour market. The term 'non-discriminatory' means that any monopsonistic employer who hires an additional worker to a new and higher wage rate will have to pay this new and higher wage rate to all previously employed and to this date less well-paid workers. This makes the so-called 'marginal costs of hiring labour curve' a steep upwards sloped line (Figure 3.12). The time horizon will be the short run, that is, we will not consider substitution effects between labour, on the one hand, and capital, energy and so on, on the other hand.

The profit of a representative monopsonistic firm π_M is given by:

$$\pi_M = p \cdot X(L) - Lw(L) \tag{3.39}$$

where p is the producer price, X stands for the output, L for labour input, w equals the nominal wage rate. Labour supply is specified for reasons of simplicity as a linear function (see Sell and Kermer 2013, p. 286):

$$w = \frac{1}{b}[L + a] \text{ or } L = wb - a; \ a, b > 0 \tag{3.40}$$

The production function is linear as well and reads, if α is taken as a productivity parameter:

$$X(L) = \alpha L \tag{3.41}$$

Combining the labour supply function with the production function and the profit equation yields:

$$\pi_M = p(\alpha L) - L\left(\frac{1}{b}[L + a]\right) \tag{3.42}$$

The first order condition for a profit maximum is then given by:

$$\frac{\partial \pi_M}{\partial L} = p\alpha - \frac{1}{b}(2L + a) = 0 \tag{3.43}$$

Solving for L generates the optimal size of employment for the monopsonistic firm:

$$L_M^* = \frac{1}{2}(bp\alpha - a) \tag{3.44}$$

Inserting this result into the labour supply function gives us the monopsonistic wage rate:

$$w_M^* = \frac{1}{2}p\alpha + \frac{a}{2b} \tag{3.45}$$

$$\pi_M = p\left[\alpha\frac{1}{2}(bp\alpha - a)\right] - \frac{1}{2}[bp\alpha - a]\left(\frac{1}{b}\left[\frac{1}{2}(bp\alpha - a) + a\right]\right) > 0 \tag{3.46}$$

In comparison, a competitive labour market will render different results. The profit of the representative firm reads:

$$\pi_C = p(\alpha L) - Lw \tag{3.47}$$

The first order condition is now:

$$\frac{\partial \pi_C}{\partial L} = p\alpha - w = 0 \tag{3.48}$$

$$w_C^* = p\alpha; \ L_C^* = bp\alpha - a \tag{3.49}$$

$$\pi_C = p\alpha(\alpha bp - a) - p\alpha(bp\alpha - a) = 0 \tag{3.50}$$

Employment, hence, is higher under full competition and so is the wage rate provided that

$$\frac{a}{2b} < \frac{1}{2}p\alpha \tag{3.51}$$

If a monopsonistic labour market/firm is regulated by a minimum wage, the profit equation becomes:

$$\overline{\pi}_M = p(\alpha\overline{L}) - \overline{L}\left(\frac{1}{b}[\overline{L} + a]\right) \tag{3.52}$$

$$\overline{\pi}_M = p(\alpha\overline{L}) - \frac{1}{b}\overline{L}^2 - \frac{a}{b}\overline{L} \tag{3.53}$$

$$\overline{w} = \frac{1}{b}(\overline{L} + a) \tag{3.54}$$

$$\overline{L} = b\overline{w} - a \tag{3.55}$$

$$\overline{\pi}_M = p\alpha(b\overline{w} - a) - (b\overline{w} - a)\overline{w} = (b\overline{w} - a)(p\alpha - \overline{w}) \tag{3.56}$$

This profit will fall short of the 'pure' monopsonistic profit, but will be positive as long as

$$\overline{w} > \frac{a}{b} \text{ and } p > \frac{w}{\alpha} \tag{3.57}$$

The first condition is always fulfilled (see below). For the second condition it is important to realize that there are two cases embodied in the profit equation: as long as the minimum wage is below the equilibrium wage rate,

$$w_C^* = p\alpha > \overline{w} = \frac{1}{b}(\overline{L} + a) = \frac{a}{b} + \frac{\overline{L}}{b} \tag{3.58}$$

profits of the monopsonistic firm will be positive. But if the minimum wage is 'really' binding,

$$w_C^* = p\alpha < \overline{w} = \frac{1}{b}(\overline{L} + a) = \frac{a}{b} + \frac{\overline{L}}{b} \tag{3.59}$$

the representative firm incurs losses if it continues to plan along the labour supply curve. Then, the above profit equation is no longer valid: the monopsonistic firm will now behave like any other firm under perfect competition and equate the minimum wage with the MVL:

$$\overline{\pi} = p(\alpha L) - L\overline{w} \tag{3.60}$$

The first order condition is now:

$$\frac{\partial \pi_C}{\partial L} = p\alpha - \overline{w} = 0 \tag{3.61}$$

$$\overline{w} = p\alpha; L = \overline{w}b - a = bp\alpha - a \tag{3.62}$$

$$\overline{\pi} = p\alpha(\alpha bp - a) - p\alpha(bp\alpha - a) = 0 \tag{3.63}$$

Figure 3.12 shows all five situations.

With no minimum wage legislation installed, the monopsonistic firm will choose the wage rate w_M^* and the corresponding labour input L_M^*. In the alternative competitive setting, employers will choose w_C^* and L_C^*. In the

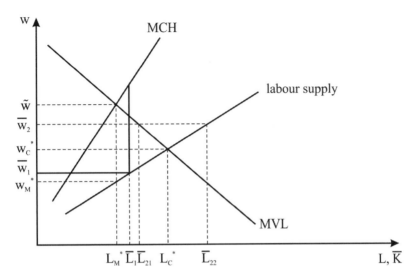

Source: Author.

*Figure 3.12   Optimal wages and optimal employment in a
            non- discriminatory monopsony*

case of a minimum wage, three distinct situations have to be distinguished:
At $\overline{w}_1$, the marginal costs of hiring labour curve (MCH) will become vertical
at the intersection point with the labour supply curve. The monopsonistic
firm will find the corresponding labour input on the labour supply curve at
$\overline{L}_1$. The minimum wage rate $\overline{w}_1$ is obviously below the competitive wage rate
$w_C{}^*$ and would not be binding under this scenario. If, however, the minimum
wage is set much higher, say at $\overline{w}_2$, two possibilities emerge. The monopsonistic firm could in principle continue to behave as before and find the corresponding labour input again on the labour supply curve. This would leave
us at employment $\overline{L}_{22}$. However, as shown in our algebra above, this would
incur losses to the firm and can, therefore be excluded as a viable solution.
Hence, the monopsonistic firm will now behave like any other firm under
perfect competition and equate the minimum wage rate with the MVL: as a
consequence, $\overline{L}_{21}$ is the level of employment optimally chosen. Notice that
this amount of labour input is lower than the competitive solution ($L_C{}^*$),
but still higher than the monopsonistic solution under a 'low' minimum
wage rate $\overline{w}_1$, $\overline{L}_1$. One should also realize that any minimum wage will create
employment under the regime of a monopsony, as long as $\overline{w} \leq \tilde{w}$.

Let us now turn back to our main subject, the distributional implications that accrue to the monopsony. As we have seen above, the

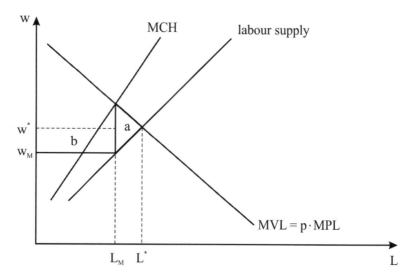

Source: Author.

Figure 3.13   A comparative static welfare evaluation of the monopsony

monopsonistic firm will in general pay lower wages and employ fewer workers than the many firms in the competitive solution. This is obviously a disadvantage for the wage share of workers. As depicted in Figure 3.13, employees transfer an amount of the area b to the employees (wage cut). Furthermore, the lower employment causes a loss of welfare to the society equivalent to the triangle a.

3.7   EMPIRICAL FACTS AND FIGURES

The model of changing wage structures (see Machin 2011, p. 140) is usually tested by estimating a relative wage equation:

$$\ln(W_S/W_U)_t = \gamma_0 + \gamma_1 \text{ trend} + \gamma_2 \ln(N_S/N_U)_t + v_t \qquad (3.64)$$

where the expression on the left-hand side is the log of the skilled to unskilled wage ratio, relative demand for skilled labour is proxied by a trend variable, relative supply is measured by the log of the ratio of the number (N) of skilled (S) to unskilled (U) workers and v is an error term.

This model fits well with the data from countries such as the UK in the period 1974 to 2007 (Machin 2011, p. 141): relative supply of skilled

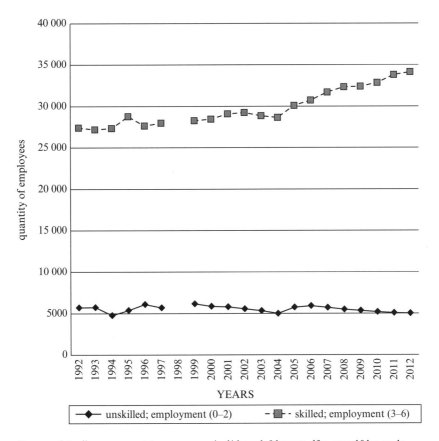

Source: http://appsso.eurostat.ec.europa.eu/nui/show.do?dataset=lfsa_egaed&lang=de.

Figure 3.14 *Employment of skilled and unskilled labour force in Germany (1992–2012)*

workers (as expected) had a negative impact on relative skilled wage while the trend variable (symbolizing the relative labour demand index) showed a positive coefficient (Machin 2011).

In the case of Germany, the database is too narrow and also too incomplete for any sort of econometric exercise. The following observations (Figures 3.14 and 3.15[7]), however, seem to be indisputable: the employment of low skilled workers has stagnated since the early 1990s, whereas there is a clear upward trend in the employment of high skilled workers. The latter (though the time period of observation is rather short in this case and commences only in 2004) has obviously been driven more by demand than by

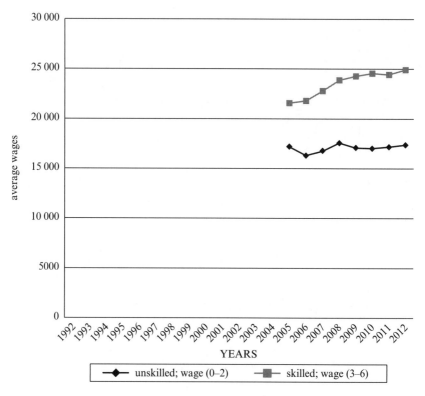

Source: http://appsso.eurostat.ec.europa.eu/nui/show.do?dataset=ilc_di08&lang=de.

*Figure 3.15   Average wages of skilled and unskilled labour force in
            Germany (2004–12)*

supply forces: wages for skilled work moved upwards, those for unskilled
remained almost constant.[8] As a result, it is fair to say that any former
hypothetical equilibrium in the income distribution between skilled work
and unskilled work has been shaken: the ratio of the wage sum for skilled
work to the wage sum of unskilled work has gone up.

We have based our quantitative plots presented in Figures 3.14 and
3.15 on data supplied by the International Standard Classification of
Education (ISCED). In doing so, we follow implicitly the systematics
provided by Francis Green (2013, p.41). His primary skill indicators are
'years of education' and 'educational qualifications' or certificates (Green
2013). Beyond the education system, there are further important factors
that affect skills such as family background, learning/training on the job
and the efficiency of the labour market (p. 28).

NOTES

1. The amount of maths used in this excursion goes beyond the level that is 'on average' present in our expositions. Readers who are not sympathetic with the algebra used may refer to the graphs, their respective verbal explanations and the final summary of results.
2. Notice that given the four possibilities for each market, there are a total of 16 combinations of real wages!
3. The 50/10 ratio stands for the ratio of the median to the tenth and hence lowest percentile (Manning 2011, p. 135). A more equal personal income distribution is associated with a fall in this ratio, *ceteris paribus*.
4. As Rodrik (2000, p. 26) explains, the demand for labour will become more elastic whenever the other factors of production (as capital) are able to react more easily to changes in their economic environment, for example, by moving to foreign countries. This effect seems more likely under the conditions of globalization (Vannoorenberghe and Janeba 2013, p. 6).
5. One should realize that changes in the nominal wage costs per unit of production do possibly reflect changes in competitiveness. Better indicators for the competitiveness of firms/economies are, however, the real exchange rate and even Tobin's q (see, for example, Maass and Sell 1998).
6. As long as the firm/economy of concern is hit by significant unemployment (often caused by a lack of demand for goods and services), it is labour demand that represents the 'shorter market side' and hence determines the (labour) market outcome. This point is often overlooked by Keynesian economists notwithstanding their special relationship with the 'demand side'.
7. We have used the International Standard Classification of Education (ISCED) that distinguishes between the following levels of education. Level 0: pre-primary education – the initial stage of organized instruction; it is school- or centre-based and is designed for children aged at least three years of age. Level 1: primary education – begins between five and seven years of age, is the start of compulsory education where it exists and generally covers six years of full-time schooling. Level 2: lower secondary education – continues the basic programmes of the primary level, although teaching is typically more subject focused. Usually, the end of this level coincides with the end of compulsory education. Level 3: upper secondary education – generally begins at the end of compulsory education. The entrance age is typically 15 or 16 years. Entrance qualifications (end of compulsory education) and other minimum entry requirements are usually needed. Instruction is often more subject oriented than at ISCED level 2. The typical duration of ISCED level 3 varies from two to five years. Level 4: post-secondary non-tertiary education – between upper secondary and tertiary education. This level serves to broaden the knowledge of ISCED level 3 graduates. Typical examples are programmes designed to prepare pupils for studies at level 5 or programmes designed to prepare pupils for direct labour market entry. Level 5: tertiary education (first stage) – entry to these programmes normally requires the successful completion of ISCED level 3 or 4. This includes tertiary programmes with academic orientation (type A), which are largely theoretical and tertiary programmes with an occupational orientation (type B). The latter are typically shorter than type A programmes and aimed at preparing students for the labour market. Level 6: tertiary education (second stage) – reserved for tertiary studies that lead to an advanced research qualification (PhD or doctorate).
8. When skilled and unskilled work are classified not by qualifications but by abilities, the database of EUROSTAT shows – again for the case of Germany – a mild upward trend in the wages of unskilled work. However, the vertical distance between the level of skilled wages and unskilled wages has grown as well. The picture of both employment schedules resembles those of Figure 3.14.

4. Income distribution and the capital market

4.1 INTRODUCTION

The European debt crisis has made it clear that the struggle on the capital markets is between investors and savers: low (high) interest rates punish savers (investors) and help investors (savers).

More than that, at the same time we can observe a contest between creditor countries, that is, the so-called 'GANL' (Germany, Austria, Netherlands, Luxembourg) in the northern core of the Eurozone confronted with opposing interests of debtor countries in the southern periphery of Europe, that is, the so-called 'GIIPSC' (Greece, Italy, Ireland, Portugal, Spain, Cyprus) or 'GIIPS' (when Cyprus is omitted). For this reason, we dedicate a special section to the balance of payments disequilibrium and the role of Target2 balances within the European debt crisis.

In this chapter, we want to again apply the order of analysis proposed earlier and explained in detail in Chapter 2: we stick to our premise that the outcomes of markets, of negotiations and of elections (or of any results of voting) in democratic and pluralistic societies are driven by the distributional contest. Now that the capital market is in focus, our main interest is in the distribution of capital income.

The chapter is organized as follows. In Section 4.2, we deal with 'simple market solutions'. Here, the concept of the investor's and the saver's rent gives interesting insights into the contest between these two groups of economic agents. The section includes an excursion that puts the European balance of payments crisis within the framework of the New Austrian Business Cycle Theory (ABCT) at the centre of the analysis. Section 4.3 is dedicated to bargaining solutions between creditors and debtors. Here, we apply both neoclassical 'Edgeworth box type' tools as well as a simultaneous two-person game framework. Section 4.4 deals with the political economy of the capital market. Our primary interest here is in the behaviour of small and large stockholders. A fifth, empirical section concludes the chapter.

4.2 SIMPLE MARKET SOLUTIONS

4.2.1 Introduction

We start with a discussion of the simple macroeconomic investment savings framework known from classical economics. The distributional contest between savers and investors can be represented by the continuous struggle for the investors' rent vis-à-vis the savers' rent. A key aspect of this type of analysis is the curvature/slope of the savings function. Unlike the investment demand function, which is usually taken to fall as a negative function of the interest rate, visualized as a more or less steep line, the savings function may first rise with the (still low or moderate) interest rate, but, at higher interest rates, the slope may become horizontal or even negative. This is what used to be called 'perverse savings' by economists or as the 'backward bending savings curve' (Brakman et al. 2006, p. 255). As we shall show in the following, the backward bending savings curve has significant consequences for the distribution of the rent balance between savers and investors.

Details can be observed with the help of Figure 4.1. In the left part of the diagram, we have depicted savings and investment as a function of R

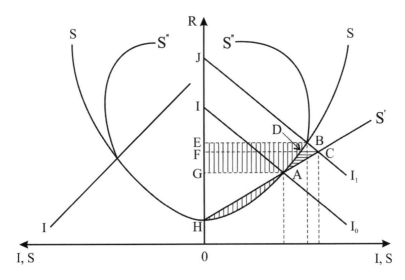

Figure 4.1   *Rent distribution on the capital market between savers and investors*

or likewise $(1 + r)$, that is, the market gross interest rate. Already we can see here that saving decreases in response to higher interest rates. Why is this result conceivable? 'An increasing R influences your response in two ways. First, future consumption is cheaper in terms of current consumption, which should encourage you to consume later and save more now. A second effect, as long as you are a creditor, of a higher interest rate makes you richer and pushes you toward consuming more now and later. It is entirely possible that the second effect may predominate. In this case, the supply curve will decline confronted with a higher R' (Fabozzi and Modigliani 2009, pp. 357–8). This explanation is sort of 'traditional'. Rational expectations economics highlights further reasons: given asymmetric information, savers will infer from higher interest rates that these will make it all the more difficult for investors to pay back their loans. 'In this case the suppliers of funds could be worse off if the interest rate increases and they would be therefore be inclined to save less' (Brakman et al. 2006, p. 255). A third underpinning can be traced back to information economics (see Arnold 2006, pp. 231–46): when banks act as intermediates between borrowers and savers, the information asymmetry between banks and borrowers will also have adverse selection effects. Borrowers will then be confronted with a backward bending supply function of the banking sector.

If S and not S'^1 is then the relevant supply curve on the capital market, point A stands for the initial equilibrium when investment demand is low (I_0). In comparison, the rent of savers is obviously higher in the case of the backward bending supply curve shown by the shaded area between H and A – at a given investors' rent IAG. In a second scenario of a high investment demand (I_1), the rent of savers accounts for the area HEB in the case of the backward bending supply curve and is clearly higher than before investment expanded (GHA). It is higher than in the case of the linear supply curve shown by the area EFDB, but smaller by the triangle ADC. As ADC will always fall short of EFDB, the backward bending supply curve renders the rent balance more favourable than the case of the linear supply curve. The new investors' rent is now JEB, which is definitely more than it was before (IAG). But it is less than what it could have been at a linear supply curve on the capital market: the net loss equals $JFC - JEB = EBCF = EFDB + DBC$. Hence, we account for a net gain of rent in favour of savers *and* investors in the amount of ADC/DBC.

In other words, the more pronounced the income effects of higher interest rates, the effects of anticipating future debt, the effects of adverse selection and hence the more backward bending the savings' supply function is, the higher will be the gains for savers in their distributional contest with

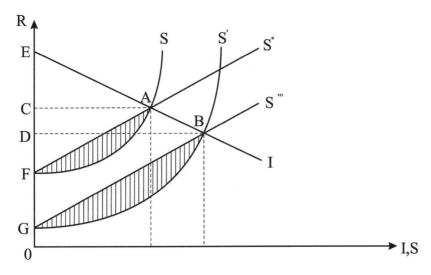

Source: Author.

Figure 4.2 The impact of an expansion in savings on the capital market

investors, whenever there is an expansion of private and/or government demand on the capital market.

In Figure 4.2, we discuss the distribution of rents subject to the case of an exogenous outward shift of the savings function. What about the effect of higher savings (due to changes in time preference and the like) on the rent distribution between savers and investors? The details can be taken from Figure 4.2. Firstly, we can observe as above a higher rent of savers when the supply curve is backward bending in comparison to a linear supply curve. The shaded area between F and A denotes the difference. When the savings function shifts to the right, this area increases, *ceteris paribus*, to the 'lens' between G and B. Investors' rent will rise due to an outward shift of savings supply from ECA to EDB, that is, by the area ABCD; savers' rent will also go up from FAC to its new level GBD. In a way, what we observe is a 'win-win' constellation for savers and investors as the size of the pie (transactions on the capital market) increases. This result replicates a long-standing insight that (economic) growth in conjunction with stable or even lower prices tends to reduce the distributional conflict.

4.2.2   Excursion: The New Austrian Business Cycle Theory (ABCT) of the Capital Market and its Application to the European Debt Crisis

4.2.2.1   Introduction: the one country equilibrium case

The New ABCT has already demonstrated its capability to provide an excellent framework for the explanation of the financial crisis (see, for example, Alonso et al. 2011; Bagus and Howden 2011) that started in 2007. Also, some recent methodological criticism against pitfalls of the new Austrian approach has been successfully rejected (Salerno 2011). In this subsection, we intend to demonstrate the explanatory power of New Austrian economics in the field of the ongoing Euro crisis and its implications for the distributional contest between creditor and debtor countries.

The three diagrams in Figure 4.3 depict the situation of a single closed economy in total equilibrium as follows from the New ABCT:[2]

At the bottom, we have the classical market for loanable funds where the intersection between savings S(i) and investment I(i) determines the interest rate in equilibrium, i* (the natural rate of interest). Above this diagram, we find the overall production possibility frontier (PPF). Point A denotes the current division of production between investment goods and consumer goods. The last diagram on the left side represents Von Hayek's famous triangle.[3] The horizontal leg of this triangle measures (read from left to right) 'goods in process moving through time from the inception to the completion of the production process' (Garrison 2001, p. 46). It can also be seen to represent 'the separate stages of production' (Garrison 2001, ibid.), starting with the early and ending with the final stages. The vertical leg stands for the output of consumer goods that can be produced once the beginning of the production process (point A on the horizontal leg) is defined. The surface between the hypotenuse of Von Hayek's triangle, the vertical leg, and the horizontal leg measures the output of intermediate goods engaged – together with the original factors of production, labour and land – in the production of consumer goods. The angle α is hence a proxy for the productivity of the intermediate goods and equals in equilibrium the natural rate of interest, i*.

The logic of the diagrams has to be understood from the bottom to the top and then from the right to the left. In the first place, the capital market determines the equilibrium size of savings and investment and the equilibrium rate of interest. Given the PPF, the amount of available consumer goods is then determined. Given the equilibrium rate of interest and hence, by and large, the angle α, the point A is determined in Von Hayek's triangle, which stands for the implicit length of the production process.[4] Now let us assume that the original equilibrium is destroyed as a result of a positive change in the time preference of households. The savings

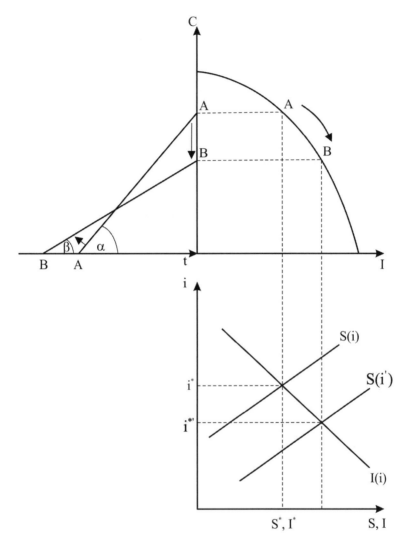

Source: Garrison (2001, p. 62).

Figure 4.3   Hayek's triangle, the production possibilities frontier and the capital market

function shifts to the right (S (i′)), the equilibrium interest rate decreases down to its new level i*′, investment rises according to point B on the PPF. The output of consumer goods necessarily falls; the now lower interest rate 'favors relatively long-term investment. Resources are bid away from late stages of production, where demand is weak because of the currently low consumption, and into early stages, where demand is strong because of the lower rate of interest' (Garrison 2001, p. 46). Correspondingly, the new point B on the horizontal leg of the triangle is located to the left of point A and the new angle β is smaller than α. This is about the same statement as recognizing that the natural rate of interest has fallen on the capital market and/or that the productivity of intermediate goods is now lower than it was before, as in the 'classical world' consumers postpone part of their current demand for consumer goods to the future by saving more today. By doing so, they expect to receive more of the durable and high quality consumer goods in the future. This matches the shift of the production process towards the early (or lengthier) stages. This is why the point A on the horizontal axis of the Hayekian triangle now moves towards the new point B. Notice that the growth rate of the economy will be higher after the capital restructuring than it was before (Garrison 2001).

These 'macroeconomics of capital structure' will now be extended in order to analyse the effects of Target2 balances on Euro countries. To do so, we will create a two countries/two areas framework, a task that, to our knowledge, introduces an innovation into the diagrammatic framework of the New Austrian model of economics.

4.2.2.2   The two countries disequilibrium case

Only in recent years has the ABCT been considered for open economies (see, for example, Cachanosky 2012 and the literature cited therein). In the following exposition, we present our ideas in the framework of two regions.

There are two areas within the Euro countries' zone, one (on the left side of Figure 4.4) that is characterized by high interest rates, low domestic savings and a high potential for commercial capital imports and a second one (on the right side of Figure 4.4) with inverse properties. In the following, we analyse the three scenarios that are relevant for our subject: (i) the years 1999 to mid 2007; (ii) the years mid 2007 to 2012 if Target2 would not have been operative; (iii) the years mid 2007 to 2012 with Target2 being operative and effective.

Initially, as was the case in the period between 1999 and mid 2007, Target2 (or likewise its predecessor Target) played no significant credit role for central bank money flows between the two areas. Instead, commercial capital flows satisfied the demand to finance each country's current account deficit/surplus. The excess demand for savings in the left part of the diagram matches the excess supply of savings in the right section. This corresponds to the (bilateral) current account deficit (ED) in the GIIPS/ current account surplus (ES) in the GLNF countries. As interest rates

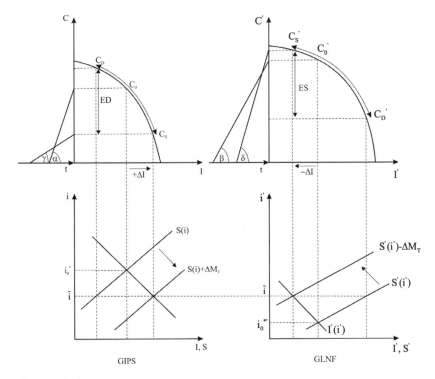

Source: Author.

Figure 4.4 How the Target2 mechanism enforces a shift of purchasing power from the GANL to the GIIPS countries

tended to converge at $\tilde{\imath}$ (with interest rates coming down from a higher level i_0^* in the GIIPS countries and rising from a lower level $i_0^{*\prime}$ in the GLNF countries), the consumption production point, CS (CS′), of the GIIPS (GLNF) countries moved downwards (upwards) to the right (left), the consumption demand point, CD (CD′), of the GIIPS (GLNF, that is, Germany, Luxembourg, Netherlands, Finland) countries moved upwards to the left (downwards to the right) as investment was expanded (reduced). In Von Hayek's triangle, the capital structure was reorganized in favour of long-term (short-term) investment in the GIIPS (GLNF) countries. Intermediate goods were bid away from late (early) stages of production, where demand was weak because of the currently low consumption (investment), and into early (late) stages, where demand was strong because of the lower (higher) rate of interest.

This phase is characterized by a (mal-)investment boom, a lower production of consumption goods and above average (but unsustainable) growth in the GIIPS countries along with weak investment, a higher production of consumption goods and little if any economic growth in the GLNF countries.

The hypothetical scenario of 'autarky' in both regions (where the relevant variables show the subscript '0') reveals a relatively high (low) natural rate of interest in the GIIPS (GLNF) countries. The equilibrium points on the respective PPFs are C_0 and C_0', the equilibrium interest rates are i_0^* and $i_0^{*\prime}$. This scenario is not so unusual as one may expect because it also represents quite well the virtual situation after 2007 if Target2 would not have been operative and effective (see above). As Sinn and Wollmershäuser (2011) argue, voluntary capital exports from the GLNF countries to the GIIPS countries fell to values close to zero after the Lehman Brothers collapse. The GIIPS countries were, so to say, no longer able to generate a deficit of their current account financed by commercial capital flows.

They were, however, unable to generate a surplus in their balance of the current account either for the reason that earlier investment expenditures were not steered into sectors where the countries involved could hold comparative advantages, but were concentrated primarily in the sector of non-tradeables (such as housing, local bank services and so on). Notice that under this scenario the capital structure in both regions would have experienced notable changes vis-à-vis the first scenario: the natural rate of interest is now high (low) in the GIIPS (GLNF) countries, the production of consumption goods is relatively high (low) in the GIIPS (GLNF) countries, whereas investment expenditures are weak (strong). Under this scenario, hence, the GIIPS (GLNF) countries could have moved towards later (earlier) stages of investment and towards less external imbalances.

In sharp contrast, the very real Target2 scenario after 2008 drives a wedge between the preferences of consumers and the production decisions of entrepreneurs. In both regions, a new internal and external disequilibrium emerges: 'Toward the end of 2010 . . . accumulated imports [of the GIIPS countries] amounted to . . . 44 billion Euros. This was 12% of the entire capital requirement created by the current account deficit. Fully 88% was evidently financed by the Target balances, i.e. by the money-printing press' (Sinn and Wollmershäuser 2011, p. 32). For the sake of simplicity we assume that 100 per cent of the current account deficit was financed by the Target balances as this assumption does not change the general results of our subsequent analysis significantly.

Due to the expansionary (contractive) effects of Target2 liabilities (claims) on the original monetary base in the GIIPS (GLNF) countries, the effective market rate of interest falls (rises) below (above) the natural rate in the GIIPS (GLNF) countries. It is an increased (lowered) supply of loanable funds that causes the effective market interest rate to fall (rise). Obviously, this is not the money market interest rate, but the effective rate commercial banks charge borrowers for credits in the respective area or region. Put this way, if it would not be an effective rate of interest charged to the borrowing real sector of the economy, it would be inconceivable to observe higher imports (likewise exports) than ordinary capital flows can explain. The newly created central bank money through Target2 (ΔMT) drives a wedge between savings and investments. Consumers in the GIIPS (GLNF) countries take their decisions according to their respective savings function, investors analogously according to their respective overall investment function. The new savings curve S(i) $\pm$ ΔMT symbolizes the respective supply of loanable funds in the GIIPS/GLNF countries including the credit supply provided by Target2. There is now an excess demand ED (excess supply ES) for consumer goods in the GIIPS (GNLF) area. As Figure 4.4 demonstrates, the concomitant excess demand (supply) of consumer goods in the GIIPS (GLNF) countries together with the increase, $+\Delta$I (drop, $-\Delta$I), in investment expenditures in the GIIPS (GLNF) countries matches the increase in Target2 liabilities (claims) respectively. The impact on Von Hayek's triangle and the structure of capital is about the same as in scenario (i), but quite different to that first scenario, the impact on the capital structure in the GLNF countries is now 'involuntary', mildly spoken.[5] Notice also that the productivity of intermediate goods as measured previously by the angle α (β) is now lower (higher) in the GIIPS (GLNF) countries as $\gamma < \alpha$ ($\delta > \beta$).[6]

Opposite to the first scenario, the impact of the now functioning Target2 mechanism forces the GLNF countries into an involuntary excess supply in the production of consumer goods along with a reduction of their domestic investment expenditures. In other words, the GIIPS countries are now in the position to enforce in their own economies – via the Target2 operations – an excess demand for consumer goods along with an increase in investment expenditures.

4.2.2.3 A static welfare evaluation of Target balances
In Figure 4.5, we now have the possibility to compare our three scenarios (with rearranged numbering) in terms of static welfare, that is, rent units:[7]

1. The years mid 2007 to 2012 if Target2 would not have been operative (former scenario (ii)) are represented by the equilibria 'in autarky' G and G'; these solutions serve henceforth as a reference for the subsequent welfare evaluation.

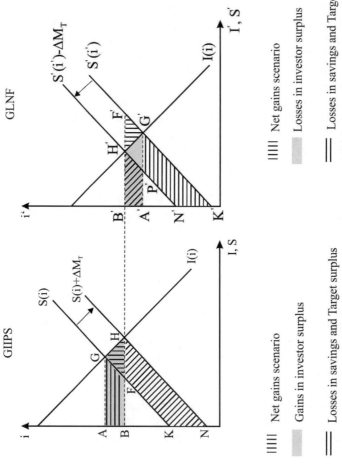

Source: Author.

Figure 4.5 The rent shift from GANL to GIIPS countries via the Target2 mechanism

2. The years 1999 to mid 2007 (former scenario (i)) led to capital inflows (outflows) in the size of FH (H′F′); in both economic clusters we record a net welfare gain corresponding to the triangles FGH and H′F′G′ (vertically dashed), a result that is very well known from economic textbooks. In the GIIPS countries, the gains in investors' rent (grey shaded) outweigh the losses in savers' rent (AGFB) while in the GLNF countries the gains in savers' rent (B′F′G′A′) outweigh the losses in investors' rent (grey shaded). We are aware of the fact that this welfare balance is somewhat optimistic.
3. The years mid 2007 to 2012 with Target2 being operative and effective are somewhat more complicated to be evaluated (former scenario (iii)). Starting with the GIIPS countries, there are gains in investors' rent to an amount of AGHB (grey shaded, identical with scenario (ii)). At the same time, there are now gains in rent that accrue both to savers but also to the Target2 mechanism corresponding to the difference between the area KFHN (diagonally dashed) and the area AGFB (horizontally dashed). Overall, we find gains in savers' and Target2 rent so that the Target2 scenario leads to net welfare gains for the GIIPS countries that exceed the gains of the second scenario.

In contrast, the GLNF countries suffer from net welfare losses due to the Target2 mechanism: the small area of gains that accrue to savers and Target2 B′H′P′A′ (diagonally dashed) are outweighed by the losses of investors' rent B′H′G′A′ (grey shaded, identical with scenario (ii)) and the large area of losses that accrue to savers and Target2 N′P′G′K′ (horizontally dashed). Notice that the Target2 scenario hence produces a net welfare transfer from the GLNF countries to the GIIPS countries where the overall welfare balance for both clusters of countries should converge to zero. That is, what we find is a zero-sum game with the GLNF countries losing in this distributional contest and the GIIPs countries winning. This result matches the earlier finding that the aggregated effects of the Target2 balances on the monetary base add up to nil at the ECB level.

4.2.3 The Distributional Conflict in an Imperfect Capital Market

Brakman et al. (2006) have objected that the 'naive' construction of market equilibria for savings and investment does not take into account the insights won by modern capital market theory. The latter advises economists to consider the phenomenon of asymmetric information that can be divided into the so-called adverse selection and the moral hazard problem (Brakman et al. 2006, p. 211). In the following, we especially highlight the effects that accrue to the existence of asymmetric information.

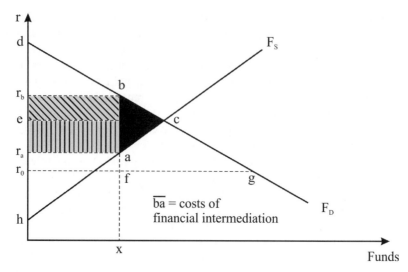

Source: Author's compilation based on Brakman et al. (2006).

Figure 4.6   Equilibrium on the imperfect capital market

In Figure 4.6 we show the details. On the x axis we measure total supply and demand for Funds on the capital market, on the y axis we have the real rate of interest, r. The slope of the demand function (F_D) is negative and assumed to be linear. The supply function may be horizontal as long as (only) firms finance investment with internal sources (retained profits) with implicit costs of size r_0, which correspond to the risk-free return on government bonds. In such a risk-free world, we would expect capital market equilibrium at point g. Once firms run out of internal finance, they depend on the upward supply curve section of F_s, which will be steeper, *ceteris paribus*, the more pronounced asymmetric information is between borrowers and lenders. Notice that the horizontal part of the supply curve only represents the total economy if savings of private households are neglected. However, the results to be derived do not hinge upon the assumption of a horizontal supply curve. The latter could well start at h and behave 'normally'. The existence of financial intermediation costs drives a wedge between the effective costs for investors (r_b) and the effective yield for savers (r_a). This wedge will be lower (higher) the less (more) significant adverse selection and moral hazard among borrowers are. The wedge is also affected negatively by the efficiency of the banking sector. The latter, in turn, should be a function of the degree of competition prevailing in this sector.

At financial intermediation costs of size ba, no more than x will materialize as the amount of investment financed in the economy. This is not surprising at all; the interesting aspect for us is that the banking sector now becomes a strategic actor in the distributional contest between savers and investors. Again, the rent concept gives us important hints. At the hypothetical equilibrium located in point c, savers and investors would distribute total rent (triangle dce for investors and triangle ech for savers) within themselves. In the case of existing financial intermediation costs, investors' rent is reduced to the triangle dbr_b, and savers' rent to the area har_a. The banking sector now appropriates the income bar_br_a. This is their compensation for bearing the risks associated with adverse selection and moral hazard and for undertaking the different transformation tasks typical for the financial sector (risk transformation, maturity transformation and so on). Notice also that the economy as a whole loses welfare to the amount of the triangle abc.

4.3   BARGAINING SOLUTIONS IN THE CAPITAL MARKET

The European debt crisis is probably a good example for the struggle between borrowers and lenders on the capital market. Borrowing countries are located in the periphery of the Eurozone, on the one hand, and lending countries in the core of the Eurozone, the rest of the EU and, ultimately, in the rest of the world (ROW), on the other hand. Borrowing countries will hope to keep the interest rate level low in order to protect their overall liquidity and solvency. Lending countries, however, have their own incentives for charging high interest rates to the borrowing countries. The price of the credit, in their view, should reflect the risk of a default.

An appropriate setting to demonstrate the contest on the terms of the credit in a two-person environment is the well-known inter-temporal consumption choice model. There are two households/agents, each can choose between alternative bundles of homogeneous consumption goods available in the present or in the future period. In the beginning, each household is provided with an initial endowment of future and present consumption goods. However, any of the two households may depart from their initial endowment point by entering into an exchange with the other household. This is likely, for example, when one of the households has a high time preference and wants to exchange some of its future consumption goods for present consumption goods. This, in turn, is only viable if the household signs an obligation/credit contract in which it promises to pay back the equivalent of the present consumption goods – including an interest rate element – in the future to the other household. Assuming for reasons of simplicity an additive inter-temporal utility function, we have:

$$U(C_t, C_{t+1}) = U[C_t] + U\left[\frac{C_{t+1}}{1+\rho}\right] \tag{4.1}$$

where $(1 / 1+\rho)$ equals the discount factor applied to future consumption and ρ is the symbol for the time preference. In our example, we assume household 1 to have a high time preference; it is willing to borrow present consumption goods from household 2 at a maximum interest rate of 10 per cent. In other words, household 1 is willing to exchange (for example) 100 units of present consumption (to borrow) goods against 110 units of future consumption goods (to pay back). The marginal rate of substitution (MRS) of the respective household is given by:

$$\left.\frac{dC_2}{dC_1}\right|_{\overline{U}^1} = MRS^1_{C_1,C_2} = -\frac{110}{100} = -(1+r) = -1.10 \tag{4.2}$$

For the second household we assume:

$$\left.\frac{dC_2}{dC_1}\right|_{\overline{U}^2} = MRS^2_{C_1,C_2} = -\frac{105}{100} = -(1+r) = -1.05 \tag{4.3}$$

Household 2, hence, is willing to give up 100 units of present consumption goods in exchange for 105 units of future consumption goods. Its implicit interest rate thus amounts to a minimum of 5 per cent. How can both households get to seal a deal? This is obviously the case whenever household 2 receives an interest rate of or higher than 5 per cent, and if household 1 is willing to pay an interest rate of or lower than 10 per cent. In the bargaining equilibrium, an exchange of goods and hence an implicit credit contract will be agreed on by the two households at a unique real rate of interest (which, by the way, must equal the marginal productivity of capital) and at identical marginal rates of substitution between future and present consumption goods for the two households. The distributional conflict hence is embodied in the interest rate margin, which is in the range between 5 and 10 per cent. A sort of equal distribution of risks between the borrower and the lender would imply an interest rate of 7.5 per cent.

In Figure 4.7, we find the graphical solution to the problem well known from textbooks: Y stands for the arbitrarily chosen 'endowment point' in the beginning. The corresponding inter-temporal indifference curves build the famous 'lens' known from any other Edgeworth box. At Y, the MRS differ between the households. This is visualized in the figure by the different angles (tan α > tan β) that the tangents have at the respective indifference curves. A possible equilibrium that enables an exchange of goods is at Z; here, the interest rate factor $(1 + r)$ and the marginal rates

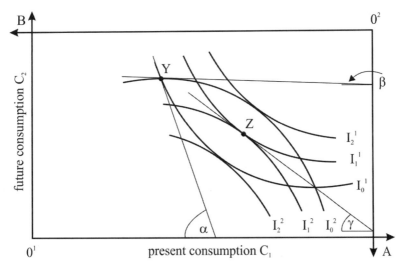

Source: Author.

Figure 4.7 Lending and borrowing in the inter-temporal consumption choice model

of substitution of the two households do harmonize (tan γ). Compared to point Y, household 1 and household 2 achieve higher levels of utility. Household 1 (2) realizes a higher (lower) consumption in the present in exchange for a lower (higher) consumption in the future period. A possible numerical case for point Z could be:

$$\left.\frac{dC_2}{dC_1}\right|_{\bar{U}^1} = \left.\frac{dC_2}{dC_1}\right|_{\bar{U}^2} = \text{MRS}^1_{C_1,C_2} = \text{MRS}^2_{C_1,C_2} = -\frac{107}{100} = -(1+r) = -1.07 \tag{4.4}$$

Hence, the creditor and the debtor household sign a credit contract with a (real) interest rate of 7 per cent, which is less than what initially household 1 was prepared to pay, but more than household 2 was inclined to ask for. From a distributional perspective, the interest rate of 7 per cent gives a small (dis)advantage to the (lender) borrower.

Figure 4.8 goes beyond the insights gained from Figure 4.7. As well known from traditional Edgeworth box analysis, Z is not the only possible exchange outcome between the two agents. If 'market power' is not divided equally between the two involved parties, agent 1 (agent 2) may enforce an exploitation solution as depicted in point X (U). Inactivity (Y), however,

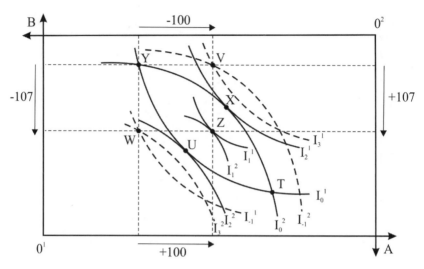

Source: Author.

Figure 4.8   Fraud in the inter-temporal consumption choice model

is already an inferior solution, as agent 1 (agent 2) – at a given utility level of agent 2 (agent 1) – cannot gain higher utility levels as opposed to the exploitation alternative. The latter solution, in turn, will give rise to a strong interest in searching for ways to disentangle/destroy the obvious market power on the other side. What happens when we come to comment on points such as V or W? In the first case (V), agent 1 would appropriate 100 units of present consumption goods for himself without handing out the obligation/security to agent 2, which, being an enforceable contract, promises the delivery of 107 units of future consumption goods in the next period. In the second case (W), agent 2 would appropriate the mentioned security without delivering in exchange the promised amount of present consumption goods (100 units).

Realizations such as the points V or W do not only represent the actions of perpetrator and victim in a (personal) fraud scenario, they should also shake the overall trust in the feasibility of exchange transactions on the credit market. The utility levels achieved by either agent 2 in the case of V or agent 1 in case of W are far below those utility levels achievable by inactivity (Y) and also below those 'produced' by exploitation (U, X). Hence, they give incentives to abstain from exchange transactions in the future and prevent agents from repeating successful bilateral exchange.

Graphical models such as those depicted in Figures 4.7 and 4.8 are able

Table 4.1 Nash equilibria in the simultaneous creditor-debtor game

	C	E	D
C	(+100, +100) (y→z)	(+ 90, 110) (y→u)	(−100, +100) (y→w)
E	(110, + 90) (y→x)	(0.5 x 110 + ** 0.5 x 90; 100 0.5 x 90 + 0.5 x 110) 100	(−100, +90) (y→ v; y→x)
D	(+100, −100) (y → v)	(+90, −110) (y→u; y→w)	(−100, −100)* (y→v; y→w)

Source: Author.

to reveal possible solutions on the credit market that reflect the distributional conflict between borrowers and lenders, but not necessarily the likely
outcomes. The latter, in turn, can be obtained from a careful game-theoretic
analysis of the above puzzle. For that we have designed a simultaneous
matrix game between creditor and debtor (Table 4.1). Each player has three
strategies: cooperate (C), exploit (E) and defect (D). All payoffs represent
either actual payments or present values of future payments. Hence, point
Z could be characterized by (100, 100) because the present value of 107
units for the lending party is: $107/(1 + 0.07) = 100$. All payoffs seem to be
clear and plausible with the exception of the combination E/E: when both
agents intend to exploit the contesting other agent, two results may emerge.
We may find ourselves left with the alternative of inactivity, which stands
for no exchange at all. This would give us the payoffs (0, 0). A different reasoning seems more plausible. Both players intend to exploit their adversary
(110), but take the risk of being exploited themselves (90). Each of these
outcomes has a probability of 0.5 if we refer to the 'principle of insufficient

reason'. Hence the expected payoff for each agent is 0.5 × 110 + 0.5 × 90 = 100. All other payoffs in Table 4.1 are almost self-explanatory. Where then is the equilibrium in the creditor-debtor game? As the reader may easily confirm, for each player there do not exist even (weak) dominant strategies. Making use of the cell-by-cell inspection technique, we find two non-cooperative Nash equilibria: one is located in the very centre of the matrix at the combination of strategies E/E (two stars). The other material-izes at the combination D/D (one star). Notice also that there is equivalence between the payoffs of C/C and E/E: mutual cooperation is not worse in terms of payoffs than the expected value of exploitation/being exploited. But as mutual cooperation is not Nash equilibrium, only banking supervi-sion is capable to enforce fair contracts in the credit market!

4.4   THE POLITICAL ECONOMY OF THE CAPITAL MARKET

The dividend irrelevance proposition goes back to Modigliani and Miller (1958). Modigliani and Miller state that stockholders are indifferent about receiving dividends or acknowledging a price appreciation (increase in the capital value) of their shares. In fact, 'paying out earnings as dividends or retaining them to finance new investment is strictly equivalent from the point of view of shareholder wealth' (Howells and Bain 2007, p. 178):

$$\overline{K} = \frac{D_1}{P_0} + g \ \text{ or } \ P_0 = \frac{D_1}{\overline{K} - g} \tag{4.5}$$

The first equation explains the rate of return $(\overline{K})$ one can expect from investing in shares. The latter can be disaggregated in the real rate of return from dividends D_1 / P_0, and the percentage increase in the value of capital:

$$g = \frac{P_1 - P_0}{P_0} \tag{4.6}$$

where P_t (where $t = 0,1$) stands for the price of the share (Howells and Bain 2008, p. 360) in period t.

What is the rationale of the irrelevance theorem? In the following, we present Gordon's version (see Brennan 1962, pp. 1116–17), which is slightly different from the original presented by Modigliani and Miller. Assume that the representative firm retains a constant fraction of its earnings per share $\lambda = (1-\phi)$ with ϕ = payout ratio and earns a constant average rate ω on its investment. If there is no outside finance, then

$$g = [\omega(1 - \phi)] = \omega\lambda, \text{ for } \lambda = (1 - \phi) \tag{4.7}$$

Let us define the current amount of dividends as the product of the payout ratio and the current amount of profits:

$$D_1 = \phi\pi \tag{4.8}$$

Substituting for g and D in the above formula for the share price gives:

$$P_0 = \frac{\phi\pi}{\overline{K} - (1 - \phi)\omega} \tag{4.9}$$

What is the effect of alternative retention ratios on the price of a share?

$$\frac{\partial P_0}{\partial (1 - \phi)} = \frac{(\omega - \overline{K})\pi}{[\overline{K} - (1 - \phi)\omega]^2} \tag{4.10}$$

Dividend policy is irrelevant and the value of the firm is independent of the dividend payment (McGowan 2005, p. 122) when the differentiation of the share price with regard to the payout ratio is zero. This is the case, as the numerator in the right-hand side of the equation shows, whenever the average rate of return ω equals the discount rate $\overline{K}$. In this case, all 'dividend policies are optimal because all [of them] imply identical stockholder wealth and so the choice among them is irrelevant' (De Angelo et al. 2006, p. 294).

However, this theorem is not interested in the structure or likewise composition of stockholders. The latter can be important though. Assume the following stylized facts:

- There are two groups of shareholders: many owning small shares and not so many provided with large shares.
- The many small stockholders have to face transaction costs when selling or buying shares.
- Furthermore, they have a high marginal propensity to consume, say between 0.5 and 1.
- The not so many stockholders with large shares have a low propensity to consume, say between 0 and 0.5, and face no transaction costs.
- Given these differences, there exists an intrinsic distributional conflict between the two groups of shareholders: the owners of small pieces of the firm definitely prefer dividends while the owners of large pieces prefer an increase in the capital value.
- From this setting with controversial interests we can deduct a rational partisan scenario.

- Shareholders' voting weights correspond to the value of their shares. Firms will choose a policy offering a high payout ratio (retention ratio) when there is a majority of votes assigned to stockholders with small (large) shares.

As a result, increases in the value of capital and the payment of dividends are incomplete and hence not fully equivalent substitutes. Let us explain our argument in more detail.

For this, we now turn to a less perfect, but perhaps more realistic view of the world. Both types (small, large) of shareholders will have a utility function of the form:

$$U = U(g, D_1/P_0) = U(g, d) \text{ for } d = D_1/P_0 \qquad (4.11)$$

Notice that in this setting, small (large) shareholders have a higher (lower) preference for dividends and a lower (higher) preference for increases in the value of capital:

$$U^s(g, d) = g^{\alpha_s} d^{\beta_s} \qquad (4.12)$$

$$U^l(g, d) = g^{\alpha_l} d^{\beta_l} \qquad (4.13)$$

$$\text{with } \alpha_1 > \alpha_s; \beta_s > \beta_1$$

Utility maximization requires the following Lagrange functions:

$$L^s(g, d) = g^{\alpha_s} d^{\beta_s} + \lambda[\overline{K} - d - g] \qquad (4.14)$$

$$L^l(g, d) = g^{\alpha_l} d^{\beta_l} + \lambda[\overline{K} - d - g] \qquad (4.15)$$

The first order conditions for the small shareholders are:

$$\frac{\partial L^s(g, d)}{\partial g} = \alpha_s g^{\alpha_s - 1} d^{\beta_s} - \lambda = 0 \qquad (4.16)$$

$$\frac{\partial L^s(g, d)}{\partial d} = \beta_s g^{\alpha_s} d^{\beta_s - 1} - \lambda = 0 \qquad (4.17)$$

$$\frac{\partial L^s(g, d)}{\partial \lambda} = \overline{K} - d - g = 0 \qquad (4.18)$$

Combining the first and the second first order condition leads to:

$$\beta_s g^{\alpha_s} d^{\beta_s - 1} = \alpha_s g^{\alpha_s - 1} d^{\beta_s} \qquad (4.19)$$

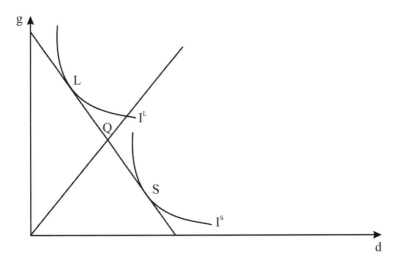

Source: Author.

Figure 4.9 The partisan model for payout and retention policies

$$\frac{\alpha_s}{\beta_s} = \frac{g^{\alpha_s} d^{\beta_s - 1}}{g^{\alpha_s - 1} d^{\beta_s}} = \frac{g^{\alpha_s}}{g^{\alpha_s - 1}} \cdot \frac{d^{\beta_s}}{d^{\beta_s - 1}} = \frac{g}{d} \qquad (4.20)$$

Analogous conditions exist for the large shareholders. If each group of shareholders could vote alone, Figure 4.9 shows the alternative optima (L, S) and the respective combinations of g and d. If the voting power is distributed equally among large and small shareholders, the firm's management will have to offer a compromise as in Q. Notice that such an outcome can be the result of a 'large coalition' between the two grand parties of the political spectrum existing among shareholders.

What is then the political economy of the capital market issue related to the distributional conflict? An important aspect is related to the payout vis-à-vis retention policies of firms quoted on the stock exchange.

Firms in Germany (Adler and Schmid 2012, p. 8) tend to offer rather stable payout levels/dividend payments. That is, when the size of profits falls (rises), the payout ratio is adjusted upwards (downwards). This is a strong hint that backs the hypothesis that the associated firms act as partisans for (this time in favour of) the group of small stockholders: stabilizing dividend payments to become a foreseeable stream of income helps the small stockholders to smooth their consumption expenditures (Kibet et al. 2010, p. 73).[8]

Large and small stockholders accumulate wealth not only when the capital value of the firm increases but also when they save to a different extent the payouts of the firm (see above). A small numerical example can illustrate the case. Assume each group of stockholders (as an aggregate) receives dividends per period to an amount of 100; while the large stockholders have on average, say, a savings ratio of 0.5, the small stockholders' savings ratio is 0.25. After 20 periods – without any interest effects taken into account and assuming saved money to be invested outside the company – the derived wealth of large stockholders amounts to 1000 while the small stockholders' non-company wealth sums up to only 500. Hence, *ceteris paribus*, large stockholders account for two thirds of total non-company wealth after a rather short period of observation.

4.5   EMPIRICAL FACTS AND FIGURES

We know already from the Modigliani-Miller theorem that realized capital gains are more or less perfect substitutes for dividend payments. Given the assumptions from above, we would expect the (not so) wealthy stockholders to have a slight preference for (dividends) realized capital gains. In countries like Sweden (Roine and Waldenström 2011), one can observe since the early 1980s declining dividend and interest income (as a share of total income) whereas realized capital gains (as a share of total income) have increased considerably. This development went alongside a rising share of top income earners (as a percentage of GDP). Hence, it seems to be here that realized capital gains have or at least signal a regressive impact on the distribution of incomes.

An important empirical question that addresses directly (and not indirectly as in the Swedish exercise above) the distribution of wealth in the capital market is: how strong is the concentration of company stock holdings? In the case of Germany, the findings point to a concentration of company stock holdings, as an 'increase of undistributed profits is likely to imply rising values of business assets and may lead to increasing capital income of stock holders in the future. Given a comparably high concentration of company stock holdings within the population, this may result in an increase of the concentration of [capital] market income' (Adler and Schmid 2012, p. 18).

In order to test the validity of the political economy approach, we investigate in the following on a national level for Germany the development of corporate profits, payouts and profit retentions in the years 1991 to 2010. In Figure 4.10, we can observe an upward trend in the evolution of corporate profits (left scale), only interrupted by the worldwide economic crisis during 2007–09. At the same time, the payout quota (right scale) exhibits a cyclical pattern. This impression tends to foster the hypothesis that firms have favoured planned payouts vis-à-vis *planned* retentions of profits.

To get a more accurate impression, we have calculated (Figure 4.11)

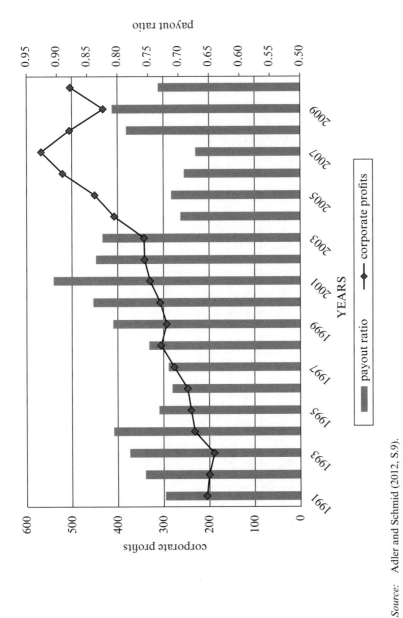

Source: Adler and Schmid (2012, S.9).

Figure 4.10 Corporate profits and payout ratio in Germany (1991–2010)

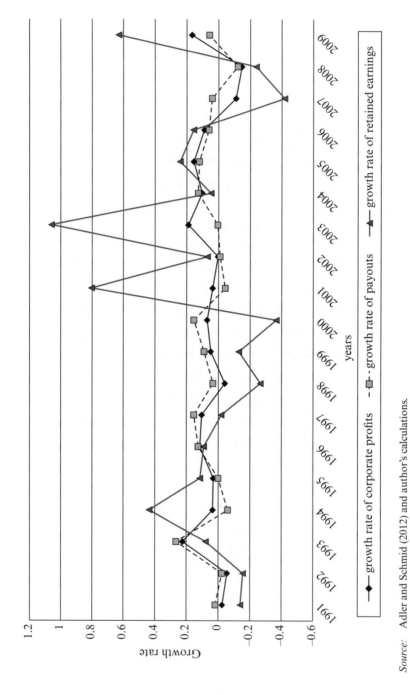

Source: Adler and Schmid (2012) and author's calculations.

Figure 4.11   The growth rate of corporate profits, payouts and retained earnings in Germany (1991–2009)

the growth rates for all of the three relevant variables: profits, retentions of profits and payouts. It is fair to say that the correlation between the growth rates of corporate profits and payouts is far ahead of the correlation between the growth rate of profits and retentions. This finding again supports the idea that retentions play a residual role whereas payouts are planned.

NOTES

1. Notice that even a much more backward bending supply curve such as S″ is theoretically feasible, but will not be considered in the balance of rents.
2. For reasons of simplicity, we disregard the backward bending phenomenon in the savings curve.
3. A more detailed description of the ABCT can be found in Garrison (2001), De Soto (2009) and Ravier (2001).
4. Notice that 'the slope of the hypotenuse of the Hayekian triangle reflects the market-clearing rate of interest in the market for loanable funds. "Reflects" is a strong . . . a connection as can be made here . . . the slope of the hypotenuse and the market-clearing rate of interest will move in the same direction' (Garrison 2001, pp. 47–8).
5. As a matter of fact, under the Target2 scenario being effective, capital exports from GLNF countries become involuntary. Instead of direct financial claims against GIIPS countries, the GLNF countries only acquire claims against the ECB and the European System of Central Banks respectively.
6. Notice that the angles γ and δ are not identical although market interest rates converge to $\tilde{i}$; this is not necessary (see above). It suffices that the angles must rise in the exporting countries and decrease in the importing countries.
7. The following analysis differs in at least two aspects from Sinn (2010). Firstly, we model flows of savings/investments instead of flows of capital goods. Secondly, we disregard the 'overheating effects' that are associated with the financing of investment expenditures by the GLNF countries in the GIIPS countries. As Sinn shows, such overshooting of capital outflows creates losses in GDP per capita terms for the capital exporting countries.
8. The tax effect is, in turn, the strongest argument in favour of low dividends. See Kibet et al. (2010, p. 77).

5. Income distribution and the business cycle

5.1 INTRODUCTION

Business cycle theory and policy came under fire during and after the Dotcom Boom of the information and communication technology at the beginning of the new millennium. Most respected economists and/or econometricians such as Clive W.J. Granger pointed out that the traditional cycle of economic activity was in principle over and, so to say, replaced by rather small variability in the (always positive) growth rates. He traced back this presumed development to the dynamics of the services or non-tradeables sector in all advanced economies that evolved and expanded to the detriment of the (tradeable) industrialized sector. In many of the well-known textbooks on macroeconomics, earlier chapters on the business cycle simply faded away. Famous macroeconomists made statements such as that of Robert E. Lucas Jr at the convention of the American Economic Association in the year 2002: 'Its central problem of depression prevention has been solved, for all practical purposes, and has been solved for many decades.' At the same conference, Edward Cristian Prescott advanced the argument that 'business cycle theory . . . provides little guidance to policy except for the important implication that a stabilization effort will have either no effects or a perverse effect'.

This optimism was, if anything, premature as the deep and worldwide economic crisis in 2008/09 showed dramatically. But even without this event, the 'classical' industry cycle with its typical length of four to seven years and its four phases (upswing, boom, downswing and recession) proved to be rather robust. This observation can be reconciled with the above-mentioned point made by Clive W.J. Granger. When non-tradeables are to a large extent complements to and not substitutes of tradeables, a cycle of the tradeables will induce a cycle of the non-tradeables as well. Another stylized fact has proved to be robust too: during the phases of upswing and boom, the overall income distribution tends to change in favour of profits, while during the phases of downswing and recession the opposite is true, that is, income distribution tends to change in favour of labour income.

The chapter is organized as follows. In the next section, we model this process first as a 'market mechanism' in a two and then in a three persons or similar classes framework. Thereafter, we address the question of how the business cycle affects the bargaining between entrepreneurs and unions and the resulting income distribution between profits and wages. Finally, we present a political economy model of the business cycle where the concentration of personal incomes is endogenized.

5.2 THE MARKET MECHANISM

Let us assume that our economy consists of two individuals ($1 = $ earner of profits and $2 = $ earner of wages) with the following consumption functions:

$$C_1 = c_1 y_1 + e \tag{5.1}$$

and

$$C_2 = c_2 y_2 + e_2 \tag{5.2}$$

with $c_i = $ marginal propensity to consume and $e_i = $ autonomous consumption.

Via aggregation we achieve:

$$C = C_1 + C_2 = c_1 y_1 + c_2 y_2 + e_1 + e_2 \tag{5.3}$$

If the marginal rates of consumption are identical, we have: $c_1 = c_2 = c$. This leads to:

$$c(y_1 + y_2) + e_1 + e_2 = cY + e \tag{5.4}$$

Notice that $Y = y_1 + y_2$ and $e = e_1 + e_2$.

If, however, the marginal rates of consumption are different ($c_1 \neq c_2$) and if both incomes are proportional to one another ($y_2 = v y_1$), then we can calculate:

$$Y = y_1 + y_2 = y_1 + v y_1 = (1 + v) y_1 \text{ or } y_1 = Y/(1 + v) \tag{5.5}$$

which implies:

$$C = C_1 + C_2 = c_1 y_1 + c_2 y_2 + e_1 + e_2 = (c_1 + v c_2) y_1 + e_1 + e_2 \tag{5.6}$$

Solving for total consumption gives:

$$C = \frac{c_1 + vc_2}{1 + v}Y + e = cY + e \qquad (5.7)$$

If not all marginal rates of consumption are identical, the macroeconomic or aggregate marginal rate of consumption function (c) is a weighted average of the individual consumption rates and changes according to variations in the income distribution:

$$C = c_1y_1 + c_2y_2 + e \qquad (5.8)$$

$$\frac{dC}{dY} = c_1\frac{dy_1}{dY} + c_2\frac{dy_2}{dY} \qquad (5.9)$$

Because $Y = y_1 + y_2$, it holds that: $1 = \dfrac{dy_1}{dY} + \dfrac{dy_2}{dY}$

This has an important repercussion on the marginal rate of consumption:

$$\frac{dC}{dY} = c_1\frac{dy_1}{dY} + c_2\left[1 - \frac{dy_1}{dY}\right] \qquad (5.10)$$

We are now able to show in a simple manner that due to changes in the distribution of income during the cycle a dampening effect may result from consumption expenditures. The different incomes are no longer proportional to each other. Following Nicholas Kaldor (1955), earners of wages (profits) exhibit a higher (lower) marginal rate of consumption. Let the consumption functions of person 1 be $C_1 = 0.5y_1 + 80$ and person 2 be $C_2 = 0.8y_2 + 50$.

Initially, we assign an income of 500 to both individuals ($y_1 = y_2 = 500$), so that $Y = 1000$. Total consumption then equals:

$$C = C_1 + C_2 = 0.5 \cdot 500 + 80 + 0.8 \cdot 500 + 50 = 780 \quad (5.11)$$

Let the upswing and boom phases of the cycle now raise total income by 100 units of income (UI). Total income is now 1100. Associated with this income increase is a change in the distribution of income. Let the new individual incomes amount to $y_1 = 590$ and to $y_2 = 510$. As a result, we have:

$$C_1 = 375; C_2 = 458; C = C_1 + C_2 = 833 \qquad (5.12)$$

Although each individual rate of consumption is positive, the increase in total income by 100 units goes along with a relative decline of total consumption. This is due to the stylized change in income distribution associated with upswing and boom phases: 833/1100 < 780/1000!

During downswing and recession phases of the cycle, the opposite will occur. A decrease of total income by 100 units from 1000 to 900 goes along with a change of income distribution so that $y_1 = 410$ and $y_2 = 490$. We achieve:

$$C_1 = 285; C_2 = 442; C = C_1 + C_2 = 727 \qquad (5.13)$$

This now implies an increase in the relative size of total consumption accompanied by a decrease in total income. The reason, again, lies in the change of income distribution, this time in favour of wage earners: 727/900 > 780/1000!

However, these results still suffer from a methodological weakness and lead to some sort of unsubstantiated optimism: reality looks pretty much more like a three persons or likewise three classes society. In such a society, the middle class plays an essential role.

As is well known, what is referred to as the 'Easterlin paradox' – a doubling of absolute income will not cause satisfaction to double too – can be relatively easily explained considering that most people are mainly interested in their own status compared to that of other people. In other words, their relative status is more important to them than their absolute income position (Lewitt and Dubner 2006, p. 24). The role of comparing and being compared (in the following, cf. Sell 1982) in determining individual consumption is described in unparalleled clarity by James Duesenberry, who states that 'the dissatisfaction with his consumption standard which an individual must undergo is a function of the ratio of his expenditures to those of people with whom he associates' (Duesenberry 1967, p. 32).

If dissatisfaction – or its opposite, satisfaction – is expressed by the utility index U_i we obtain, according to Duesenberry, the following individual utility function of an arbitrary economic subject i:

$$U_i = U_i(C_i / \Sigma \alpha_j C_j) \qquad (5.14)$$

Weight α_j indicates how strong consumer i assesses the influence of consumption expenditure by individual j on his own consumption expenditures. If this utility concept, which emphasizes the interdependence of acts of purchase, is applied to the evaluation of income redistribution measures, cases may occur where 'a decrease in inequality might increase the average propensity to save' (Duesenberry 1967, p. 44). Duesenberry's ideas were taken up by Harry G. Johnson (1951, 1952a, 1952b, 1971). The latter from the very beginning intended to investigate the exact character of the interdependence of acts of purchase with a view to income redistribution measures and possible multiplier effects on income. Johnson considers the parenthesized expression in the utility function to stand for relative consumption, with the weighting factors α_j assuming decisive importance (Johnson 1951, p. 295). Let

$$C_{i \text{ relative}} = \frac{C_i}{\Sigma \alpha_j C_j} \tag{5.15}$$

so that:

$$U_i = U_i(C_{i \text{ relative}}); U_i' > 0, U_i'' < 0 \tag{5.16}$$

Using two simple numerical examples, Johnson explains two alternative characteristics of the consumer behaviour of a community consisting of three classes or three individuals. In the first case of a three-person community (A, B, C), it shall be known that in the initial condition, consumption is distributed as follows:

$$C_A = 50, \ C_B = 100, \ C_C = 150 \tag{5.17}$$

Further, 'middle income class man' B shall allocate a weight of $\alpha_{BA} = \frac{1}{4}$ to the consumption of 'lower income class man' A, whereas he allocates a weight of $\alpha_{BC} = \frac{3}{4}$ to the consumption of 'higher income class man' C for the determination of his own relative consumption:

$$C_{B \text{ relative}} = \frac{100}{\frac{1}{4}50 + \frac{3}{4}150} = 4/5 \tag{5.18}$$

Now let us do a redistribution from C to A, whereby it is assumed that B's income is not impaired. It shall be known that this is done to an extent such that

$$C_A = 75, \ C_C = 125 \tag{5.19}$$

This means that:

$$C_{B \text{ relative}} = \frac{100}{\frac{1}{4}75 + \frac{3}{4}125} = 8/9 \tag{5.20}$$

Since $8/9 > 4/5$, according to Johnson the satisfaction of B has increased, *ceteris paribus*, which will cause him to restrict his own consumption to values below 100 with his income unchanged. The exact amount can be computed:

$$4/5 = \frac{C_i^{new}}{1/4 \cdot 75 + 3/4 \cdot 125}; C_i^{new} = 90 \qquad (5.21)$$

The quantity of α_{BC} (= 3/4) is an expression of the 'middle class person' B's effort to keep up with the consumption of the higher earner C, that is, to 'emulate' him. This is the behaviour typically found in an 'emulative society' (Johnson 1971, p. 166), which is also referred to as 'keeping up with the Joneses'. If the role model restricts his consumption, his lead obviously becomes smaller. This reduces my attempts at emulating him, thus curbing my own consumption. Accordingly, in such an 'emulative society', there is the possibility that an income redistribution from rich to poor will not increase aggregate consumption of a given income, but reduce it (because 75 + 90 + 125 < 50 + 100 + 150). Note that the latter result, among other things, is fundamentally opposed to Kaldor's strongly disputed distribution theory.

In the opposite case, B orients himself more towards A, whose income is lower, that is, B wants to always have a sufficiently large lead over A with respect to the quantity and quality of the consumer goods. Then, the values are, for example, $\alpha_{BC} = 1/4$, $\alpha_{BA} = 3/4$.

Accordingly, before redistribution let:

$$C_{B\,relative} = \frac{100}{3/4 \cdot 50 + 1/4 \cdot 150} = 4/3 \qquad (5.22)$$

However, after redistribution (see above) the following applies:

$$C_{B\,relative} = \frac{100}{3/4 \cdot 75 + 1/4 \cdot 125} = 8/7 \qquad (5.23)$$

Because 4/3 > 8/7, B's feeling of utility will decrease as a result of redistribution, and his motivation to extend his own consumption will increase (see Johnson 1951, pp. 296–7). The exact amount can be computed:

$$4/3 = \frac{C_i^{new}}{3/4 \cdot 75 + 1/4 \cdot 125}; C_i^{new} = 113.33 \qquad (5.24)$$

Johnson refers to this type of behaviour as superiority (in a later paper, he uses the somewhat misleading term 'competition', cf. Johnson 1952a, p. 141), and he also uses the expression 'keeping ahead of the Smiths'. More generally speaking, this is a situation where everyone tries to maintain his lead over those who are below him in the income hierarchy. As a result, in such a 'lead-oriented society', there is the possibility that an income redistribution from rich to poor will not reduce the aggregate consumption of a given income, but increase it (because 75 + 113.33 + 125 > 50 + 100 + 150). Note that in this case the tendency of Kaldor's results is confirmed.

However, the two above examples are not pure mental exercises but quite well symbolize the downturn in the economic cycle where wage agreements that lag behind lead to a reduction in profits and profit margins. In this case, the following applies: if an attitude of 'keeping ahead of the Smiths' (superiority) prevails over emulation ('keeping up with the Joneses'), the middle class ensures that consumer demand stabilizes (is further reduced) and thus mitigates (increases) the downturn.

In the following, we shall extend the different cases distinguished by Johnson, thus also going beyond him. In doing so, we shall apply our experiment inversely to the way it was applied before, so to speak, which represents an existing upswing in the cycle. The redistribution carried out now is from A to C, whereby it is assumed that B's income is not impaired. It shall be known that this will have the following consequence:

$$C_A = 25, \ C_C = 175 \tag{5.25}$$

Further, it shall initially apply that B allocates a weight of $\alpha_{BA} = \frac{1}{4}$ to the consumption of A and a weight of $\alpha_{BC} = \frac{3}{4}$ to the consumption of C for the determination of his own relative consumption. Before redistribution, the following applies (see above): $C_{B\,relative} = 4/5$. Afterwards, the following applies:

$$C_{B\,relative} = \frac{100}{\frac{1}{4}\,25 + \frac{3}{4}\,175} = 100/137.5 \tag{5.26}$$

Since $100/137.5 < 4/5$, according to Johnson the satisfaction of B has decreased, *ceteris paribus*, which will cause him to extend his own consumption to values above 100, with his income unchanged. The exact amount can be computed:

$$4/5 = \frac{C_i^{new}}{1/4 \cdot 25 + 3/4 \cdot 175}; C_i^{new} = 110 \tag{5.27}$$

Accordingly, during times of upswing, aggregate demand is even increased in an emulative society as a result of the middle class's consumption. In the opposite case, B orients himself more towards A, whose income is lower. If so, by analogy to the above example, the values shall, for example, be: $\alpha_{BC} = \frac{1}{4}$, $\alpha_{BA} = \frac{3}{4}/4$. Accordingly, before redistribution, the following applies (see above):

Table 5.1 Consumer interdependence and the business cycle

Phase / Behaviour	'Keep up with the Joneses' dominates	'Keep ahead of the Smiths' dominates
Upswing	**Upswing is reinforced**	Cycle is being stabilized
Downswing	Downswing is reinforced	**Cycle is being stabilized**

Source: Author.

$$C_{B\,relative} = 4/3 = 1.33 \tag{5.28}$$

However, after redistribution, the following applies:

$$C_{B\,relative} = \frac{100}{\frac{3}{4}\,25 + \frac{1}{4}\,175} = 100/62.5 = 1.6 \tag{5.29}$$

Because 1.6 > 1.33, B's feeling of utility will, however, now increase as a result of redistribution, and he will be likely to reduce his own consumption. The exact amount can be computed:

$$4/3 = \frac{C_i^{new}}{3/4 \cdot 25 + 1/4 \cdot 175}; C_i^{new} = 83.33 \tag{5.30}$$

In a society characterized by the desire to 'keep ahead of the Smiths', aggregate demand will more likely be curbed by the consumption of the middle class in periods of economic upswings.

If the cases investigated by Johnson himself as well as those added and evaluated by us are analysed, the overall result is a system of effects that is certainly of interest to economic research – an overview is given in the matrix above (Table 5.1). The cells with bold text are of particular relevance. Since it is a stylized fact that income distribution changes in favour of lower (upper) income groups during the downswing (upswing) phases of the cycle, the behaviour of the middle class will be dominated by a 'keeping ahead of the Smiths' attitude in the case of a downswing and by a 'keeping up with the Joneses' attitude in the case of an upswing.[1] The latter pattern in consumption behaviour, in turn, is a signal for the existence of equity aversion as a social preference. We shall address this subject in much greater detail in Chapter 9. For the economic research on the business cycle it is a remarkable result that this social preference tends to dampen the effects of both downturns and upswings, thus smoothing the cycle.

5.3 LABOUR CONTRACTS AND THE BUSINESS CYCLE

Following the Right-to-Manage approach (see Cahuc and Zylberberg 2004, pp. 393–7), unions gain utility (U) from successful bargaining for their members. Utility increases stem from additional employment (L) and/or from higher wages (w) in comparison to the outside option of employees (w_A). If negotiations fail, the union's reservation level of utility is reduced to $(M - L) w_A$, where M is the given supply of labour:

$$U(w, L) = L \cdot w + (M - L) \cdot w_A \qquad (5.31)$$

Entrepreneurs, in turn, register an increase in profits (π) in line with the difference between revenues y (L) and labour costs wL once production in the relevant sector is started. Firms will begin with production only after signing a labour contract with the unions.

$$\pi = y(L) - w \cdot L \qquad (5.32)$$

In order to achieve the Nash solution, five prerequisites have to be fulfilled:

- Only those solutions are considered where neither unions nor firms realize losses vis-à-vis the no-bargaining situation.
- $\pi \geq \pi_0$; $U \geq U_0$, where $U_0 = Mw_A$ and $\pi_0 \geq 0$
- So-called 'invariance': any viable solution should be independent from the units in which utility is measured.
- Any solution should be independent from irrelevant alternatives.
- Pareto-efficiency is to be guaranteed.

In Figure 5.1, we have depicted (solid line) a concave 'contract possibility curve' in analogy to the well-known 'production possibility or transformation curve'. To guarantee Pareto-efficiency, only solutions on the frontier line are viable. Moving upwards or downwards on the frontier line implies solutions where an increase in the utility of unions (profits of firms) is not possible unless it goes along with lower profits of firms (utility levels of unions).

Possible solutions:

- Point A: only unions realize a net bargaining revenue.
- Point B: both unions and firms realize a net bargaining revenue.
- Point C: only firms realize a net bargaining revenue.

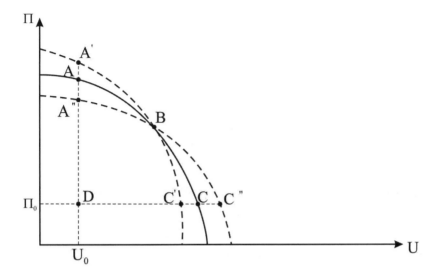

Source: Author.

Figure 5.1 The contract possibilities curve for unions and firms

- Point D: the position of the 'threatening point' is defined as the set of utilities/profits that is achievable to both parties if the negotiations fail (Π_0, U_0).
- Bargaining power of the distinct parties involved determines the point that can be reached on the frontier line.

The 'contract possibility curve', however, is not a static phenomenon: it is very much likely that it shifts according to phases of the business cycle. During upswing and boom, the dotted curve with associated points A′ and C′ becomes relevant, whereas during downswing and recession, the alternative dotted curve with associated points A″ and C″ replaces the solid frontier line. The message is clear: during upswing and boom, firms (unions) can (only) achieve higher (lower) levels of profits (utility), while in downswing and recession, unions (firms) have the potential to reach higher (only lower) levels of utility (profits).

Notice that relating total utility of unions to the total profits of the firms, one ends up with the ratio between the total wage sum (W) and total profits (Π), which is a simple measure for income distribution between labour and capital:

$$\Omega = W/\Pi = [L \cdot w + (M - L) \cdot w_A]/\Pi = Y/\Pi - 1 \qquad (5.33)$$

5.4   INCOME DISTRIBUTION AND THE POLITICAL BUSINESS CYCLE: THE VERY SPECIAL CASE OF A MONETARY UNION

5.4.1   Introduction[2]

If national politicians are no longer in a position to determine their own rate of inflation once a monetary union has been established and for the existence of the union a significant level of unbalanced growth must be guaranteed – countries that are lagging behind with regard to levels of productivity must achieve overproportional growth rates[3] until they have made up lost ground – two objectives still remain from Tinbergen's (reduced) uneasy polygon of economic policy (1963, pp. 8–12) – full employment and an equitable distribution of income. It is important to realize that targeted balances of the current accounts between member countries of a monetary union cannot be (any longer) goals for national economic policy: if balances occur, these tend to simply reflect differences in external competitiveness of the respective countries. A planned surplus in the current account vis-à-vis other member countries makes no sense, either because in the medium to long run it will result in a too low domestic investment rate or because – as could be observed in the EMU between 2007 and 2013 – it may end up in cumulating Target2 balances (claims of surplus countries vis-à-vis the ECB versus liabilities of deficit countries vis-à-vis the ECB) against the ECB. The latter aspect is addressed in more detail in Chapter 4 (see above).

The question that now arises is whether it is rational for national governments participating in a monetary union, from the standpoint of maximizing one's votes in an election, to offer voters a particular combination of employment and income distribution objectives. It is often assumed that these two objectives are compatible, as it is argued that a more even distribution of income stimulates demand and, where there is unemployment, can lead to an 'increase in employment' (Blümle 1989a, p. 723). In this case (a), there will be a positive correlation between the goals of income distribution and employment: a reasonable optimum cannot then be determined. If, however, we take into consideration the income elasticities of different categories of goods and the trends to saturation in consumption that are explained by the fact that with time the share of relatively inferior goods grows, or the vast majority of income elasticities sink, an inverse correlation is also conceivable: relatively superior goods can open up saturated markets and as articles of conspicuous consumption can encourage imitation, 'a levelling of income distribution which lowers the number of these articles per head of the leaders in consumption can lead to an overproportional fall in demand' (Blümle 1988, p. 149). At the same time, there is an increase in the significance of goods for the maintenance of demand. A policy of levelling incomes against the group of leading consumers will consequently prove particularly dangerous for the long-run growth of demand. In this case (b), there appears to be a convex relationship between employment and income distribution; optima with employment and income distribution as references are no longer excluded.

5.4.2 Inequality of Income Distribution and Aggregate Demand

The following exposition draws heavily on Blümle (1988). Consider a representative household i, equipped with an income y_i and showing a demand for commodity j, x_{ij}. Total income (Y) and population (P) of the economy under observation are assumed to be constant:

$$x_j = \sum_i^n x_{ij} \ , \ i = 1 \ldots n \tag{5.34}$$

With n being the number of individuals in the economy,

$$Y = \sum_i^n y_i \tag{5.35}$$

$$\bar{x}_j = f(\bar{y}) \text{ with } \bar{y} = \frac{Y}{P} \text{ and } \bar{x}_j = \frac{x_j}{P} \tag{5.36}$$

Personal income distribution is characterized by the mean (μ_L) and the variance (σ_L^2) of the logarithm of incomes – following the theory of Gibrat, we may state:

$$\bar{y} = e^{\mu_L + \frac{1}{2}\sigma_L^2} = e^{\mu_L} e^{\frac{1}{2}\sigma_L^2} \tag{5.37}$$

$$\ln \bar{y} = \mu_L + \frac{1}{2}\sigma_L^2 \tag{5.38}$$

$$\mu_L = \ln \bar{y} - \frac{1}{2}\sigma_L^2 \tag{5.39}$$

A semi-logarithmic specification of the demand function is given by:

$$x_{ij} = a \ln y_i + b \tag{5.40}$$

Hence,

$$\sum_i^n x_{ij} = a \sum_i^n \ln y_i + nb \tag{5.41}$$

$$\frac{1}{n}\sum_{i}^{n} x_{ij} = \bar{x}_j = b + a\mu_L; a\mu_L = a\frac{1}{n}\sum_{i}^{n} \ln y_i \qquad (5.42)$$

Making use of the above definition for μ, we achieve:

$$\bar{x}_j = b + a \ln \bar{y} - \frac{a}{2}\sigma_L^2 \qquad (5.43)$$

Alternatively, we may approximate the demand schedule by a function with the property of being iso-elastic:

$$x_{ij} = by_i^a = e^\beta y_i^a, \text{ with } b = e^\beta \qquad (5.44)$$

As the log-normal distribution is reproductive, the distribution of $e^\beta y_i^a$ is as log-normal as y. Now the parameters of the distribution change from

$$e^{\mu_L}e^{\frac{1}{2}\sigma_L^2} \text{ to } e^{\beta + a\mu_L}e^{\frac{1}{2}a^2\sigma_L^2}: \overline{e^\beta y^a} = e^{\beta + a\mu_L}e^{\frac{1}{2}a^2\sigma_L^2} = \bar{x}_j \qquad (5.45)$$

Making use of $\bar{y} = e^{\mu_L}e^{\frac{1}{2}\sigma_L^2}$ and of $\bar{x}_j = e^{\beta + a\mu_L}e^{\frac{1}{2}a^2\sigma_L^2}$ helps to eliminate μ_L:

$$\ln \bar{y} = \mu_L + \frac{1}{2}\sigma_L^2 \rightarrow \mu_L = \ln \bar{y} - \frac{1}{2}\sigma_L^2 \qquad (5.46)$$

$$\ln \bar{x}_j = \beta + a\mu_L + \frac{1}{2}a^2\sigma_L^2 = \beta + a\left[\ln \bar{y} - \frac{1}{2}a\sigma_L^2\right] - \frac{1}{2}a^2\sigma_L^2 \qquad (5.47)$$

$$\ln \bar{x}_j = \beta + a \ln \bar{y} + \frac{1}{2}a\sigma_L^2(a - 1) \qquad (5.48)$$

Hence, taking into consideration the e-function, the demand per head for commodity x_j can be written as:

$$\bar{x}_j = b\bar{y}^a e^{\frac{a\sigma_L^2(a - 1)}{2}} \qquad (5.49)$$

The parameter a in the last equation can be identified with the income elasticity of demand. The following cases should be distinguished:

1. for $a < 0$, a higher σ_L^2 (a more unequal income distribution) leads to a higher demand for commodity j
2. for $0 < a < 1$, a higher σ_L^2 leads to a lower demand for commodity j
3. for $a > 1$, a higher σ_L^2 leads to a higher demand for commodity j.

In the special cases of a = 0 and a = 1, income distribution does not exert any influence on commodity demand. With leaders (group 1) and followers (group 2) in consumption patterns existing in the economy, it can be shown that bandwagon effects tend to strengthen the demand dampening effect of a more equal personal income distribution. As Blümle (1975, p. 151) puts it, the demand of a representative household k belonging to the lower income group 2 for commodity j can, then, be taken as:

$$x_{kj2} = f_{j2}[y_{k2}, x_{ij1}; x_{i+1j1}]; k = 1 \ldots m \qquad (5.50)$$

with m being the number of individuals belonging to the lower income group 2 and

$$\frac{\partial x_{kj2}}{\partial x_{ij1}} > 0 \quad \text{(Bandwagon effect)} \qquad (5.51)$$

Choosing again an iso-elastic version, we achieve:

$$x_{kj2} = e^{\beta_2} y_{k_2}^{a_2} x_{ij1}^{b_1} x_{i+1j1}^{b+1} \qquad (5.52)$$

For

$$x_{ij1} = e^{\beta_1} y_{i1}^{a_1} \qquad (5.53)$$

Hence,

$$x_{kj2} = e^{\beta_2} y_{k_2}^{a_2} e^{\beta_1(b_1 + b_{i+1} + 1)} y_{i1}^{a_1 b_i} y_{i+1j1}^{a_1 b_i + 1} \qquad (5.54)$$

Regarding, again, the average consumption per head (of group 2) leads to:

$$\bar{x}_{j2} = e^{(\beta_1 + \beta_2)(b_i + b_{i+1} + 1)} \bar{y}_2^{a_2} \bar{y}_1^{a_1(b_i + b_{i+1} + 1)} e^{\frac{1}{2} a_2^2 \sigma^2 (a_2 - 1)} e^{\frac{1}{2}(a_1 - 1)(b_1 + b_{i+1} + 1)} \qquad (5.55)$$

For positive values of b and constant values of $\bar{y}_1$ and $\bar{y}_2$ income elasticities of a_1 that are either negative or larger than one lead to a stimulation of demand – and so of employment – at a more unequal distribution of income within group 1 of consumers. While in the first case, a higher demand for the inferior goods makes this good progressively acceptable for group 2 as well, the second case shows an increasing demand for the luxury good, boosted by the example given by group 1 to group 2. Notice that in the terminology of the new theory of social preferences (Fehr and Schmidt 1999; Bolton and Ockenfels 2000), the motivation for group 2 to follow group 1 is intimately linked to the above introduced 'keep up with the Joneses' behaviour that signals inequity aversion.

5.4.3 Economic Targets During Monetary Union

The aggregate national voting functions – once a monetary union has been set up – may read as follows:

$$V_{1Mt} = g_{1m}(U_{1t}, \sigma_{L1t}) \tag{5.56}$$

$$V_{2Mt} = g_{2m}(U_{2t}, \sigma_{L2t}) \tag{5.57}$$

We define

$$\widetilde{W}_{1M} = \int_0^\infty g_{1M}(U_{1t}, \sigma_{L1t}) e^{-\mu_{1t}} dt \tag{5.58}$$

$$\widetilde{W}_{2M} = \int_0^\infty g_{2M}(U_{2t}, \sigma_{L2t}) e^{-\mu_{2t}} dt \tag{5.59}$$

as the respective social welfare functions during monetary union in both countries and μ_{it} as the discounting rate prevailing in country i, $\mu_{it} > 0$. The social welfare function is subject to the following constraints and/or assumptions:

$$\sigma_{L1t} = f(U_{1t}) - \lambda_1 \sigma_{L1t}^e \tag{5.60}$$

$$\sigma_{L2t} = f(U_{2t}) - \lambda_2 \sigma_{L2t}^e \tag{5.61}$$

with

$$\frac{\partial \sigma_{Lit}}{\partial U_{it}} = \frac{\partial f(U_{it})}{\partial U_{it}} = f'(U_{it}) < 0 \tag{5.62}$$

and

$$\dot{\sigma}_{L1t}^e = \gamma_1 [\sigma_{L1t} - \sigma_{L1t}^*] \tag{5.63}$$

$$\dot{\sigma}_{L2t}^e = \gamma_2 [\sigma_{L2t} - \sigma_{L2t}^*] \tag{5.64}$$

where

σ^*_{Lit} = natural standard deviation of logarithm of incomes; $\gamma_t < 0$
and

$$\dot{x} = \frac{dx}{dt}; \lambda_i, \gamma_i = \text{coefficients of reaction} \tag{5.65}$$

The first two equations from above (5.60 and 5.61) follow the formulation of the short-run Phillips curve, defining the trade-off between the new variables U_{it} and σ_{Lit}. The third and the fourth relationships (5.63 and 5.64) are at the centrepiece of our approach: they state that if the real (natural) slope of income distribution is greater than the natural (real) one, economic subjects, then, will expect a levelling of personal income distribution. It is not our intention here to consider what institutional, sociological and economic factors determine the 'natural' slope of personal income distribution. Many explanatory works are available for consultation (see Blümle 1975, especially pp. 47–99). The concept of a 'natural' slope of personal income distribution goes back to the classical contributions of V. Pareto (1895). He considered the great stability of his 'α' within time series and cross-section analysis to reflect a long-run equilibrium in personal income distribution. Moreover, he used the notion of 'normal values' of income distribution towards which a society – after exogenous changes – tends to move back. Private agents will – pretty much as in the theory of rational expectations – anticipate correctly the slope of personal income distribution only on average, that is, in the long run. The type of expectations formation hypothesis in this paper can be labelled as 'consistent' rather than adaptive: given the long-run invariance of the natural distribution of income, agents anticipate the direction of short-run changes in income distribution correctly. This feature of our model is quite different from Nordhaus (1975) and other contributions, where 'higher inflation leads agents to expect higher inflation in the future' (Nordhaus 1975, p. 170).

Short-run expectations of income distribution (changes) do influence the trade-off relationship between the income distribution goal and the (high) employment goal in the following manner: if the actual personal income distribution of today appears to be quite unequal, then leaders in consumption will anticipate a levelling process in the near future; hence, they will adjust their consumer behaviour today and reduce expenditures on consumption. In the case that those who imitate the leading consumers in their consumptive behaviour reduce their own consumptive purchases as well, then, for any given slope of income distribution, there is a higher rate of unemployment associated, *ceteris paribus*. The short-run trade-off relationship shifts. In the long run, the following holds:

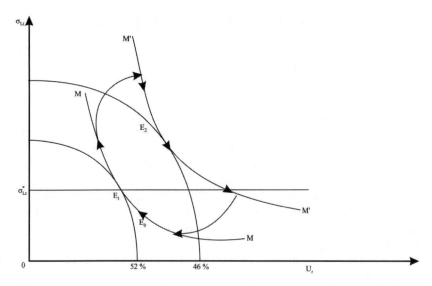

Source: Author.

Figure 5.2   The political business cycle in a monetary union

$$\sigma_{Lt}^e = \sigma_{Lt} = \sigma_{Lt}^* \qquad (5.66)$$

hence,

$$\sigma_{Lit} = \frac{1}{1 + \lambda_i} f(U_{it}) \text{ for } 0 < \lambda_i < 1 \qquad (5.67)$$

$$U_{it} = \overline{U} \text{ for } \lambda_i = 1 \qquad (5.68)$$

As

$$\frac{1}{1 + \lambda_i} < 1 \qquad (5.69)$$

the long-run trade-off relationship is flatter than the short run. What economic implications does this result have? In the long run, policies aiming at levelling the slope of income distribution will have much more negative repercussions on the (un)employment rate than in the short run. Figure 5.2 depicts the short-run trade-off relationship (MM) between σ_{Lt} and U_t.

The 'political dynamics' of the model are the following. The national politicians – now constrained by the economic implications of a monetary union – are still responsible for steering their economies but now they only have at their disposal fiscal instruments (taxation, government expenditures). They will apply these instruments before the election in such a way that they can hopefully attain a satisfactory ($50\% + \varepsilon$) iso-vote curve (given the short-run trade-off relationship MM) on election day. An optimal strategy is to reduce unemployment to a lower level by election day and to accept a more unequal distribution of income that will be associated with this policy. As soon as there are expectations of a more equal distribution, the short-run trade-off curve shifts outwards and the government loses its majority (E_2). During the election period the government will endeavour to dampen expectations of a more even income distribution. This is only possible (along the curve $M'M'$) by means of a policy of fiscal contraction (such as heavy taxation of leading consumers) that will be associated with rising levels of unemployment. As a result, the relationship $M'M'$ shifts (back) to MM. Immediately before the election the government distributes its 'presents' to leading consumers and thus succeeds in pushing demand and reaching the optimal point E_1 again. In Figure 5.2, the natural income distribution situation σ_{Lt}^* is drawn as a horizontal line running through the optimal point E_1. Finally, we shall examine the relationship between σ_{Lt}^e and σ_{Lt} that holds in the long run:

$$\dot{\sigma}_{Lt}^e = \gamma \sigma_{Lt} - \gamma \sigma_{Lt} = 0 \qquad (5.70)$$

In the long-run equilibrium there will accordingly be neither positive nor negative expectations with regard to the redistribution of income. As in the Nordhaus model, the private sector will not give rise to any endogenous business cycles; a deciding factor here is that measures taken closer to election day have more weight than those implemented earlier. Notice that the change in income distribution during the business cycle depicted in Figure 5.3 – inequality of income (measured by σ_{Lt}) increases in phases of upswing and boom while it decreases in phases of downswing and recession – matches exactly the stylized facts that we pretend to be sure of (see also Section 5.5 on empirical facts and figures).

In the following, we specify the social welfare function and the trade-off relationship in the economic system so that optimal control theory can be applied. The explanation given for the expected income redistribution serves as a boundary condition.

Preference function

$$W_t = -\frac{\alpha}{2} U_t^2 - \beta \sigma_{Lt} \qquad \alpha, \beta > 0 \qquad (5.71)$$

Economic system

$$\sigma_{Lt} = \sigma_0 - \sigma_1 U_1 - \lambda \sigma_{Lt}^e \quad \sigma_0, \sigma_1, \lambda > 0 \tag{5.72}$$

Boundary condition

$$\dot{\sigma}_{Lt}^e = \gamma(\sigma_{Lt} - \sigma_L^*) \quad \gamma < 0 \tag{5.73}$$

The maximum to be found is also restricted to interior solutions ($U_t > 0$). Only these are relevant because the case $U_t = 0$ is neither feasible (job finding and separation, structural unemployment, see Barro and Grilli 1994, pp. 257–60) nor necessarily superior from a welfare point of view (see Barro and Gordon 1983b, pp. 593–4). The three equations represent the basic elements to evaluate a current value Hamiltonian.

Current value Hamiltonian:

$$K = He^{\rho t} = -2\frac{\alpha}{2}U_t^2 - \beta(\sigma_0 - \sigma_1 U_1 - \lambda\sigma_{Lt}^e) + e^{\rho t}\psi_t\gamma(\sigma_0 - \sigma_1 U_t - \lambda\sigma_{Lt}^e - \sigma_L^*); \rho > 0 \tag{5.74}$$

where σ_{Lt}^e – state variable, U_t – control variable, ρt – rate of decay of voters' memories, $e^{\rho t}\psi_t$ – current value co-state

Differentiating K with respect to the current value co-state variable, the state variable and the control variable leads to:

State equation:

$$\frac{\partial K}{\partial e^{\rho t}\psi_t} = \gamma(\sigma_0 - \sigma_1 U_t - \lambda\sigma_{Lt}^e - \sigma_L^*) = \sigma_{Lt}^e \tag{5.75}$$

Co-state equation:

$$\frac{\partial K}{\partial \sigma_{Lt}^e} = \beta\lambda + \beta\sigma_1 - e^{\rho t}\psi_t\gamma\lambda = \rho e^{\rho t}\psi_t - (e^{\rho t}\dot{\psi}_t) \tag{5.76}$$

Optimality condition:

$$\frac{\partial K}{\partial U_t} = -\alpha U_t + \beta\sigma_1 - e^{\rho t}\psi_t\gamma\sigma_1 = 0 \tag{5.77}$$

The analytical steps for solving the state, the co-state equation and the optimality condition are presented in the mathematical Annex; for the control variable, U_t, two results emerge:

$$U_t = \frac{(\rho - \gamma\sigma_1)\sigma_1\beta}{\alpha[(\gamma\lambda + \rho)]} \tag{5.78}$$

which is the particular solution of the inhomogeneous problem ($\dot{U}_t = 0$) and

$$U_t = de^{(\gamma\lambda + \rho)t} \tag{5.79}$$

which is the general solution of the homogenous problem. Putting both solution parts together, we arrive at the total solution of the differential equation, which is:

$$U_t = \frac{(\rho - \gamma\sigma_1)\sigma_1\beta}{\alpha(\gamma\lambda + \rho)} + de^{(\gamma\lambda + \rho)t} \tag{5.80}$$

After some manipulations to express d as a function of other parameters, the final result is given by:

$$U_t = -\frac{B}{A} + e^{(\gamma\lambda + \rho)(t-T)}\left[\frac{\beta\sigma_1}{\alpha} + \frac{B}{A}\right] \tag{5.81}$$

for

$$A = \alpha(\gamma\lambda + \rho) \quad \text{and} \quad B = -\sigma_1\beta(\rho - \gamma\sigma_1) \tag{5.82}$$

The solution of the dynamic optimization problem has two main economic components: the stationary equilibrium value for the unemployment rate is higher (lower),

- the more (less) costly a skewed income distribution is perceived by the society (β)
- the less (more) a high rate of unemployment causes social welfare losses (α)
- the less (more) income (re)distribution expectations influence the employment/income distribution trade-off (γ).

The total analytical solution defines the optimal policy trajectory. Note that, quite similar to the Nordhaus model, when an election approaches, U tends to $\beta\sigma_1 / \alpha$ The unemployment rate must be falling over the entire electoral regime. 'It will fall relatively faster at the end or beginning depending on whether A is positive or negative, respectively' (Nordhaus 1975, p. 184).

5.5   EMPIRICAL FACTS AND FIGURES

A number of important studies (see Van Burkhauser et al. 1999; Van Burkhauser et al. 2006) confirm that there is 'strong evidence that the overall income distribution is sensitive to the business cycle' (Van Burkhauser et al. 1999, p. 265). 'Moreover, [the income frequency density] . . . shifted significantly leftward between peak-to-trough years (that is, in phases of downswing and recession) and significantly rightward between trough and peak years (that is, in phases of upswing and boom) . . .' (p. 265). This finding also matches our analysis of the log-normal distribution of wages in Chapter 3.

While there exist numerous models – for example, the seminal paper provided by Forster and Steinmüller in 1976 – that confirm the stylized fact that the wage share tends to be low during the boom and high during recession (Forster and Steinmüller 1976, p. 226) – recent empirical investigations on this issue are rare. One important exception is the paper elaborated by Fichtner et al. 2012). For Germany (and these results will apply for many OECD countries too) they found that the increase of salaries and wages is far behind the increase of profits since the beginning of the millennium. They also found for the years 1995–2010 a strong correlation between the height of the savings ratio, on the one hand, and the wealth/income of the corresponding households, on the other hand. Given that the top 5 per cent of wealthy households of the sample under review received 45 per cent of profit incomes, this points to the relevance of our simple two-class model from above in the tradition of Nicholas Kaldor. If profit income rises overproportionally (see above), this will contribute to an increase of the overall savings ratio. Based on micro-data of 2005 collected by the SOEP, the authors estimated a savings function revealing that an increasing share of total income for a specific income group is associated with a higher savings ratio for that group.

These findings, however, do not put into doubt the three-class approach in the tradition of Johnson (1951, 1952a, 1971) discussed above. On the contrary, a further study of the DIW, cited by Faigle (2011), shows the development of the higher, the middle and the lower incomes between 1999 and 2010 according to the sample of the SOEP. While the higher (lower) incomes experienced a dramatic increase (decrease), the middle incomes stagnated on their initial level. This matches exactly the assumptions made earlier in Chapter 4!

Figure 5.3 gives an impressive picture of the cyclicality of personal income distribution, measured adequately by the Gini coefficient out of market incomes. It seems to be a stylized fact that comparatively high values of the business climate index – provided by the Munich IFO

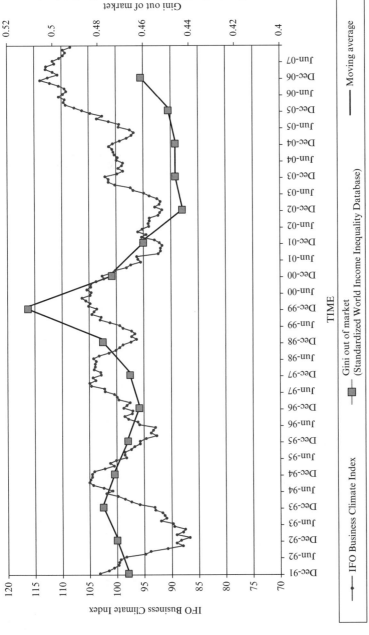

Source: OECD and CES.

Figure 5.3   Business cycle and personal income distribution: empirical evidence for Germany (1992–2007)

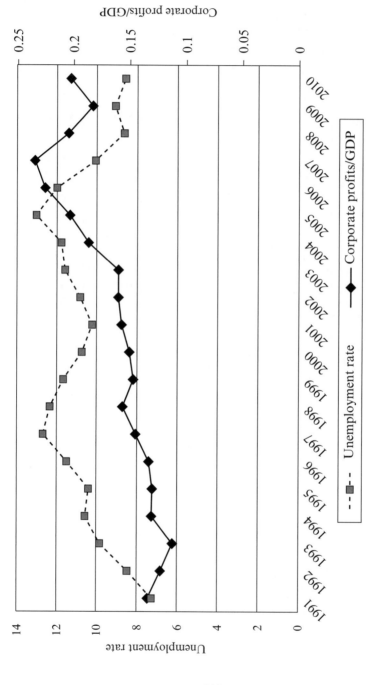

Figure 5.4   Unemployment rates and corporate profit quotas for Germany (1991–2010)

Institute – (during upswing and boom) is accompanied by relatively high rates of income concentration. Conversely, comparatively low values of the business climate index (during downswing and recession) seem to go along with lower rates of income concentration. During the years of observation (1992–2007), there is one exception. Between 1992 and 1994, Germany suffered a considerable drop in economic activity, as correctly predicted by the IFO Business Climate Index. This was, however, accompanied not by a fall but an increase in income concentration as measured by the Gini index out of market incomes.

Figure 5.4 shows the development of the IFO Business Climate Index and the evolution of the corporate profit quota in Germany (1991–2010). In this case, the corporate profit quota matches on average quite well the course in the value of the IFO Business Climate Index. But again, there are sub-periods (see, for example, 2001–02), where theory and the IFO Business Climate Index (see above) predict a fall instead of an increase in the corporate profit quota.

NOTES

1. I would like to thank Olof Johansson Stenman for his comment given at the 2009 ESA conference on a joint paper with Felix Stratmann (see also Sell and Stratmann 2009) that despite the symmetry of the matrix one should not expect the different effects to be of equal size and hence importance.
2. The following exposition closely follows Sell (1997).
3. There will tend to be a migration of labour into the country with a higher level of real wages or productivity; insofar as the participating countries will find the costs of emigration and immigration to be unacceptably high, a prospective equalization of productivity levels calls for unequal growth.

MATHEMATICAL ANNEX

Taking logarithms of

$$e^{\rho t}\psi_t = \frac{-\alpha U_t + \beta \sigma_1}{\gamma \sigma_1} \tag{5A.1}$$

and differentiating with respect to time yields:

$$\frac{d \ln \psi_t}{dt} + \rho = \frac{d \ln (-\alpha U_t + \beta \sigma_1)}{dt} \tag{5A.2}$$

It follows:

$$(e^{\rho t}\dot{\psi}_t) = \rho e^{\rho t}\psi_t - \beta\lambda - \beta\sigma_1 + e^{\rho t}\psi_t\gamma\lambda \quad |:e^{\rho t}\psi_t \tag{5A.3}$$

$$\frac{(e^{\rho t}\dot{\psi}_t)}{e^{\rho t}\psi_t} = \frac{d \ln (e^{\rho t}\psi_t)}{dt} = \frac{d \ln \psi_t}{dt} + \rho = \frac{-\beta\lambda - \beta\sigma_1}{e^{\rho t}\psi_t} + \gamma\lambda + \rho \tag{5A.4}$$

This results in:

$$\frac{d \ln (-\alpha U_t + \beta\sigma_1)}{dt} = \gamma\lambda + \rho - \frac{\beta\lambda + \beta\sigma_1}{e^{\rho t}\psi_t} \tag{5A.5}$$

Then, we obtain:

$$\frac{d \ln (-\alpha U_t + \beta\sigma_1)}{dt} = \gamma\lambda + \rho - \frac{\beta\lambda + \beta\sigma_1}{\dfrac{-\alpha U_t + \beta\sigma_1}{\gamma\sigma_1}} \tag{5A.6}$$

$$\frac{\alpha}{\alpha U_t - \beta\sigma_1} \frac{dU_t}{dt} = \gamma\lambda + \rho + \frac{\gamma\sigma_1(\beta\gamma + \beta\sigma_1)}{\alpha U_t - \beta\sigma_1} \tag{5A.7}$$

$$\dot{U}_t = \frac{dU_t}{dt} = \frac{\gamma\lambda + \rho + \dfrac{\gamma\sigma_1(\beta\lambda + \beta\sigma_1)}{\alpha U_t - \beta\sigma_1}}{\dfrac{\alpha}{\alpha U_t - \beta\sigma_1}} \tag{5A.8}$$

$$\dot{U}_t = (\gamma\lambda + \rho) + \frac{(\gamma\sigma_1 - \rho)\sigma_1\beta}{\alpha} \tag{5A.9}$$

For the particular solution of the inhomogeneous part ($\dot{U}_t = 0$) we obtain:

$$U_t = \frac{(\rho - \gamma\sigma_1)\sigma_1\beta}{\alpha(\gamma\lambda + \rho)} \tag{5A.10}$$

The general solution of the homogeneous part can be calculated by:

$$\dot{U}_t - (\gamma\lambda + \rho)U_t = 0 \tag{5A.11}$$

$$w_U = \frac{\dot{U}_t}{U_t} = \gamma\lambda + \rho \Leftrightarrow U_t = de^{(\gamma\lambda + \rho)t} \tag{5A.12}$$

Therefore, the solution of the differential equation is:

$$U_t = \frac{(\rho - \gamma\sigma_1)\sigma_1\beta}{\alpha(\gamma\lambda + \rho)} + de^{(\gamma\lambda + \rho)t} \tag{5A.13}$$

Determination of d from the limiting value: $\lim_{t \to T} \psi_t = 0$:

$$U_T = \frac{\beta\sigma_1}{\alpha} \tag{5A.14}$$

where T is the length of the electoral period. Combining the last two equations yields:

$$\frac{\beta\sigma_1}{\alpha} = \frac{(\rho - \gamma\sigma_1)\sigma_1\beta}{\alpha(\gamma\lambda + \rho)} + de^{(\gamma\lambda + \rho)T} \tag{5A.15}$$

Therefore, d can be expressed as:

$$d = \frac{\dfrac{\beta\sigma_1}{\alpha} - \dfrac{(\rho - \gamma\sigma_1)\sigma_1\beta}{\alpha(\gamma\lambda + \rho)}}{e^{(\gamma\lambda + \rho)T}} \tag{5A.16}$$

Inserting this equation, one obtains the following solution for U_t:

$$U_t = \frac{(\rho - \gamma\sigma_1)\sigma_1\beta}{\alpha(\gamma\lambda + \rho)} + \frac{\dfrac{\beta\sigma_1}{\alpha} - \dfrac{(\rho - \gamma\sigma_1)\sigma_1\beta}{\alpha(\gamma\lambda + \rho)}}{e^{(\gamma\lambda + \rho)T}}e^{(\gamma\lambda + \rho)t} \tag{5A.17}$$

$$U_t = \frac{(\rho - \gamma\sigma_1)\sigma_1\beta}{\alpha(\gamma\lambda + \rho)} + \frac{\beta\sigma_1(\gamma\lambda + \rho) - \sigma_1\beta(\rho - \gamma\lambda)}{\alpha(\gamma\lambda + \rho)e^{(\gamma\lambda + \rho)T}}e^{(\gamma\lambda + \rho)t} \tag{5A.18}$$

$$U_t = \frac{(\rho - \gamma\sigma_1)\sigma_1\beta}{\alpha(\gamma\lambda + \rho)} + \frac{\beta\sigma_1(\gamma\lambda + \rho)}{\alpha(\gamma\lambda + \rho)} e^{-(\gamma\lambda+p)T} e^{(\gamma\lambda+p)t} - \frac{\sigma_1\beta(\rho - \gamma\sigma_1)}{\alpha(\gamma\lambda + \rho)} e^{-(\gamma\lambda+p)T} e^{(\gamma\lambda+p)t}$$

(5A.19)

$$U_t = \frac{(\rho - \gamma\sigma_1)\sigma_1\beta}{\alpha(\gamma\lambda + \rho)} + e^{(\gamma\lambda+\rho)(t-T)}\left[\frac{\sigma_1\beta}{\alpha} - \frac{\sigma_1\beta(\rho - \gamma\sigma_1)}{\alpha(\gamma\lambda + \rho)}\right]$$ (5A.20)

$$U_t = -\frac{B}{A} + e^{(\gamma\lambda+\rho)(t-T)}\left[\frac{\beta\sigma_1}{\alpha} + \frac{B}{A}\right]$$ (5A.21)

for

$$A = \alpha(\gamma\lambda + \rho) \quad \text{and} \quad B = -\sigma_1\beta(\rho - \gamma\sigma_1)$$ (5A.22)

6. Income distribution and economic growth*

6.1 INTRODUCTION

There is an enormous body of literature on the subject of growth versus equity (or likewise on the subject of efficiency versus equity) that started to grow in the 1980s (see Sell 1982). This chapter will deal with this topic using both theoretical and empirical arguments. In particular, we address in this chapter the relationship between the concentration of income (measured by the Gini coefficient), or likewise specific income forms such as profits, on the one hand, and the real rate of per capita (or likewise absolute) economic growth, on the other hand.

It will, however, also include a reappraisal of the famous inverted U-curve firstly put forward by Simon Kuznets (see Sell 2001a, pp. 74–5). As well known, in the Kuznets framework there exists a non-linear (shaped like an inverted U) relationship between the per capita income, on the one hand, and the concentration of income measured by the Gini coefficient, on the other hand.

As reported by Ostry et al. (2014, pp. 7–8) and, as stated above, there exists a huge amount of literature dealing with the issue of (in)equality and economic growth. Basically there are two strands of views on this issue. One emphasizes the positive incentives that inequality can create towards economic growth: inequality may provide incentives for innovation and entrepreneurship, raise savings and may at least allow a few individuals the 'minimum needed to start businesses and get a good education' (Ostry et al. 2014, p. 8). The other view stresses that inequality may be harmful for the health status of many people and for human capital accumulation, for the maintenance of political stability and for the social consensus required to absorb 'shocks and to sustain growth' (p. 8).

The following section combines insights from biology with models of capital accumulation and the dispersion of profits. We shall show how market processes (for example, market entry and market exit of firms) create disequilibria – in the sense of the famous Schumpeterian creative destruction – and push the dynamics of investment behaviour, on the one hand, and determine size and distribution of profits, on the other hand. Hereafter, we shed some light on the bargaining process.

The final theoretical section is dedicated to the political (or likewise 'social climate') economy of growth and (personal) income distribution under the conditions of the welfare state. In this framework, a majority within the society sympathizes with inequity aversion in the vein of Sen's welfare function (1974). Social welfare can be increased either by higher per capita economic growth, given the Gini coefficient, or by a lower Gini coefficient, given the rate of per capita economic growth. The 'economic law' that has to be respected relates per capita economic growth in a non-linear way to the dispersion of personal incomes. The rationale behind this formulation is that there can be presumed an incentive and hence growth maximizing dispersion of incomes (see Sell 2014). Deviations from below or from above create economic costs. These costs consist in lower rates of per capita economic growth as compared with the unconstrained rate of per capita economic growth explained by approaches of the 'new growth theory'.

6.2   INTEGRATING COMPETITION, ECONOMIC GROWTH AND INCOME DISTRIBUTION INTO THE MARKET: THE HUNTER-PREY MODEL

The main contribution in explaining the interdependence between entrepreneurial competition – in the sense of Joseph Schumpeter and Israel M. Kirzner, that is, capital accumulation and changes in the distribution of profits – stems from Blümle (1989b). In his book chapter of 1989 – by analogy with findings provided by the theories of evolution as a part of the science of biology which hold that population numbers of hunters and prey are always anticyclical – and in line with the assumptions of Joseph Schumpeter, he described the competitive process within a closed national economy as an interaction between innovators (advancing prey) and pursuing imitators (pursuing hunters). Both groups of market players make investments, but the imitators are given the role of ensuring that the (new) technological knowledge created by the innovators is being diffused. In this context, it is of particular merit that Blümle modelled the relationship between the disparity of income distribution and the competitive process: innovators see to it that their own production methods are more cost-effective, thus causing a profit disparity among vendors (the famous curve provided by Enrico Barone). This attracts imitators into the market whose investments cause the new knowledge to be diffused while also triggering an erosion of the profit disparity that existed before. However, with the disappearance of 'difference profits', real investment decreases too, and financial investment becomes more attractive. This means that there is a positive relationship between the growth rate of the investment quota (g_{IQ} as the dependent variable), on the one hand, and the profit dispersion (v stands for the variance of the logarithm of profits per unit of production and serves as the independent variable), on the other hand. If the dispersion of profits follows by and large a log-normal distribution, the total size of 'difference profits' correlates positively with the variance of profits. Hence, one may expect a high attractiveness for real investment. If we assume a linear relationship, we obtain (for I/Y = IQ = investment quota):

$$g_{IQ} = \frac{dIQ/dt}{IQ} = -a_1 + a_2 v \tag{6.1}$$

Once the 'difference profits' disappear, real investment is no longer profitable (IQ↓) and entrepreneurs will most likely switch to financial investments:

$$v = 0 \Rightarrow g_{IQ} = -a_1 \tag{6.2}$$

Stationarity is achieved when the growth rate of the investment quota IQ becomes zero,

$$g_{IQ} = 0 \Rightarrow v^* = \frac{a_1}{a_2} \tag{6.3}$$

which enables us to calculate the stationary value of the profit dispersion. Both growth equations can be taken together as an example for the Lotka-Volterra equations model (Blümle 1989b, p. 27).

Figure 6.1 depicts the graphical interpretation of the investment function.

At the same time, there is a negative relationship between the growth rate of profit dispersion, g_v (the dependent variable) and the investment quota, IQ (the independent variable). This is due to the behaviour of imitators or likewise hunters in the model: the higher and the longer they invest in the relevant market production, the more will profit concentration and profit differences fade away.

$$g_v = \frac{dv/dt}{v} = b_1 - b_2 IQ \tag{6.4}$$

Even when the IQ falls to a level of zero, there exists always an autonomous rate of technological progress (b_1) that causes 'difference profits':

$$IQ = 0 \Rightarrow g_v = b_1 \tag{6.5}$$

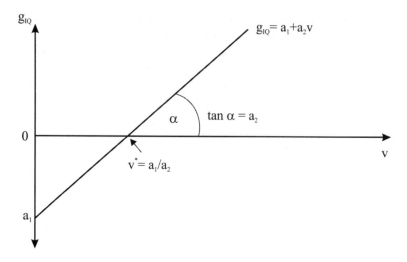

Source: Blümle (1989b).

Figure 6.1 The investment function in the hunter-prey model

Once the growth rate of profit dispersion reaches a level of zero,

$$g_v = 0 \Rightarrow IQ^* = \frac{b_1}{b_2} \tag{6.6}$$

we are able to calculate the stationary value of the investment quota. Figure 6.2 depicts the graphical interpretation of the profit dispersion function.

We may now analyse how the change in time of the investment quota relates to the change in time of the dispersion of profits. We obtain the following differential equation:

$$\frac{dIQ/dt}{dv/dt} = \frac{dIQ}{dv} = \frac{(-a_1 + a_2 v)IQ}{(b_1 - b_2 IQ)v} \tag{6.7}$$

By separating variables, we achieve:

$$(b_1/IQ - b_2)dIQ = (-a_1/v + a_2)dv \tag{6.8}$$

Taking the indeterminate integral of both sides gives:

$$\int (b_1/IQ - b_2)dIQ = \int (-a_1/v + a_2)dv \tag{6.9}$$

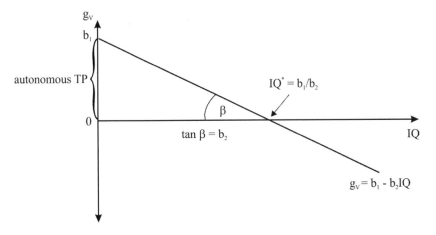

Source: Author's elaboration.

Figure 6.2   *The profit dispersion function in the hunter-prey model*

$$b_1 \ln IQ - b_2 IQ = -a_1 \ln v + a_2 v + c \qquad (6.10)$$

or

$$\exp(b_1 \ln IQ - b_2 IQ) = \exp(-a_1 \ln v + a_2 v + c) \qquad (6.11)$$

which can also be written as

$$IQ^{b_1} e^{-b_2 IQ} = v^{-a_1} e^{a_2 v} e^c \qquad (6.12)$$

where $IQ^{b_1} = e^{b_1 \ln IQ}$ and c is an integration constant. The graphical interpretation of our result is a closed, elliptic curve depicted in Figure 6.3. The stationary equilibrium is reached in P* where:

$$g_{IQ} = 0 \Rightarrow v^* = \frac{a_1}{a_2} \qquad (6.13)$$

and

$$g_v = 0 \Rightarrow IQ^* = \frac{b_1}{b_2} \qquad (6.14)$$

Figure 6.3 demonstrates the following. On the axes, the overall economic investment quota (IQ) and the variance of profits per unit of production, v (profit dispersion) are marked off; there is a central position where the stationary equilibrium is located (at P*). Profit dispersion

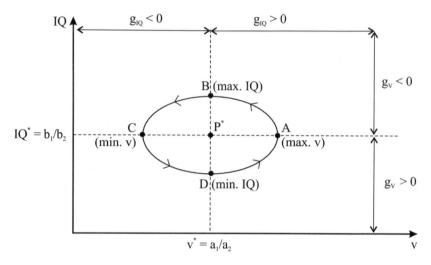

Source: Blümle (1989b).

Figure 6.3   The full investment-profit cycle in the hunter-prey model

assumes the value $v^* = a_1/a_2$ there: the smaller the inclination to financial investments a_1 and the higher the arbitrage intensity on the commodity markets a_2, the faster profit differences will be reduced. At equilibrium, the investment quota is determined by $IQ^* = b_1/b_2$: the bigger autonomous technological progress b_1 and the smaller the profit erosion speed by imitations b_2, the longer it will take for innovation leads to be reduced by investment.

At point A, profit dispersion is at its maximum and, accordingly, the incentive for risky innovations is high: IQ increases. Now, initial imitators appear, IQ continues to rise, but profit dispersion v decreases – until the maximum IQ is reached at point B. The decreasing profit dispersion v and the slowing down of the diffusion process cause IQ to drop until a minimum dispersion of profits is reached at point C; still existing profit differences are no longer being reduced. If difference profits increase again due to the occurrence of autonomous technological progress, profit dispersion v will, as a result, increase again. The system moves into the direction of point D where a minimum is reached in the real investment quota. From there on, the investment quota will increase again as a result of high pioneer profits and increases in profit dispersion.

What are the long-run implications of the model? With $I = \Delta K$, we may define the investment quota in stationary equilibrium as:

$$IQ = \frac{I}{Y} = \frac{b_1}{b_2} = \frac{\Delta K}{Y} \qquad (6.15)$$

The relationship between output (Y) and the capital stock (K) reads:

$$Y = \frac{K}{v}; \; v \equiv \text{capital coefficient} \qquad (6.16)$$

Hence, in stationary equilibrium, we have:

$$\frac{b_1}{b_2} = \underbrace{\frac{\Delta K}{K}}_{g_K} v \qquad (6.17)$$

The rate of growth of the capital stock, in turn, is given by:

$$g_K = \frac{\Delta K}{K} = \frac{\dot{K}}{K} = \frac{b_1}{b_2 v} \qquad (6.18)$$

The rate of change of the capital stock is given by:

$$\dot{K} = \frac{dK}{dt} = g_K \cdot K = \frac{b_1}{b_2 v} \cdot K \qquad (6.19)$$

In per capita or per employee terms we achieve:

$$\frac{\dot{K}}{L} = \frac{b_1}{b_2 v} \cdot \frac{K}{L} \qquad (6.20)$$

A widespread formula for the change in the capital intensity of production reads:

$$\dot{k} = \frac{dk}{dt} = \frac{\dot{K}}{L} - \frac{L}{L}k = \frac{\dot{K}}{L} - g_L \cdot k \qquad (6.21)$$

An equivalent formulation is:

$$\dot{k} = \frac{b_1}{b_2 \cdot v} \cdot k - g_L \cdot k \qquad (6.22)$$

Hence, the growth rate of capital intensity is given by:

$$g_k = \frac{\dot{k}}{k} = \frac{b_1}{b_2 v} - g_L \qquad (6.23)$$

A synonymous formulation (substituting v by k/Y) is:

$$g_k = \frac{b_1}{b_2} \cdot \frac{y(k)}{k} - w_A \qquad (6.24)$$

At steady state, it holds that:

$$\frac{b_1}{b_2} \cdot \frac{y(k)}{k} = w_A \qquad (6.25)$$

As a result, we may summarize (see Figure 6.4 for the details): the higher capital intensity is in the steady state, the higher the rate of autonomous technical progress, b_1, and the lower b_2. The latter means that the lead in innovations of Schumpeterian entrepreneurs will be eroded at a comparatively low speed by the investment behaviour of imitators. Accordingly, given an initial low capital intensity k_0, the larger the distance to one's own steady state, the higher b_1 and the lower b_2.

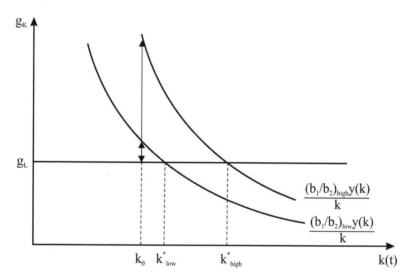

Source: Author's elaboration.

Figure 6.4   The growth rate of capital intensity in the hunter-prey model

6.3 HUNTER AND PREY IN AN INTERNATIONAL CONTEXT

Without directly referring to Blümle (1989b), Barro and Sala-i-Martin (2004) basically developed further and applied his ideas to the situation of open national economies in the world economy whose per capita incomes are on different levels. Their approach states that in the end, threshold countries are able to catch up with industrialized nations because the imitation and implementation of new developments (originating elsewhere) typically is cheaper than innovations (p. 349). A new aspect is that the imitator, that is, the person who, through product piracy, is the only one in his own country to possess the new intermediate product developed in the industrialized country, also becomes a monopolist (that is, for the relevant novel intermediate product) within the borders of his home country. The imitator will, as a rule, always (only) be able to copy a certain subset N_2 of the overall stock of innovations N_1. In this context, it shall apply that the copying costs are an increasing function of the ratio between N_2 and N_1:

$$v_2(t) = v_2(N_2/N_1); v_2' > 0 \qquad (6.26)$$

These imitation costs will be below the innovation costs v_2 as long as the ratio is $(N_2 / N_1) < 1$ (at least normally, for in exceptional cases it may even be cheaper to finance innovations oneself instead of initiating complex imitations). See Figure 6.5 for the details.

A sensible interpretation of the model by Barro and Sala-i-Martin implies that the industrialized countries will again and again succeed in expanding innovations N_1 such that the growth rate of N_1 never falls below that of N_2, and that for the representative threshold country, a balanced and constant relationship of $0 < (N_2 / N_1)^* < 1$ develops, with associated costs v_2^*. In the process, both the innovator in the industrialized country and the imitator in the threshold country achieve temporary monopoly positions as described in the hunter-prey model by Blümle, ensuring that a distance is maintained to (internal) pursuers. However, the threshold country will not be able to completely catch up with the industrialized nations and to reach their output per worker through imitation alone. This in any case applies as long as the overall productivity index A remains behind that of the country groups mentioned (Barro and Sala-i-Martin 2004, p. 358). However, this index may be raised in the threshold country by improving economic and political institutions (p. 372).

The – not totally unimportant – question remains whether the characteristics described are to be allocated to different individuals or may also be found within the very same person. For the consumer, there seems to be a

cost of increasing N

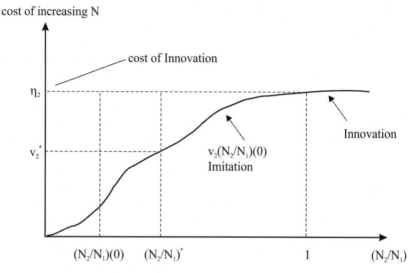

Source: Barro and Sala-i-Martin (2004, p. 354).

Figure 6.5   *The process of innovations and imitations in an international context*

positive answer to this question: if he does not happen to be at the top or bottom of the income pyramid, he will always want to both catch up with and keep ahead of other consumers (see Chapter 5). It is basically the same for the entrepreneur. Firstly, an imitator (inventor) can quickly turn into an inventor (imitator). As Barro and Sala-i-Martin demonstrated, I can temporarily be a monopolist as well as an imitator, which will give me a motivation to keep competitors at a distance. It might be added that even among innovators, there will be a desire to keep up, considering the fact that for innovations, a ladder of productivity increases exists.

6.4   BARGAINING FOR GROWTH AND EQUITY

Bargaining is always an issue between unions and entrepreneurs or likewise firms. As above, we are interested in identifying an efficient contract between these two parties.[1] The utility function of unions may have the following form: utility increases with the growth rate of wages (g_w); at the same time, it decreases with a too high dispersion of wage increases (σ_{g_w}):

$$U^u = U^u(g_w, \sigma_{g_w}) \tag{6.27}$$

with $U^u_{g_w} > 0$; $U^u_{g_w g_w} < 0$ and $U^u_{\sigma_{g_w}} < 0$; $U^u_{\sigma_{g_w} \sigma_{g_w}} > 0$

It is interesting to stay for a moment with the second derivatives from above: while the first (negative) one simply refers to the law of diminishing marginal returns of utility, the second stands for the 'law of diminishing marginal increases of damage' (see Sell and Stratmann 2013, p. 79).

Unions, hence, have a preference for a high growth rate of wages, but dislike a considerable dispersion of wage increases (see Chapter 3). This is, among other things, due to fairness considerations (Grund and Westergaard-Nielsen 2008, p. 492): perceived inequity of wage increases may signal in their view a lack of fairness in the wage structure (p. 486).

Taking total derivatives of the utility function and, then, deducting for the iso-utility functions of unions the marginal rate of substitution between the growth of nominal wages and the dispersion of wage increases, gives:

$$\frac{dg_w}{d\sigma_{g_w}} = -\frac{\partial U^u}{\partial \sigma_{g_w}} : \frac{\partial U^u}{\partial g_w} > 0 \qquad (6.28)$$

with:

$$\frac{d^2 g_w}{d\sigma_{g_w}^2} = -\left\{ \frac{U^u_{\sigma_{g_w} \sigma_{g_w}} U^u_{g_w} - U^u_{\sigma_{g_w}} U^u_{g_w g_w}}{[U^u_{g_w}]^2} \right\} > 0 \qquad (6.29)$$

Indifference curves of the unions have a positive and increasing curvature. By contrast, firms will have – with regard to their profits – a preference for a considerable dispersion of wage increases, as they presume that such a wage structure fits well the dispersion of abilities and capabilities (Sell 2001, 2014) and dispersion of wage increases is 'a better proxy for the extent of monetary incentives in the firm' (Grund and Westergaard-Nielsen 2008, p. 497). 'In general, however, firms with larger wage dispersion have higher levels of value added' (p. 492). Also, they will dislike a high growth rate of (nominal) wages, given their expectance of productivity growth and of future inflation rates. Under these conditions, a high growth rate of nominal wages leads to a high growth rate of marginal costs of labour. Hence,

$$\Pi^f = \Pi^f(g_w, \sigma_{g_w}) \qquad (6.30)$$

with $\Pi^f_{g_w} < 0$; $\Pi^f_{g_w g_w} > 0$ and $\Pi^f_{\sigma_{g_w}} > 0$; $\Pi^f_{\sigma_{g_w} \sigma_{g_w}} < 0$

Taking total derivatives of the profit function and then deducting for the iso-profit functions of firms the marginal rate of substitution between the growth of nominal wages and the dispersion of wage increases, gives:

$$\frac{dg_w}{d\sigma_{g_w}} = -\frac{\partial \Pi^f}{\partial \sigma_{g_w}} : \frac{\partial \Pi^f}{\partial g_w} > 0 \tag{6.31}$$

with:

$$\frac{d^2 g_w}{d\sigma_{g_w}^2} = -\left\{\frac{\Pi^f_{\sigma_{g_w}\sigma_{g_w}} \Pi^f_{g_w} - \Pi^f_{\sigma_{g_w}} \Pi^f_{g_w g_w}}{[\Pi^f_{g_w}]^2}\right\} < 0 \tag{6.32}$$

In addition, the assumption of a positive impact stemming from a higher dispersion of wage increases on the profits of the firm can be substantiated further by making use of an analogy to the theory of efficient wages. 'It is dispersion of wage increases that would be expected to induce workers to exert effort' (Grund and Westergaard-Nielsen 2008, p.487). In the following, l stands for labour input and e for effort:

$$\Pi(w, l) = P \cdot f[e(\sigma_{g_w}) \cdot l] - wl; \text{ with } P = 1 \tag{6.33}$$

We assume further, following the theory of efficient wages:

$$f' = \frac{\partial f}{\partial(el)} > 0, f'' < 0, e' = \frac{\partial e}{\partial \sigma_{g_w}} = e'(\sigma_{g_w}) > 0, \frac{\partial^2 e}{\partial \sigma_{g_w}^2} = e'' < 0 \tag{6.34}$$

Let's stay again for a moment with the rationale of these first and second derivatives: $f' > 0$ is the traditional assumption that effective labour input has a positive but diminishing ($f'' < 0$) impact on output; $e' > 0$ modifies the standard assumption of the theory of effective wages, where higher (average) wages have a positive impact on effort. In our context, it is a higher wage increase dispersion that better represents and gives monetary incentives (p. 487) to unequal abilities and capabilities and therefore pushes the efforts of the labour force. This effect, again, goes along with diminishing returns. Notice that, given a left-steep, oblique to the right distribution of wages, as is the case for a log-normal distribution, the average wage will increase in line with a higher dispersion of wage increases.

The two first order conditions are:

$$\frac{\partial \Pi}{\partial \sigma_{gw}} = f'[e(\sigma_{gw}) \cdot 1] \cdot e'(\sigma_{gw})1 - \frac{\partial w}{\partial \sigma_{gw}}1 \overset{!}{=} 0 \qquad (6.35)$$

$$f'[e(\sigma_{gw}) \cdot 1] = \frac{1 \cdot \dfrac{\partial w}{\partial \sigma_{gw}}}{e'(\sigma_{gw})1} = \frac{\dfrac{\partial w}{\partial \sigma_{gw}}}{e'(\sigma_{gw})} \qquad (6.36)$$

$$\frac{\partial \Pi}{\partial l} = f'[e(\sigma_{gw}) \cdot 1] \cdot e(\sigma_{gw}) - w \overset{!}{=} 0 \qquad (6.37)$$

$$f'[e(\sigma_{gw}) \cdot 1] = \frac{w}{e(\sigma_{gw})} \qquad (6.38)$$

Putting these two results together, gives:

$$\frac{\dfrac{\partial w}{\partial \sigma_{gw}}}{e'(\sigma_{gw})} = \frac{w}{e(\sigma_{gw})} \qquad (6.39)$$

or

$$\frac{e'(\sigma_{gw})w}{e(\sigma_{gw})} = \frac{\partial w}{\partial \sigma_{gw}} > 0 \qquad (6.40)$$

This is a sort of a modified Solow condition. It fully converges with the Solow condition for:

$$\frac{e'(\sigma_{gw})w}{e(\sigma_{gw})} = \frac{\partial w}{\partial \sigma_{gw}} = 1 \qquad (6.41)$$

In Figure 6.6, we have depicted the bargaining equilibrium between firms and unions: the higher, *ceteris paribus*, the bargaining power of unions (firms), the more will the equilibrium be located to the left (right) of the diagram.

Notice that a 'contract line' that combines all relevant tangential solutions of the bargaining process must not necessarily be a falling line as one may suspect from first glance in Figure 6.6. It could also well behave like an inverse U-shaped relationship between the growth rate of wages and the dispersion of wage increases (see also Grund and Westergaard-Nielsen 2008, p. 494).

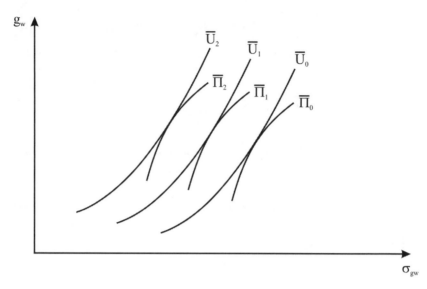

Figure 6.6   *Bargaining for wage increases and wage increase dispersion between unions and firms*

6.5   A POLITICAL ECONOMY APPROACH OF OPTIMAL PERSONAL INCOME DISTRIBUTION AND GROWTH

6.5.1   Introduction

'Des riches, il en fuadra toujours. Sans eux, tu peux me dire comment feraient les pauvres?'[2]

In the crisis regions of Europe, national governments are actually pursuing restrictive fiscal policies in order to meet the criteria set by the Troika (IMF, EU Commission and ECB). These 'austerity programmes' primarily consist in cutting public expenditures on social security and thereby narrowing the gap between the consumer and the producer wage rate. Hence, a secondary effect aimed at by the respective politicians is to gain (or to regain) competitiveness and to foster the preconditions for economic per capita growth in the framework of the globalization of markets.

However, a side effect of these measures is a considerable shift in the distribution of functional and personal incomes in favour of earnings not stemming from labour. It is not clear how such changes in personal income distribution, on the other hand, will affect the economy's per capita growth rate. One may argue that each economy/society strives – at different degrees of consciousness – for an individual, more or less stable combination between the per capita growth rate to be achieved and the income distribution prevailing. If there are economic reasons to find a concave relationship between the per capita growth rate and the distribution[3] of personal incomes, the optimization puzzle requires the existence of a social preference function, where social utility increases by a higher per capita growth rate and/or by a more equal income distribution. We believe that our social optimization model can help to understand 'how income distribution and economic growth are jointly determined in political equilibrium' (Persson and Tabellini 1994, p. 618).

Recent contributions on the links from income distribution to growth[4] are mainly characterized by three approaches (see Alesina and Perotti 1994 for a still valid survey): (1) those stressing purely economic links from income distribution to growth (incentives for the accumulation of physical or human capital and so on); (2) those pointing at political channels (rent seeking, fiscal policy and political instability aspects) that inter-link income inequality and growth; and (3) Benabou's (1996a, 1996b) admirable approach to integrate political economy/socio-political theories and imperfect capital markets/property rights theories. Our own approach is eclectic – drawing on all of the directions of research[5] mentioned and hence giving a survey on many of these as well – but at the same time clearly biased towards the first option as our explanations will rely much more on purely economic arguments than on political economy considerations, on the one hand, and on integrating theories – which stress the advantages of redistribution – on the other hand.

6.5.2 Personal Income Distribution as a Determinant of Economic Growth

In the first place, we should discuss how inequality in personal income distribution gives (dis)incentives to income generation. Thereafter, one may shed light on the impact of income (in)equality on the pattern of income use of different income groups, where an aggregate consideration of personal income distribution can ensue in general. Finally, we shall briefly discuss the reciprocal relationship between personal income distribution and economic growth within the broader framework of the social climate of a society.

When analysing the relation between income distribution and per capita economic growth, the impact of income distribution on the national savings rate is mostly under discussion. In the majority of cases, it is argued – following macroeconomic models of economic growth – according to aggregates of the functional income distribution. As opposed to this, we concentrate here on the issue of personal income distribution. First of all, our aim is to investigate the relationship that exists between the diffusion of individual incomes and economic growth, expressed by the growth rate of per capita income.

Simon Kuznets (1955) formulated, based on the analysis of time series, an inverted U-Hypothesis, according to which the equality of personal income distribution decreases first and later increases during the process of development. Our own approach is a bit different: the main question we ask is how different income distribution scenarios will effect economic growth per capita in a cross-section view. It seems to be quite obvious that both a quite equal as well as an extremely unequal distribution of personal incomes are a disadvantage to economic growth. We now proceed to explain the different issues in more detail.

1. Let us begin by discussing the incentive compatibility conditions of income generation. Net incomes should be decisive for the incentive effects in income generation. The evaluation of incentive effects of income generation has to be conducted on a disaggregated level with regard to the income distribution of employed persons (workers, managers) and the income distribution of self-employed-persons; the latter being incomes generated as a sort of 'compensation to the dispositive factor' within business activity. In principle, we would need a theory on how to aggregate these two or better three income distributions in order to deduct the overall supply-side effects of personal income distribution.

    With regard to the personal income distribution of employed persons, Tinbergen[6] has derived an equilibrium in personal income distribution that clears the different markets in concern. He makes use of a utility function, where income, the amount of personal faculties of the respective individuals, the special requirements of the jobs of concern and the difficulties to work on them serve as arguments. In this way, he succeeds in explaining a log-normal distribution of personal incomes under certain conditions. Concerning the relationship between economic growth per capita and personal income distribution, we can conclude – according to the reasoning of Tinbergen – that during the process of economic growth, a certain income distribution is responsible for the characteristic requirements that special places of employment harmonize with the wishes and abilities of specific employees. During economic growth, the requirements of qualification change permanently and, therefore, this adjustment process is of great importance.

An equitable wage structure likely means that poorly qualified employees receive a higher wage than they deserve corresponding to their marginal revenue product. Once they become unemployed, they will charge the social system, ask for common national funds built for public consumption purposes and reduce, thereby, the possibilities for investment by the public sector. On the one hand, the readiness of qualified persons to educational investment is reduced through an equitable income distribution because human capital is paid less interest.[7] On the other hand, a very uneven personal income distribution with very low wages for the less qualified persons doesn't produce incentives to realize rationalization investments and, so, to increase productivity. In a like manner, such a distribution of incomes lowers the possibility and the readiness to endeavour with success and, at the same time, creates a hostile climate for economic growth. Plato[8] knew about this problem:

> If a potter has become rich, do you think that he will care about his skill any longer? In no way. But, instead, he will become more and more idle and careless; hence, he will become a bad potter. But also, if he cannot afford to buy his instruments or anything else belonging to his arts and crafts because of being poor, he, then, will do his job worse than he might do it under other conditions and he will educate also his sons or any other person being apprenticed to him to work badly. So in the end both, poverty and wealth, will make the work as well as the worker himself worse.

Hence, personal income distribution has both the function to force one to work as well as to motivate to achieve good results, whereby an extreme equality as well as a marked inequality are disadvantageous and make the necessary processes of adjustment and improvement during economic growth more difficult.

When it comes to discussing the innovative aspects of the economic growth process, in general, the so-called 'dispositive factor' (or entrepreneurial activity) is attributed with special importance. However, it neglects to consider the fact that the 'dispositive factor' cannot be found only in the field of self-employed business. With regard to the leading employees of management (upper income groups), Lydall[9] recalls that there exists a significant difference in the distribution of personal incomes among market-oriented and socialist countries. In comparison, he finds a higher frequency of elevated incomes, which is attributed to the higher responsibility of managers, in the market system. 'Responsibility' is measured indirectly by the income sum devoted to the subordinates. Obviously, special incentives are necessary for qualified persons who want to expose themselves to the stress and risk of occupations with great responsibility. Again, we should take into consideration that a certain degree of income differentiation is necessary in order to have, on the one hand, managers feeling compensated adequately for their output. The latter, in turn, is difficult to control. On the other hand, there should simultaneously be enough incentives for the managers to prove successful in their work in order to make progress.

The simple explanation for a log-normal distribution of personal incomes given by Wijk[10] is more obvious for the lower income groups of employed persons than for other individuals. He argues as follows. In the case of a utility function of the Weber-Fechner type, a log-normal distribution of incomes results in a normal distribution of incentives. A certain sense of justice, which has developed historically and which, therefore, should evolve differently on the international level, seems to be decisive for motivating effects. In contrast to this, we expect among the management a strong(er) commitment to the economic success of the firm. This goes along with a close orientation towards the income distribution of wealth. This is an explanation for the fact that the distribution of personal incomes among the higher income groups of employed persons as well as the distribution of wealth resembles the picture of a Pareto distribution.

With regard to the incomes of self-employed persons, we find that their incomes have a higher mean and a greater variance in comparison with employed persons. As far as the readiness to bear risk and the presence of professional skills are concerned, the occupations of the latter can be considered to be substitutes for the work done by the self-employed. Accordingly, Bronfenbrenner[11] has developed his 'theory of normal profits' as a supply-demand model for business output, where special risk aspects of any self-employed activity, however, should be taken additionally into consideration.[12]

With regard to economic wealth, it is possible to deduce a Pareto distribution if a process of accumulation (of assets) and dying off (of individuals) is considered.[13] It can be shown that such a distribution of wealth becomes more unequal, the higher the average interest rate is; hence, the distribution of wealth is – at least in the long run – a function of the interest rate. The role of the interest rate is twofold. On the one hand, a higher interest rate is conducive to the accumulation of wealth. On the other hand, a higher interest rate will make long-term arrangements less profitable as is the case with investments in research and development where market success can only be expected in the long run; yet they are decisive for the rate of economic growth. Furthermore, one can establish substitutability between risky and less risky or risk-free assets (with a constant rate of return) among the owners of wealth. Thus, not only the level of the average interest rate, but also a certain dispersion of interest rates will determine the portfolio decisions of wealth holders and, consequently, contribute to an optimal provision of the economy with risk capital.

Most likely, the distribution of wealth will have a normative impact on the income differentials among the managers of the firm(s). Notwithstanding the correct view of an increasing disconnection between the functions of management and capital ownership, managers and shareholders have similar positions in society and also during the decision-making process in the economy. Hence, this makes comparable income differentials within each group necessary if a trustful cooperation is to become possible and if managers and capital owners strive for common goals.

As far as the distribution of wealth between employed persons and self-employed persons is concerned, Aristophanes has stressed its great significance for economic development in criticizing the claims for an equal distribution. He has made his point in favour of the advantages of a skewed distribution of wealth in the following way: 'the rich man is enabled by his means to establish and to run a business; poverty, on the other hand, forces the poor man to work in the rich man's businesses.'[14]

2. A second issue concerns the expenditure behaviour of different income groups. We have explained above the role of income elasticities of different classes of goods, the significance of leaders and followers in consumption. However, are these arguments restricted to rich countries? It is not established that the double fold orientation of the 'middle class' towards the 'Joneses' and the 'Smiths' bandwagon effects is of less importance in poor than in rich countries, provided that income distribution is neither too equal nor too skewed.[15] Murphy et al. (1989) argue in the same vein that in poor countries, 'extreme equality could mean equal distribution of misery, as no sectors industrialize for lack of demand. Similarly, oligarchical income distributions could pose problems for industrialization, as the small number of property owners demand goods whose production could not possibly be profitably industrialized' (Murphy et al. 1989, p. 554).

Finally, it remains to be said that an existing group of high(er) income earners is actually often a prerequisite for the introduction of new goods and is, hence, motivating incentives for innovations. One should notice that not only goods for final consumption receive support for production; for example, it has been observed in the electronics sector that similar techniques are being applied in the consumer goods as well as capital goods production. The achievement of economies of scale will promote a development – beyond the sector of consumption goods – which helps to afford competition in large markets, and is beneficial to international competitiveness. Also, on the cost side, resource saving and productivity increasing processes are to be expected that lead to a higher growth rate as well.

3.   A last point to consider is the likely effect of a negative social climate – created by and large by a distorted distribution of personal incomes – on per capita economic growth. The analysis of the collapse of socialism in Eastern Europe helps to understand a simple mechanism: when personal income is distributed equally among the members of a society (that is, with a Gini coefficient (G) that is zero at the margin) individual incentives for gaining some extra will be near to zero. This is because any extras achieved in terms of consumer goods or hoarded precious metals suffer from two shortcomings. As no property rights are defined, these items are totally unprotected against confiscation by the government; at the same time, it is to be expected that neighbouring households will be 'green with envy'. Both aspects work as very negative incentives for total factor productivity gains and/or per capita income growth (g) in the economy/society as a whole. As Benabou puts it, 'growth is reduced through a decline in the expected return on investment, due to a higher threat of expropriation' (1996b, pp. 4–5). However, contrary to him, we believe that not only greater inequality but also too much equality increases such a threat. At the other extreme (the one that is primarily if not only stressed by the literature highlighting the political instability channel, see Alesina and Perotti 1994, p. 362) – that is, approaching on the margin a Gini coefficient of 1 – more social instability in a country has to be expected (Sachs 1989; Benhabib and Rustichini 1991) if it is not the whole social consensus in the economy that is to disappear imminently; strong forces push the society, then, towards more instability or even revolutionary changes,[16] a fact that, economically, is at least reflected in a reduction of investment (see Alesina and Perotti 1996, pp. 1203–28) and/ or the growth rate or, in extremis, an almost total lack of total factor productivity gains: 'The political consensus necessary for efficient growth may not be attainable if income inequality is too severe' (Benhabib and Rustichini 1991, p. 5). It is also argued (Alesina and Rodrik 1994) that a rising number of poor citizens leads to increased pressure for redistributive policies, which reduce incentives for the accumulation of human and physical capital. Roland Benabou (1996a, 1996b), however, does not share this view entirely; according to him, when capital and insurance markets are imperfect, redistributing

wealth from richer to poorer agents can have a positive effect on economic growth because it relaxes the latter's credit and/or liquidity constraints and reduces the number of people who do not have the collateral required to become an entrepreneur, thus enhancing social mobility.

Regarding the history of personal income distribution theory, it can be said that a first milestone was achieved when V. Pareto discovered the relationship corresponding to his 'law', but one should keep in mind that Pareto (and with him Davis), furthermore, conceived a specific magnitude of his a (near 1.5) as an expression for social stability.[17] At first glance, this fact seems to be surprising as (see above), traditionally, a quite uneven distribution of incomes was perceived as a problem for social stability, but very seldom an almost equal one. This former way of thinking did, however, not take into account enough the social phenomenon of envy and jealousy. As Mandeville[18] pointed out, envy is a phenomenon of social nearness. Among very homogeneous societies a 'rule of envy'[19] may become reality, which – as can also be observed empirically[20] – is able to paralyse any stimulus to particular efforts in a competitive environment. The reason is that the existence of envy tends to make people afraid of having success because being successful may produce envy among other people. As far as the relationship between economic growth and the distribution of personal incomes is concerned, one is inclined to speak of a 'trap of envy'.

A main function of economic growth is – as has been stressed quite often – that it tends to work as a 'social damper'.[21] During economic development, necessary redistributions of income are more easily implemented in the social environment if this process is not a zero-sum game: in this case, only additional incomes are redistributed. A too equal distribution of incomes lowers, as we have shown, the growth prospects of an economy because it makes the incentive structure suboptimal. At the same time, a lower rate of economic growth leads most likely to stronger feelings of envy, a fact that tends to hinder the evolution of incentives and makes it more difficult again to reach a high(er) rate of economic growth. In this context, it is important to observe that the social climate can even improve during a process of economic growth coupled with an income distribution that is becoming more uneven – whenever the society of concern is not (or no longer) captivated by feelings of envy. Namely, looking at rising incomes among others can embody a 'factor of hope'[22] for the rest of the economy: if they, the less lucky people, can hope for an improvement in their own economic situation, a positive reaction towards the wealthier people seems possible. Only if the (re)distribution of incomes continues to become more uneven during economic growth, then social instability may emerge.[23]

Thus, the conclusion of these arguments leads, again, to the concept of an optimal distribution of incomes with regard to economic growth, if we consider how the social climate in a society affects the growth prospects of the economy. The relationship between the social climate and the economic growth rate is also determined by traditions and norms that have been developed historically. Due to large differentials in this respect among the total of countries in the world economy, one cannot expect this relationship, hence, to be (always) stable in a cross-section analysis (see below).

In the following, we therefore postulate the existence of a strictly concave function (see Chiang 1984) that relates economic growth per capita to a measure of personal income distribution, similar to the Gini coefficient.[24] As in the following equation, per capita economic growth is 'explained' by an autonomous component c – the latter is exogenous for us, while it has been founded extensively by the new growth theories – and the society is penalized by growth losses whenever the actual personal income distribution (G) undergoes or surpasses the incentive maximizing income distribution, b. Notice that G, when it comes to measuring this variable empirically, has to be calculated from net incomes and not from market incomes. Otherwise, it is inconceivable to investigate a social equilibrium. In order to be symmetric, a quadratic form has to be given to the losses in terms of the per capita growth rate:

$$g = -a[G - b]^2 + c \qquad (6.42)$$

with: $a, b, c, \geq 0$, and $0 < b \leq 1$

Differentiating this equation with respect to the Gini coefficient, we may conclude that optimal solutions are only defined for a positive slope of the social indifference curve; the slope itself is endogenous as it decreases according to a higher Gini coefficient (a more unequal personal income distribution):

$$\frac{dg}{dG} = -2a[G - b] > 0 \text{ for } G < b \qquad (6.43)$$

with

$$\frac{d^2g}{dG^2} = -2a < 0 \qquad (6.44)$$

It is reasonable to assume that modern welfare states that are doing fairly well do so because – among other things – they have deliberately chosen combinations of personal income distribution and per capita economic growth that are desirable for a stable and viable society. Hence, there exists a social welfare function (W), one that deserves this classification (!), which assigns higher social welfare values to a more equal income distribution at a given growth rate of per capita income and to higher growth rates of per capita income at a given distribution of personal income:[25]

$$W = W(g, G) \qquad (6.45)$$

with $W_g > 0$ and $W_G < 0$

Notice that when it comes to testing the model empirically, the Gini coefficient that enters the welfare function must be the Gini coefficient for disposable income (market income minus direct taxes plus cash transfers) and not the Gini coefficient for market income (Bastagli et al. 2012, p. 6). Taking total derivatives and then deducting the marginal rate of substitution between per capita growth and the skewness of personal income distribution gives:

$$\frac{dg}{dG} = -\frac{\partial W}{\partial G} : \frac{\partial W}{\partial g} > 0 \qquad (6.46)$$

As above, we assume:

$$\frac{d^2g}{dG^2} = -\left\{ \frac{W_{GG} W_g - W_G W_{gg}}{[W_g]^2} \right\} > 0 \qquad (6.47)$$

The maximization of the social welfare function, constrained by the non-linear growth-income distribution relationship from above, yields a corresponding Lagrange function that reads:

$$L = W(g, G) + \lambda[g + a(G - b)^2 - c] \Rightarrow \text{max!} \qquad (6.48)$$

The first order optimality conditions (FOOC), then, are:

$$\frac{\partial L}{\partial g} = \frac{\partial W}{\partial g} + \lambda = 0 \qquad (6.49)$$

$$\frac{\partial L}{\partial G} = \frac{\partial W}{\partial G} + 2a\lambda[G - b] = 0 \qquad (6.50)$$

$$\frac{\partial L}{\partial \lambda} = g + a(G - b)^2 - c = 0 \qquad (6.51)$$

From the first FOOC, we can deduce that

$$\lambda = -\frac{\partial W}{\partial g} \qquad (6.52)$$

which can be introduced into the second FOOC and gives:

$$\frac{\partial W}{\partial G} - 2a\frac{\partial W}{\partial g}[G - b] = 0 \qquad (6.53)$$

Solving this equation for G gives us the optimal personal income distribution (G*):

$$G^* = \frac{\dfrac{\partial W}{\partial G}}{\dfrac{\partial W}{\partial g}} \cdot \frac{1}{2a} + b \qquad (6.54)$$

In the same vein, we can use this result for solving the third FOOC to obtain the optimal per capita growth rate:

$$g^* = c - a(G^* - b)^2 \qquad (6.55)$$

$$g^* = c - \frac{1}{4a}\left[\frac{\dfrac{\partial W}{\partial G}}{\dfrac{\partial W}{\partial g}}\right]^2 \qquad (6.56)$$

A graphical illustration of the optimization problem is given in Figure 6.7. It shows possible curvatures of the quadratic function together with hypothetic tangential situations. Notice that – to the best of my knowledge – the first version of this non-linear relationship between inequality and growth was published in Blümle and Sell (1998), that is, a bit before the contribution of Benhabib (2003) to whom Ostry et al. (2014) erroneously attribute such novelty. As can be seen from Figure 6.7, under 'normal' conditions, no society will choose a maximal rate of economic growth, given the economic 'law' represented by the quadratic function.

A priori, we don't know which of the three alternative concave functions, $g_0(G)$, $g_1(G)$, $g_2(G)$, is achievable by the society of concern. Let us first assume that it is the less favourable function, $g_0(G)$: b is then the respective Gini coefficient that maximizes the growth rate of per capita income (c); however, society will not choose the coordinates (b; c). Instead,

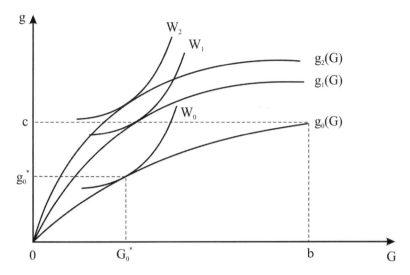

Source: Blümle and Sell (1998).

Figure 6.7   Optimal growth and income distribution in the social climate approach

given the social welfare function explained above, the tangential solution between the concave growth function $g_0(G)$ and a social indifference curve W_0 explains the 'social optimum' with the coordinates $(g_0^*;G_0^*)$. Notice that the horizontal distance between G_0^* and b reflects some degree of inequity aversion, which is typical for the social climate within a welfare state. Notice also that the existing inequity aversion has to be traded off against the loss of per capita economic growth reflected in the vertical distance between c and g_0^*.

6.6   EMPIRICAL FACTS AND FIGURES

Authors like Rodrik (1999) and Pritchett (2000) for a long time dominated the 'mainstream' contributions to the subject of income inequality and economic growth: 'Income inequality enters with a highly significant negative coefficient and raises the explanatory power of the regression' (Rodrik 1999, p. 395), which is intended to explain the growth differential between two sub-periods, 1960 to 1975 and 1975 to 1989 for a large sample of countries. Using the Gini coefficient as a proxy for latent social conflicts (p. 399), however, may be highly disputable.

It was, however, Forbes's paper of 2000 – after a number of theoretical contributions, among them Blümle and Sell (1998), who argued also on an empirical basis, and postulated an at least sectionally positive relationship between income inequality and economic growth – which set a new standard in the empirical investigation of the relationship between growth and equity and questioned chosen estimation techniques as well as the data basis in many of the previously published papers. The latter, Blümle and Sell (1998), it seemed, had confirmed a semi-strong but significant negative relationship between income inequality and economic growth (Forbes 2000, pp. 870–71). In her own empirical estimates, Forbes finds 'that in the short and medium term, an increase in a country's level of income inequality has a strong positive correlation with subsequent economic growth' (p. 871). Different from the majority of other studies – which utilize cross-country growth regressions – Forbes inspected the short- and medium-term relationship between income inequality and average annual economic growth within individual countries. She admits that the positive relationship found 'could diminish (or even reverse) over significantly longer periods' (p. 885). Scully's study of 2002 somewhat backs the results achieved by Forbes: using data from the World Bank with country observations (Gini coefficient, growth of per capita income) for the years 1975, 1980, 1985 and 1990, he also found 'a *positive* but relatively small trade-off between growth and income inequality' (Scully 2002, p. 90, emphasis added). In our own empirical cross-country regression, we (Blümle and Sell 1998, p. 347) found a non-linear relationship between today's income inequality and subsequent economic growth, which confirms the theoretical model from above. The data set was provided by the World Bank and the regression related mid-1980s Gini coefficients to average annual per capita growth rates of GDP between 1985 and 1994, including information on a broad range of formerly socialist and then transforming-into-a-market-economy countries (p. 347).

Banerjee and Duflo (2003, 2008), in the first place, heavily criticize the usage of linear models when testing the relationship between income inequality and economic growth, especially when theory is yet unclear about what type of relationship can be assumed (Banerjee and Duflo 2003, p. 290). Basically, their empirical finding is that 'the relation between the level of inequality and future growth for the economy . . . is U-shaped . . . i.e., there is less growth when inequality is either high or very low' (p. 277). These findings are totally in line with the results presented by Blümle and Sell (1998).

Ostry et al. (2014) highlight a further important methodological issue, already raised briefly above. The authors point to the necessity to distinguish (see above) between the market income Gini and the disposable income Gini coefficient. In the first case, coefficients are calculated out of market incomes and in the second case out of net or disposable incomes. Ostry et al. already incorporate the impact of redistribution policies. They find that 'the average redistribution, and the associated reduction in inequality, is . . . associated with higher and more durable growth' (Ostry et al. 2014, p. 26). As far as the Gini in net income is concerned, the authors find in their own empirical analysis a negative correlation with per capita economic growth in the next ten years (p. 16).

The following empirical analysis is based on the graphical inspection presented in Sell (2001a, p. 78). Figure 6.8 contains four quadrants. In the first one (counting counter-clockwise), we have depicted a stylized version of the Kuznets curve;[26] the fourth quadrant relates per capita income to subsequent per capita growth rates (g) of real income (GDP), and, hence,

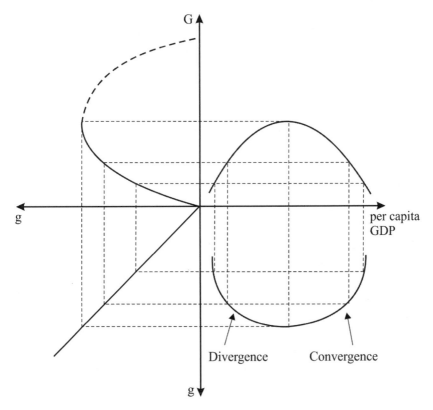

Source: Sell (2001).

Figure 6.8 A graphical interpretation of the divergence-convergence puzzle

The new economics of income distribution

serves to symbolize possible convergence/divergence in the data. As many previous empirical studies have shown, it is difficult to find either unconditional convergence or divergence. In the majority of cases, one finds conditional convergence for a 'club of rich countries' (like the OECD) and conditional divergence for a 'club of poor countries' (in Africa, Asia and so on).[27] In between, there is a range of per capita incomes where the evidence is at least inconclusive. These stylized facts sort of motivate the curvature of the 'convergence-divergence' function in quadrant four. Quadrant three is a 45 degree line that only helps to transfer coordinates from quadrant four into quadrant two: the resulting relationship between the Gini coefficient (G), on the one hand, and the per capita growth rate of real GDP (g), on the other hand, yields a non-linear function that looks pretty much like the quadratic function which emerged from the Blümle-Sell approach (Blümle and Sell 1998, see above).

The empirical test for our approach stands somehow in contrast to conventional 'growth-equity empiricism'. Instead of estimating or likewise plotting a bunch of Gini coefficients against a huge and undifferentiated sample of per capita economic growth rates stemming from a large sample of developed and developing countries, we prefer to go by pieces. We first identify the empirical relevance of the Kuznets curve in Figure 6.9 considering both 'poor' and 'rich' countries. Thereafter, we look for conditional convergence among 'rich countries' (Figure 6.10) and conditional

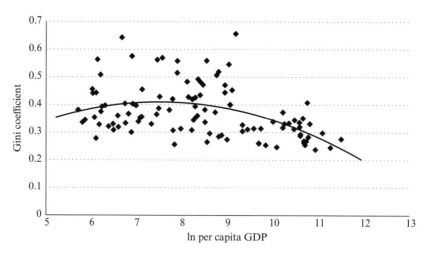

Source: OECD and CES.

Figure 6.9   The Kuznets curve: 80 developed and developing countries in the year 2009

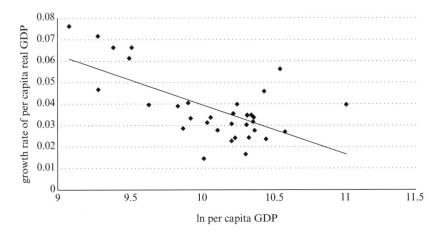

Source: OECD and author's calculations.

Figure 6.10 Convergence for the club of rich countries (34 countries, 2003–12)

divergence for 'poor countries' (Figure 6.11). If each of these pieces confirms the underlying theory (see above), we suggest that the empirical findings do not contradict the Blümle-Sell (1998) hypothesis of a non-linear relationship between the Gini coefficient, on the one hand, and the per capita real growth rate of income, on the other hand.

Figure 6.9 tests the existence of the Kuznets curve for a large sample of 80 countries, where all the information was collected in 2009, the most recent year for which a maximum amount of data was available. It turns out that the relationship is close to an inverted U, which is precisely the prediction of the Kuznets curve! This cross-section evidence stands in sharp contrast to Thomas Piketty's heavy criticism against this concept (Piketty 2014, pp. 13–15). Note that Lee's (2006) empirical investigation of the Kuznets curve – covering 14 countries in the EU over a period of 42 years (1951–92) – confirms our own findings: 'The result . . . supports the Kuznets' hypothesis . . . i. e., the inequality is likely to be increasing with development level in the EU before the turning point' (p. 794).

In Figure 6.10, we have used the most recent data set to test for conditional convergence among rich (being almost identical with the group of OECD countries) economies. The base year for per capita income is 2003 and we plot those incomes against the average growth rate of real per capita income between 2003 and 2012. As can be seen, there is an undisputable conditional convergence among this club of countries. Note that

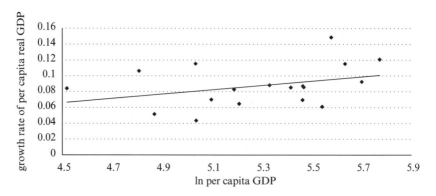

Source: OECD and author's calculations.

Figure 6.11   *Divergence for the club of poor countries (18 countries, 2000–12)*

the idea of a 'club convergence' has recently received strong interest again in growth theory (Irmen 2008, p. 24): 'In a world with closed and open economies, club convergence in growth rates occurs among open economies. Hence, the world income distribution may exhibit club convergence with some countries trapped in a stationary steady state while others experience steady growth' (p. 27).

Finally, in Figure 6.11, we have collected for the years 2000–12 data from the 18 poorest countries in the world economy. Here again, there is clear empirical evidence, this time in favour of the conditional divergence hypothesis. Notice that the existence of such a picture is explained in development economics by vicious circles and the 'trap of poverty' (Sell 1993).

NOTES

*   This chapter is based on the contribution of Blümle and Sell (1998). The original paper was presented at the time at several conferences and was well received. As I remember, helpful comments were provided by Josef Baumgartner, Michele Boldrin, Silke Gehle, Uwe Greiner, Axel Jochem, Bernard Malamud, George Tolley, Matti Viren and Goran Zettergren on a first version of the paper. Additional comments were provided by participants of the 44th International Atlantic Economic Conference held at Philadelphia on 9–12 October 1997 and by the participants of the Workshop in Economic Policy and Public Finance held at the Department of Economics, University of Chicago on 17 October 1997.

1.   In his paper on union-firm bargaining, Palokangas (2004) prefers to maximize a generalized Nash product of unions' 'utility and firms' profits. This procedure, however,

corresponds to the 'Right-to Manage' approach and not to the theory of efficient contracts.

2. Viviane Forrester, *L'horreur économique*, Paris: Arthéme Fayard, 1996, p. 27.
3. Most recently, Barro (1996, pp. 2–3) has found some evidence of a non-linear relationship between the extent of democracy and economic growth.
4. According to Atkinson (1997), the subject of income distribution has been marginalized in the past, but there are strong signs that since the late 1990s it is being welcomed back.
5. We will, for example, make use of the political instability point of view and, at the same time, widen it into a social climate of the society approach.
6. See Tinbergen (1956).
7. See Fischer and Serra (1993) for an explicit modelling of externalities in human capital production and its growth repercussions.
8. Quotation according to Balaglou and Peukert (1996, p. 37).
9. See Lydall (1968, p. 127).
10. See Pen (1973, p. 254).
11. See Bronfenbrenner (1971, pp. 365–85).
12. See Friedman (1953, p. 288).
13. See Blümle (1972).
14. See Braeuer (1981, p. 50).
15. Someone interested in the Tour de France is easily convinced that you must be able to see the leader in front (being yourself a runner up) to be still dreaming of the *maillot jeaune* (yellow jersey).
16. 'A large group of impoverished citizens, facing a small and very rich group of well-off individuals, is likely to become dissatisfied with the existing socioeconomic status quo and demand radical changes. As a result, mass violence and illegal seizures of power are more likely the more unequal the distribution of income is' (Alesina and Perotti 1994, p. 362).
17. See Lange (1968, p. 146).
18. See Mandeville (1980, p. 122).
19. See Hirschmann (1989, p. 86).
20. See Schoeck (1987, pp. 81, 109).
21. See Boulding (1981, p. 208).
22. See Hirschmann (1989, p. 75).
23. See Offe (1991, pp. 279–92).
24. We admit that the Gini coefficient is by no means an optimal measure for the skewness of personal income distribution. However, it is an index for which there exists information for many countries.
25. Our social welfare function is closely related to the one put forward by Sen (1974) where $W = m (1 - G)$ and m stands for per capita income instead of per capita income growth. Generally, the concept of social economic goals and derived social welfare functions goes back to Tinbergen (1963). As a matter of fact, it would be no problem to put forward our model with the level of per capita income as an argument in the welfare function.
26. As opposed to Thomas Piketty (2014, pp. 13–15), we will show that the Kuznets curve is still a useful empirical and theoretical tool of analysis and definitely not a sort of by-product of the two world wars in the twentieth century and the decades in between and after.
27. See Sell (2001) and the literature cited therein.

7. Factor mobility and income distribution

7.1 INTRODUCTION

It is a quite well-known effect of globalization that it has a positive effect on the mobility of the factors of production. This applies to capital and to labour in a different manner: capital mobility has increased far more than labour mobility. The positive reasons are intimately linked to the liberalization and deregulation of capital markets since the 1980s, but also to the processes of financial innovation ('securitization'), and of technological revolutions in the information and in the communication sector. Negatively speaking, labour mobility was prevented from growing faster for reasons of national labour market regulations, by the still high implicit costs of migration and by existing and rather persistent differences in culture and language. The latter holds even if one acknowledges the enormous spread of English over the world as the first communicating language in the last 30 years.

The big transformation of the world economy since the early 1990s is primarily due to the increasing integration of former socialist countries and of other emerging economies into the international division of labour. All of these countries were, by and large, abundant in less qualified labour and scarce in qualified labour (human capital) and in physical capital. As a consequence, (human and physical) capital became on a world scale relatively scarcer and (less qualified) labour became relatively more abundant. This implies, at least in the medium to long run, that the ratio of real interest rates to real wages is pushed upwards.

The organization of this chapter is as follows. In the next two sections, we assess the impact of factor (labour, capital) mobility on the income distribution of the recipient and sending countries in a two-country setting. Thereafter, we put forward a bargaining approach, where the income gains of factor mobility are traded against changes in income distribution. The final section is dedicated to a political economy approach. Here, we incorporate aspects of domestic regulation into the overall picture of income distribution under the conditions of enhanced factor mobility.[1]

7.2 LABOUR MOBILITY AND INCOME DISTRIBUTION

Assume the world is represented by the less wealthy emigration country A and the more developed immigration country M. Both countries produce with the factors of production labour (L) and capital (C) a homogeneous good X. We neglect migration costs (see Sinn 2005 for a model with explicit transaction costs). The production function reads:

$$F^i(L_i, C_i); \text{ with } i = A, M \tag{7.1}$$

Figure 7.1 depicts the initial situation before migration: country A has a low wage rate of w_0^A. Efficient factor allocation demands equating the nominal wage rate with the corresponding marginal value of labour:

$$w_0^A = p_A MPL_A = p_A \frac{\partial X^A}{\partial L} = p_A F_L^A \tag{7.2}$$

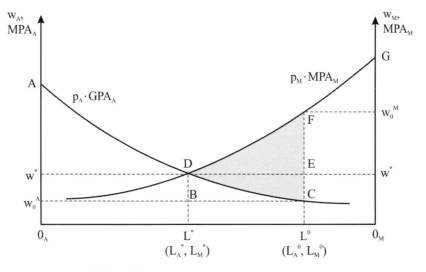

Source: Kermer (2007, p. 175).

Figure 7.1   Labour mobility in the simple factor-specific marginal productivity of two countries diagram

This leads to the total labour input of L_0^A. For reasons of simplicity, we assume a perfectly elastic labour supply, so that only labour demand determines the wage rate. In country M we observe the much higher nominal wage rate w_0^M. Also here, under the conditions of no international factor mobility, it must hold that:

$$w_0^M = p_M MPL_M = p_M \frac{\partial X^M}{\partial L} = p_M F_L^M \qquad (7.3)$$

Hence, before migration, L_A^0 workers are employed in country A and L_M^0 in country M. In a fully integrated labour market between the two areas, labour will migrate from the rich area M to the less wealthy region A. The unique wage rate converges towards w* and the respective labour inputs will now become L_A^*, L_M^*. The main effects of this labour mobility are twofold: one is a nominal output effect, the second is a distribution effect. World nominal output will be increased by the triangle DCF if migration is allowed between A and M. This output gain accrues to the different areas as follows: M increases its nominal GDP by DL*L⁰F, A renounces nominal GDP in the amount of DL*L⁰C. However, it can be shown that the gross gain DCF is divided by the two countries: country M's net gain (in units of GNP) is only DFE if we assume that the migrated labour force from A sends its earnings as 'remittances' back home. This equals the rectangle DEL*L⁰. Considering the loss of nominal output of size DL*L⁰C, country A has a net gain represented by the residual semi-triangle DEC. This is also the net gain in GNP for country A.

Even more interesting, in our context, are the distribution effects of migration: Before migration, labour (capital) income in country A is given by the area:

$$w_0^A CL^0 O_A (w_0^A AC) \qquad (7.4)$$

In country M, the respective factor incomes are:

$$w_0^M FL^0 O_M (w_0^M GF) \qquad (7.5)$$

In the new 'open frontiers' equilibrium D, income distribution changes asymmetrically in both countries. On the one hand, in country A (M), capital income is reduced (increased) by the area w*DCw_0^A(w_0^M FDw*). On the other hand, labour income will rise (fall) in country A (M) by the area w_0^Aw*EC(w_0^M FEw*).

Summing up, the graphical analysis suggests that capital owners will improve (deteriorate) their relative and absolute position in the North

(South) in the aftermath of free labour migration. Moreover, the gains of capital owners in the North ($w_0^M FDw^*$) outweigh the losses of capital owners in the South ($w^* DCw_0^A$). In contrast, owners of low and medium working qualification will deteriorate (improve) their absolute and relative position in the North (South) following a liberalization of labour flows. However, the losses for the factor of production labour in the North ($w_0^M FEw^*$) fall short of the gains achieved by labour in the South ($w_0^A w^* EC$).

Notice that 'the potential for immigration to affect the native income distribution is greater the more closed the economy is to international trade' (Blau and Kahn 2013, p. 12). The intuition is clear. Factor mobility and the free flow of goods and services are somewhat (more or less perfect) substitutes (see Wellisch and Walz 1998): immigration of unqualified work 'increases the supply of labor' (Blau and Kahn 2013, p. 13) and has, by and large, the same impact on the relative price of unskilled work as imports of goods that intensively use low qualified work in production.

This leads us to the important question of how the wage gap between high and low skill labour is affected by immigration, hence how income distribution within the labour market of the recipient country will change (see also Chapter 3). Here, we can rely on the excellent exercise by Kahanec and Zimmermann (2008, p. 30): 'skilled labour immigration has a large potential to reduce inequality in the receiving countries. An important channel is the rise in relative wages of the unskilled with respect to the wages of the skilled. Unskilled immigration seems to generally increase inequality ...'. The authors assume complementarity between skilled and unskilled labour and make a distinction between the exogenous wage (minimum or likewise union wages) and the endogenous wage regime.

Unskilled immigration depicted in Figure 7.3 affects both the market of skilled as well as the market of unskilled labour force. Initial (dis)equilibria in both markets are characterized by A^0 and B^0 respectively. Whereas there is a competitive equilibrium in the labour market of the skilled, the union wage rate w_1^0 causes unemployment of size $\overline{L}^0 - L^0$ in the market for unskilled labour. Immigration shifts labour supply of the unskilled to the right and will cause additional unemployment of size $\overline{L}^1 - \overline{L}^0$, with no consequences for the market of skilled labour. If unions were prepared to let the wage decline from w_1^0 to w_1^1, this would induce more employment of the unskilled (L^1) and, due to complementarity, also raise the demand for the skilled workers. As a result, skilled wages move upwards from w_h^0 to w_h^1, which yields a new equilibrium in point A^1. 'In sum, rising unemployment or falling wages for the poor (or both) and rising wages for the skilled workers mark a reduction in the relative position of the poor, and provide an *indication of increasing inequality*' (pp. 15–16, emphasis added) in the case of unskilled immigration.

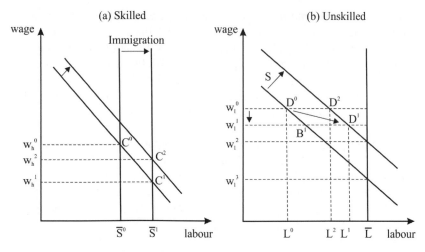

Source: Kahanec and Zimmermann (2008).

Figure 7.2   Employment and wage effects as a consequence of unskilled immigration

In Figure 7.2 (see Kahanec and Zimmermann 2008, p. 15), we have captured the analysis of immigration of the skilled workers. The shift in the supply curve from $\overline{S}^0$ to $\overline{S}^1$ will push the wage rate downwards from w_h^0 to w_h^1, with the equilibrium point now moving downwards from C^0 to C^1. Due to complementarity, the higher employment of the skilled workers will also shift the demand for unskilled workers outwards with w_l^0 as the old and w_l^1 as the new wage rate (equilibrium is removed from D^0 to D^1 or to D^2). This result holds as long as we talk about a rigid union wage regime. Employment, hence, can either increase from L^0 to L^1 or to L^2. Under the competitive scenario, (flexible) wages will rise from w_l^3 to w_l^2. Employment now stays at its competitive level $\overline{L}$. Due to complementarity, we have to take into account a 'feedback effect' on the market for skilled work: demand will shift outwards and so equilibrium moves to C^2 and wages rise up to the new level w_h^2. 'Hence, immigration of skilled labour is likely to cause a decline in skilled wages and a rise in unskilled employment, and in the case of a competitive equilibrium in the unskilled market, also a rise in low-skilled wages. This provides a strong rationale for the conjecture that *skilled immigration reduces inequality*' (p. 15, emphasis added).

Anwar (2008) comes to somewhat different results. In his simple general equilibrium approach for a small open economy, he also finds the immigration of skilled labour to deteriorate income distribution, that is, to increase wage inequality between the skilled and unskilled labour. This

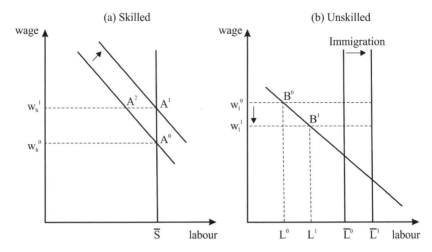

Source: Kahanec and Zimmermann (2008).

Figure 7.3   Employment and wage effects as a consequence of skilled immigration

finding stands in contrast to Kahanec and Zimmermann (2008), where the immigration of skilled labour causes wage inequality to decrease. Not surprisingly, this rather unusual finding of Anwar (2008) hinges upon one key assumption of the author: 'the inflow of . . . skilled labour increases wage inequality as long as the income share of skilled labour in the services sector [which provides a variety of producer services for the production of the industrial good] is greater than (or equal to) the income share of unskilled labour in the agricultural sector' (p. 501). This assumption makes the 'inflow of skilled labour [to] decrease both the skilled and unskilled wage rate but its impact on unskilled wage rate is larger' (Anwar 2008, p. 501). It is in the end an empirical question, whether Kahanec and Zimmermann (2008) or Anwar (2008) drew the right conclusions.

7.3   CAPITAL MOBILITY AND INCOME DISTRIBUTION

In the following, we put forward main market aspects of capital mobility basing our arguments on the contribution of Tobias Seidel (2005). We assume the world consists of two countries, Home (H) und Foreign (F). The factor intensity between capital and labour is given by:

$$k^j = \frac{K^j}{L^j}, j \in \{H,F\} \qquad (7.6)$$

Let there be the same amount of labour force in both countries, but Home shall be more endowed with capital than Foreign. This implies $k^H > k^F$. Output of Home and Foreign is given by the production function,

$$Y^j = f(K^j, L^j) \qquad (7.7)$$

which has well-known properties:

$$f_K^j > 0, f_L^j > 0 \qquad (7.8)$$

and

$$f_{KK}^j < 0, f_{LL}^j < 0 \qquad (7.9)$$

Both countries make use of the same technologies. Hence, the real wage rate (w) and the real interest rate (r) of both countries can be determined easily:

$$w^j = \lambda(k^j) \text{ with } \lambda' > 0 \qquad (7.10)$$

and

$$r^j = \mu(k^j) \text{ with } \mu' > 0 \qquad (7.11)$$

As $k^H > k^F$, it also must hold that $w^H > w^F$ and $r^H < r^F$. In Figure 7.4, we have depicted the situation where both countries run their economies under autarky (no trade, no capital flows).

The initial setting is characterized by the constellation $r_0^H < r_0^F$. Wage income in Home has the size ACr_0^H, capital income equals $r_0^H CKH$. In Foreign, wage income corresponds to DEr_0^F, capital income amounts to $Dr_0^F \overline{FK}$. Now we proceed to analyse the free flow of capital between Home and Foreign. In the first place, we deal with the case of flexible wages in each of the two countries.

7.3.1 Flexible (Real) Wages

As above in the case of the labour markets, we consider symmetry. The marginal productivity of capital is assumed to be higher in Foreign. This gives investors from Home an incentive to export capital to Foreign.

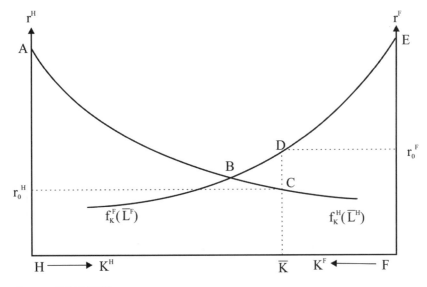

Source: Seidel (2005).

Figure 7.4 *Capital allocation in the simple factor-specific marginal productivity of two countries diagram*

In Figure 7.5, we see the following. When capital leaves Home, the real wage rate (w^H) will fall in Home, but the real interest rate ($r_0^H \rightarrow r_1^H$) will rise. The inverse will happen in Foreign.

With no capital controls existing, capital will be exported from Home to Foreign until the marginal product of capital equalizes in both countries. Hence, also the real interest rates will converge.

This reallocation of factors of production will render a positive welfare effect for the world consisting of two countries. It is equal to the triangle BDC. Before capital flowed, production amounted to the area of ACDEFH, now it is the area of ABEFH that can be produced. The world wins as a whole, but also each country is better off after the flow of capital from Home to Foreign.

Let's turn now to the accounting of GNP and GDP effects. The increase in GNP in Home can be subdivided into the gain of interest rate payments from Foreign ($BG\overline{K}\overline{K'}$) minus the loss of GDP units of size $BC\overline{K}\overline{K'}$.

Gross national income of Home rises by BCG from size $AC\overline{K}H$ to size $ABG\overline{K}H$. Hence, wage income falls in Home from ACr_0^H to ABr_1^H. Net loss hence amounts to $r_1^H BC r_0^H$. However, this loss is more than compensated by the new capital income of size $r_1^H G\overline{K}H$. Net gain of capital income hence

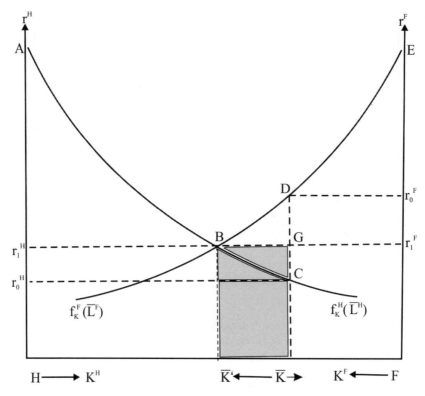

*Figure 7.5   Capital mobility with flexible (real) wages in the simple factor-
specific marginal productivity of two countries diagram*

amounts to $r_1^H GCr_0^H$. Both factors of production jointly win income by the triangle BCG!

Gross national income of Foreign increases from $DEF\overline{K}$ to $BEF\overline{K}GB$. The new gross national income is composed of the GDP of size $BEF\overline{K}$ and the (negative) interest rate payments of size $BG\overline{K}\overline{K}'$. In Foreign, however, capital income will be reduced from its earlier size $Dr_0^F F\overline{K}$ by $Dr_0^F r_1^F G$ to become $Gr_1^F F\overline{K}$. Gains in national welfare here accrue to wage income: labour wins the area $Dr_0^F r_1^F B$. Both factors of production jointly win income by the triangle BDG. Globalization, hence, tends to equalize factor prices. At the same time, domestic capital owners win more than foreign capital owners lose: $r_1^H GCr_0^H > Gr_1^F F\overline{K}$. Conversely, the domestic losses for labour are more pronounced than the gains for labour in the

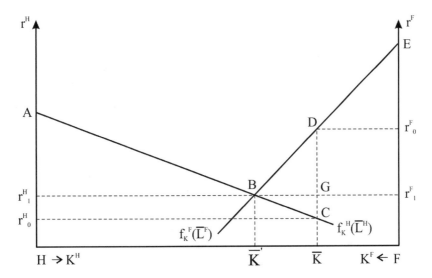

Source: Vaubel (2005).

Figure 7.6 *Capital mobility with flexible (real) wages in the simple factor-specific marginal productivity of two countries diagram (asymmetric marginal productivity curves)*

foreign country: $r_1^H BC r_0^H > Dr_0^F r_1^F B$. Therefore, it seems that the compara-tively immobile factor of production, labour, loses during globalization, while the more mobile factor of production, capital, is on the winning side.

Vaubel (2005, p. 148) objects (Figure 7.6) that these results can some-what turn into their opposite once the assumption of symmetry is given up: if the supply elasticity of human capital (the 'third factor') is larger in the North than in the South of the world economy, the marginal productivity of capital curve in Home will be much flatter than the corresponding curve in Foreign. Now it is the case that the losses for domestic labour are smaller in comparison to the gains for labour in Foreign: $r_1^H BC r_0^H < Dr_0^F r_1^F B$. On the other hand, gains for domestic owners of capital will be smaller than the losses for capital owners in Foreign: $r_1^H GC r_0^H < Gr_1^F F\overline{K}$.

Given this ambiguity in the possible theoretical results that can be achieved, Vaubel (2005, p. 148) suggests investigating empirically the supply elasticities of human capital and the possible differences to be observed in the South and in the North of the global economy.[2]

7.3.2   Rigid (Real) Wages

Seidel (2005) addresses the even more realistic case of rigid real wages in Home. If Home is reluctant to accept lower real wages as a result of capital exports to Foreign, this goal can only be achieved via stabilizing the ratio between capital input and labour input. Given the capital mobility induced by globalization, the same capital intensity of production can only be maintained at Home if labour input is reduced whenever capital exports occur. To make a numerical example: let 10 per cent of capital leave Home via capital exports, then labour input will have to be decreased by the same 10 per cent if the former capital intensity and the earlier level of the real wage is to be stabilized. This necessarily implies that 10 per cent of the active labour force becomes unemployed at Home.

In Figure 7.7, we have the following. Given that each capital import leads to unemployment, the marginal productivity of labour schedule (f_K^H) will shift downwards. A new equilibrium is reached when both marginal productivity curves (at Home and in Foreign) intersect at the old level of the domestic real interest rate. Hence, $\rightarrow r_0^H = r_2^F$.

Worldwide output (and hence total welfare) will fall from ACDEFH to A'B'EFH. Gross national income in Home will decrease from its old level $AC\overline{K}H$ to its new level $A'B'C\overline{K}H$. Gross national income at Home can be subdivided into GDP of $AB\overline{K}'H$ plus the interest rate payments stemming from Foreign ($B'C\overline{K}\,\overline{K}''$). As a consequence, globalization is associated with welfare losses for Home in the presence of rigid wages. While the old loss for wage income $r_1^HBCr_0^H$ seems to be larger than the new one $r_1^HB''B'r_0^H$, now we have to account for U as the number of unemployed and for the fact that GDP has fallen.

Gross national income in Foreign will rise from its former level $ED\overline{K}F$ to its new level $EB'C\overline{K}F$ by B'DC. Hence, the process of globalization is favourable to Foreign. Gross national income of Foreign consists of GDP of size $EB'\overline{K}''F$ minus the interest rate payments to Home ($B'C\overline{K}\,\overline{K}''$). As opposed to the scenario of flexible wages, capital owners in Foreign lose more now than before as $Dr_0^Fr_1^FG < Dr_0^Fr_2^FF$. On the other hand, the labour force gains $DB'r_2^Fr_0^F$, which is definitely more than $Dr_0^Fr_1^FB$.

In the case of rigid wages, the North (Home) will clearly lose welfare, whereas the South (Foreign) still profits from the new division of labour in the world economy. The interesting implication is that rigid wages at Home make autarky more profitable than free trade/free flow of capital goods. Quite opposed to this, Foreign profits from rigid wages at Home and prefers globalization in comparison to autarky. What does this imply in a two-country world? If one of the two countries prefers autarky over globalization, the second country will most likely have to renounce the

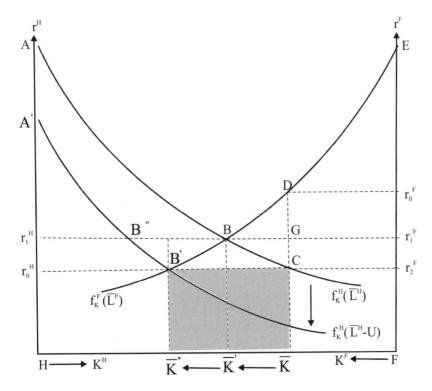

Source: Seidel (2005).

Figure 7.7 *Capital mobility with rigid (real) wages in the simple factor-specific marginal productivity of two countries diagram*

advantages of globalization, although the latter would put it in a better position.

This means ultimately that the aim to protect workers in the North of the world economy against the pitfalls of globalization causes welfare losses not only on the national but also the world scale level. Yet, we may summarize that protectionism and/or the scenario of autarky will not lead us to optimal solutions. The alternative scenario of free capital flows with flexible wages in all the participating countries can create welfare gains for everybody.

However, the scenario of flexible wages is also not free of costs. As we have seen above, in the North of the world economy, wages will suffer from severe income losses, which can create a bunch of social problems. One possibility to prevent this dilemma consists of avoiding minimum wages in conjunction with high social transfers for those who thereby lose their job in favour of wage subsidies. These could be granted up to a specific income frontier.

To sum up, for the (domestic) countries in the North of the world economy, factor mobility seems to have – via market forces – the following major effects. Due to free immigration, labour income and the wage rate will fall, the outflow of capital (and the rise in the interest rate), in turn, will make domestic wage income suffer too. In the case of immigration – assuming that capital is homogeneous – we have, however, to distinguish between the case of unskilled and skilled labour force. Whereas skilled immigration reduces inequality within total wage income (and lets the wages for skilled work fall), the opposite occurs with unskilled immigration. There are strong indicators that this sort of factor mobility goes together with an increasing inequality (and with falling wages for unskilled labour) in the recipient countries.

One should, however, add to our analysis – both for flexible and rigid wages – an important differentiation provided by William Easterly et al. (2004): the results achieved so far stem from what Easterly calls 'the factor world', that is, the neoclassical school of international economics that highlights the differences in the (relative) endowment with production factors across the countries in the world. As Easterly points out, there is in fact an important competing view which he calls 'the productivity world', an approach that can be easily linked to the classical school of economics in the vein of David Ricardo and his theory of comparative advantage. The conclusions with regard to the effects of a free movement of factors of production will now become quite different (Easterly et al. 2004, p. 42).

Suppose countries in the North have an absolute productivity advantage in both sectors of their economy vis-à-vis the South of the global economy: 'Now both capital and labour will want to move to the [North], unlike the predictions of opposite flows (see above) in the factor world model' (Easterly et al. 2004). The final outcome would be – at least if we disregard frictions in the capital market, immigration barriers and so on – that 'all capital and labour moves to the rich country to take advantage of the superior productivity' (p. 42). Easterly's arguments can also be put forward with some easy algebra. Consider a macroeconomic production function with constant returns to scale: $Y_i = K_i^\alpha (A_i L_i)^{1-\alpha}$; where Y_i, A_i, K_i and L_i stand for output, labour augmenting productivity, capital and labour, respectively, in country I, which can either stem from the North (N) or from the South (S). Let $k_i = K_i / L_i$ and $y_i = Y_i / L_i$. In the productivity world, the marginal productivities of capital will be equated:

$$r_N = \frac{\partial Y_N}{\partial K_N} = \alpha k_N^{\alpha-1} A_N^{1-\alpha} = \frac{\partial Y_S}{\partial K_S} = \alpha k_S^{\alpha-1} A_S^{1-\alpha} = r_S \qquad (7.12)$$

Therefore,

$$\frac{\alpha k_N^{\alpha-1}}{\alpha k_S^{\alpha-1}} = \frac{A_S^{1-\alpha}}{A_N^{1-\alpha}} = \frac{A_N^{\alpha-1}}{A_S^{\alpha-1}} \tag{7.13}$$

Hence,

$$\frac{k_N}{k_S} = \frac{A_N}{A_S}. \tag{7.14}$$

In contrast to the full productivity world, we assume governments in the North to effectively control immigration. At the margin, each area (North, South) determines the remuneration of labour under the conditions of autarky. What applies in the no immigration/free capital flows scenario to wages?

$$w_N = \frac{\partial Y_N}{\partial L_N} = (1 - \alpha) k_N^\alpha A_N^{1-\alpha} \tag{7.15}$$

$$w_S = \frac{\partial Y_S}{\partial L_S} = (1 - \alpha) k_S^\alpha A_S^{1-\alpha} \tag{7.16}$$

Therefore,

$$\frac{w_N}{w_S} = \left(\frac{k_N}{k_S}\right)^\alpha \left(\frac{A_N}{A_S}\right)^{1-\alpha} = \frac{A_N}{A_S} = \frac{y_N}{y_S} \tag{7.17}$$

What now are the implications for intra- and inter-country equality of incomes? The resulting capital flows from the South to the North will 'lower capital-labour ratios in the southern countries and raise them in northern countries' (Easterly et al. 2004, p. 43). 'Southern countries will thus have lower wages and per-capita incomes, both because of lower productivity and lower-capital-labour ratios' (p. 42). Moreover, free capital mobility increases 'the per capita income ratio between rich and poor countries, increasing international inequality. Free capital mobility would lower the rate of return to capital in rich countries and increase it in poor countries; it would increase wages in rich countries and lower them in poor countries. Therefore it would lower domestic inequality in rich countries and increase inequality in poor countries. Capital flight from poor countries increases both international inequality and domestic inequality in the poor countries' (p. 43).

7.4   BARGAINING FOR WHAT?

The subsequent analysis addresses the situation in a 'factor world'. For what could firms and unions bargain when the economy faces 'a shock that results in' (García-Penalosa and Turnovsky 2013, p. 3) lower wages, higher interest rates, a lower wage and a higher profit share due to the forces of immigration? It is a somewhat undisputed effect of globalization that labour loses and capital wins. But labour could become a 'shareholder' of the achievements of globalization if it would 'participate' in the gains of capital. Three approaches seem to be feasible:

1.   increasing the qualification of labour or accumulating more human capital
2.   increasing the propensity to save or accumulating more financial capital
3.   increasing the participation in the firm or accumulating more shares of the enterprises' physical capital.

In a way, none of these alternatives can be reached by labour alone. Capital should be willing to help. This help has the character of compensation. It reminds us of Harrod's plea (1938) in favour of English landlords after the abolition of tariffs on corn in the year 1846. This event was as exogenous as today's globalization that hurts many economic agents in the labour market.

What sort of interest could domestic capital have to compensate labour for the losses incurred by globalization? One could think of at least the following:

1.   to help avoid union directives and members of unions campaigning in favour of a higher taxation of capital income (tax competition)
2.   to stabilize the overall social climate, avoiding spite and envy
3.   to reduce the likelihood of a higher propensity to strike among unions.

The basic reasoning for economic compensation stems from Nicolas Kaldor (1939) and J.R. Hicks (1939). We attempt to visualize their thoughts with the help of Figure 7.8. In Figure 7.8, we have depicted on the two axes respectively the utility of the unions (ordinate), $U(u)$ and (abscissa) of the firms, $U(f)$. Utility of the unions depends positively, say, on total labour income (LI), while utility of the firms is positively related to total profit income (Π).

Suppose the initial equilibrium (before globalization) is given by point 1; this is located on the utility possibilities curve UPC. As shown above, the real wage and the real interest rate shock bring the economy to point 2.

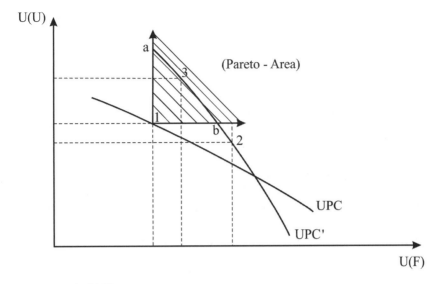

Source: Külp (1975).

Figure 7.8   Compensation strategies for utility losses due to globalization

After the shock, the new utility possibilities curve UPC′ becomes relevant. It is obvious that point 2 does not satisfy the Pareto criterion: unions do not achieve the same level of utility as in point 1. However, it is feasible to approach a new point along UPC′, say point 3. Firms can compensate unions for the losses associated with the globalization shock and are still better off than in 1. Unions, in turn, may find themselves in a much more comfortable position than in 1. Point 3, hence, fulfils the conditions of the Kaldor-Hicks criterion. For this, it is essential that the new utility possibilities curve cuts the so-called Pareto area (Figure 7.8). Moreover, as point 3 is always superior vis-à-vis point 1, not only the Kaldor-Hicks criterion but also the Scitovsky criterion is fulfilled (Külp 1975, p. 113).

But are firms the correct agent to compensate unions for wage losses? In principle, both the government and the business site have an interest in the compensation for losses due to globalization: firms have to face the trade-off between the need for international competitiveness, on the one hand, and maintaining good and workable relations with unions (see above), on the other hand. The government, in turn, has to safeguard both the attractiveness of the domestic economy for foreign investors (locational competition) and the maintenance of social peace. One way to organize the compensation is to install minimum wages. Minimum wages can either be organized politically, that is, by law, or they can be bargained between firms and unions. In the following graphical analysis, we consider minimum wages that affect directly the firms' budget constraints. Under autarky, the budget constraint reads:

$$C = r^a K + w^a L \qquad (7.18)$$

with r^a, w^a = real interest (wage) rate under autarky

As we have seen above, free mobility of factors of production will make the (real) interest rate rise and the (real) wage rate fall in the North of the world economy. The new budget constraint under the conditions of globalization is now:

$$C = r^g K + w^g L \qquad (7.19)$$

with r^g, w^g = real interest (wage) rate under globalization

$$r^g > r^a; w^g < w^a \qquad (7.20)$$

In Figure 7.9, we have depicted first the situation under autarky that is associated with the optimal solution in M and output level x^a. Under globalization, the budget constraint line will be flatter, as the new real

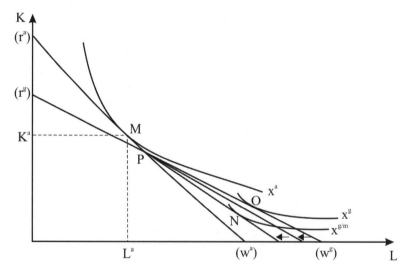

Source: Author.

Figure 7.9   *Optimal allocation of production factors under autarky and under globalization*

interest rate is now higher, and the new real wage rate is now lower than before. Output x^g would be the associated production level. Point O could, for example, represent the new equilibrium. If minimum wages are installed, the budget constraint becomes a kinked line with P as a corner. The intersection with the x axis moves leftwards (see arrows) depending on the size of the minimum wage. Now, for example, point N could become a new equilibrium with $x^{g/m}$ as the output level associated with globalization in conjunction with minimum wages. Notice that one may expect $x^{g/m}$ to fall short of x^g. This is the 'price' the economy pays for the stabilization of the social climate facing the forces of globalization and making use of minimum wages.

It is a fairly rational assumption that firms are interested in both international competitiveness as well as social peace (see above). The following model includes a further variable in our picture, namely the working conditions for the labour force, A. Higher values of A symbolize or likewise indicate 'improved quality of the physical and psychological work environment' (Daniel and Sofer 1998, p. 549). The subsequent analysis basically follows the logic of Daniel and Sofer's contribution (1998). However, their interest was primarily in the question of how firms can compensate for higher wages with more or less deficient working conditions. Our focus is just the opposite: how can firms compensate for wage decreases induced by the forces of globalization with better working conditions?

Let the revenue of the firm (R) depend on the price of the only produced good (p) and on production, f. The latter in turn depends positively on A and on labour input L. Higher values of A are associated with positive effects on the productivity of workers (Daniel and Sofer 1998, p. 548). For reasons of simplicity, we take p to be 1. L is a constant, as negotiations concern only workers already hired (p. 550); p_A is the exogenous price of a unit of working conditions. Hence,

$$\Pi = \Pi(w, A) = pR(A, L) - wL - p_A A; R'(A), R'(L) > 0 \quad (7.21)$$

Iso-profit curves of firms are characterized by:

$$d\Pi = \frac{\partial \Pi}{\partial w} dw + \frac{\partial \Pi}{\partial A} dA = 0 \quad (7.22)$$

Combining this property with the first order condition yields the marginal rate of substitution between w and A:

$$\frac{dw}{dA} = -\frac{\dfrac{\partial \Pi}{\partial A}}{\dfrac{\partial \Pi}{\partial w}} = \frac{R'_A - p_A}{L} \leq 0 \quad (7.23)$$

The slope can be positive, negative or nil.

Utility of unions (which should be identical here with the utility of each union's member) is given by:

$$U = U(w, A); U'(w) > 0; U'(A) > 0 \qquad (7.24)$$

Total differentiation gives us the slope of a representative indifference curve:

$$dU = \frac{\partial U}{\partial w} dw + \frac{\partial U}{\partial A} dA = 0 \qquad (7.25)$$

Combining this property with the first order condition yields the marginal rate of substitution between w and A:

$$\frac{dw}{dA} = -\frac{\dfrac{\partial U}{\partial A}}{\dfrac{\partial U}{\partial w}} = -\frac{U_A}{U_w} < 0 \qquad (7.26)$$

The slope will be negative. Assuming that bargaining over working conditions and wages occurs simultaneously, optima (see earlier chapters) are characterized by tangential solutions between iso-profit curves (firms) and indifference curves (unions):

$$\frac{dw}{dA} = \frac{R'_A - p_A}{L} = -\frac{U_A}{U_w} \qquad (7.27)$$

Figure 7.10 shows the graphical interpretation of possible equilibria and the position of the contract curve: 'If the union follows a policy of income redistribution between its members that takes into account the disutility of work, the contract curve is downward sloping' (Daniel and Sofer 1998, p. 548). Let the initial equilibrium ('autarky') in D be characterized by a high wage w_1 in conjunction with a low level of working conditions, A_1. Globalization will force both sides to reduce the monetary remuneration of work, especially in the case of lower/medium qualified labour. In the new equilibrium (B), firms are willing to compensate for the loss of wage income (w_2) by increasing the level/improving working conditions to A_2. As a result, the efficient contract curve CC is a downward falling line.

Notice that improving the working conditions has a positive effect on labour productivity (see above) and, hence, contributes to dampen marginal costs of labour. The latter effect gives enterprises in turn the scope for moderate wage increases in the future that accompany the process of rising GDP per capita and labour productivity in the South of the world economy.

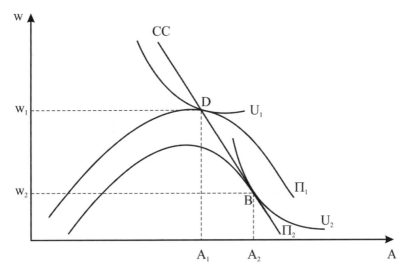

Source: Modified from Daniel and Sofer (1998).

Figure 7.10 Bargaining for wages and working conditions between unions and firms

7.5 THE POLITICAL ECONOMY OF FACTOR MOBILITY AND INCOME DISTRIBUTION

As we described above, trade and migration are to some extent substitutes and tend to have quite similar effects on income distribution. However, policy makers seem to have a clear preference for free trade and against unhindered migration (Wellisch and Walz 1998). As free factor mobility implies free movements of capital, the latter, in a sense, signals financial integration as opposed to financial autarky and goes along with free exchange of goods and services too.

Notwithstanding these facts, we want to address specifically the political economy of factor mobility and income distribution. In a 'pure market forces approach', policy makers in the North of the world economy would have to face (see above) the following: capital exports in conjunction with (skilled and unskilled) labour import, a rising share of capital income, necessarily in combination with a falling labour share in domestic GDP. For policy makers such an outcome embeds a trade-off: while the free movement of factors of production serves to maximize income (Y) and the international competitiveness of the domestic economy, the lack of regulation for labour and capital flows puts into danger a socially acceptable share for labour in national income. In contrast, the regulation of factors' mobility (capital export controls, immigration laws) can help to better achieve the distributional goal, but have to be paid by losses in allocative efficiency and hence in output.

Voters want the government to solve the trade-off by exploring the optimal quality and size of the regulation instrument. In the subsequent, initial and quite simple model, we compare two scenarios: the totally regulated economy, which allows no capital exports and no immigration, on the one hand, and the totally unregulated economy with equilibrium capital exports and immigration of foreign labour force, on the other. The different gross national incomes amount to:

$$\Pi^u = Y[\overline{K} - K^*, L^* + \overline{L}] + \Pi - LR \qquad (7.28)$$

$$\Pi^r = Y[\overline{K}, \overline{L}] \qquad (7.29)$$

with Π = interest income from abroad and LR = labour remittances. As we saw above, $\Pi^u > \Pi^r$ and $LIS^u < LIS^r$, where LIS = labour income share. The simple voting function reads:

$$V = V(\Pi, LIS); V'(\Pi) > 0; V'(LIS) > 0 \qquad (7.30)$$

In a Π/LIS diagram (Figure 7.11), we can at least identify the coordinates of the regulated and unregulated economy: as suggested above, if the domestic economy renounces installing export and immigration quotas, total income Π^u of the unregulated economy will exceed income in the regulated income, Π^r. In contrast, the labour income share in the unregulated economy, LIS^u, falls short of the corresponding share in the regulated economy, LIS^r.

If we interconnect these coordinates, and sort of interpolate the empty space in between, we get a dotted line. The latter can be virtually a tangent to an indifference or likewise iso-voting curve $\overline{V}_0$ in point P. The closer P is to the coordinates of the unregulated (regulated) economy, the higher (lower) domestic income (gross national income = GNI), but the lower (higher) the labour income share.

David E. Wildasin (2006) has put forward a framework (not yet a model) of fiscal competition that can also serve as a conduit for a political economy approach: 'a jurisdiction adapts its policies so as to attract mobile resources that produce net fiscal benefits and to repel those that impose net fiscal burdens' (p. 82). The instruments at the disposition of the jurisdiction are taxation and the provision of public services. It is easy

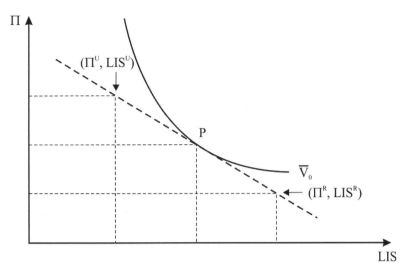

Source: Author.

Figure 7.11 *The political economy model of factor mobility*

to transfer this thought to unskilled ('to repel') and to skilled labour ('to attract') as well as to physical capital (sort of limit the outflow to a fiscal optimum, see below). The outcome of the optimization problem for the government should fulfil the conditions of political economy equilibrium if it portrays the electorate's criteria for a sound level of immigration and capital outflows.

More precisely, the optimality criterion for each (incoming!) mobile resource reads that the 'marginal net fiscal benefit' (MNFB) to the jurisdiction from attracting additional units of that resource, that is, the difference between additional fiscal contributions through the revenue system $(\Delta T)^3$ net of marginal cost (MC) of providing public services, will be driven to zero:

$$MNFB = \Delta T - MC = 0 \qquad (7.31)$$

To give an example for situations outside equilibrium. A too high (low) taxation of skilled immigrating labour in comparison to the additional costs of providing public services: $\Delta T > MC$ ($\Delta T < MC$) will lower (increase) immigration to an undesired small (high) level. The equilibrium for the jurisdiction is also a political economy equilibrium because domestic residents will consider taxation of immigrants appropriate to enhance the supply of public services to avoid congestion effects. Moreover, one has to consider as well outgoing mobile factors of production. This aspect is missing in Wildasin's equilibrium analysis.

As we saw above, at least the factor world point of view (Easterly) suggests that the North of the world economy will have incentives to export physical capital to the South. Is there no fiscal optimality condition for outgoing factors? Of course, there is one: now the jurisdiction should safeguard that the marginal loss ($-\Delta T$) of fiscal contributions (part of earlier domestic capital is no longer due to taxation) does not exceed the marginal cost reduction of providing public services (MCR):

$$MNFC = MCR - \Delta T = 0 \qquad (7.32)$$

Then, and only then, 'marginal net fiscal costs' (MNFC) will be driven down to zero. However, it may well be that the Wildasin solution corresponds more to the will of a social planner than to the one of the majority of the electorate/to the will of the median voter. The different views can be explained with the help of Figure 7.12.

It is obvious from the above calculus that the social optimal solution is given in point C, where marginal costs of providing public services to immigrants equal the marginal tax earnings due to immigration (for reasons of simplicity, we leave out in this case the issue of capital exports). Any solution on the x axis beyond point D/D9 is sub-optimal and would be repelled from the viewpoint of the social planner(s), but it may well be that a majority of the electorate prefers some point between D (D9) and E (E9). This scenario is the more likely, for example, the higher the share of former immigrants in the electorate of the receiving country. Take the large community of Turks in Germany as a clear example. The consequences for income distribution seem to be quite clear. Under the political economy scenario of immigration, the marginal costs of public services offered to immigrants exceed the marginal tax earnings one can expect. As social welfare programmes belong to the major expenditure categories of public spending, one may expect that the Gini coefficient out of net incomes is lowered in the political economy equilibrium in comparison to the social planner equilibrium.[4]

7.6   EMPIRICAL FACTS AND FIGURES

Recent empirically oriented papers, such as Delogu et al. (2013), confirm the results achieved above in our 'market analysis': 'liberalization [an increase of labour mobility] decreases the average level of GDP per worker in receiving (developed) countries, and increases it in the sending (developing countries)' (Delogu et al. 2013, p. 31). Their analysis goes beyond our own

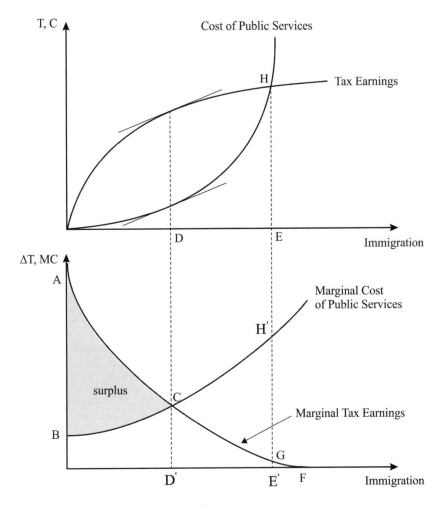

Source: Engelkamp and Sell (2013, p. 497).

Figure 7.12 Optimizing the size of immigration

in that they not only consider the pure 'migration shock' but in addition they consider what the authors call the 'human capital response' to the migration shock: 'main winners are future generations of people originating from poor countries', whereas the losers are 'current generations of low-skilled nationals in high-income countries' (p. 32).

Dustmann and Görlach (2014) address, among other things, the immigrants' earnings careers after their arrival in the destination country. This

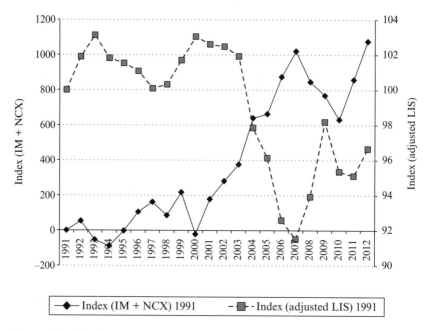

Note: IM = immigration, NCX = net capital exports.

Source: Deutsche Bundesbank and German Federal Bureau of Statistics.

Figure 7.13   *Adjusted labour share in national income for Germany
(1991–2012) matched with an immigration plus net capital
exports index*

implies observing not only the mean earnings of entry cohorts but also
identifying their wage progression in the host country (p. 2). The diffi-
culty in accurately measuring wage progression empirically is due to the
fact that if one entire cohort enters the host country at one point in time,
one part of that cohort may – at a later point in time – have returned into
their country of origin, while a second part belongs to the permanent
immigrants. For the OECD, there is increasing evidence that permanent
migrations are rather the exception than the rule. Moreover, outmigration
may not be a random process, but a selective one. In the latter case, for
example, 'only the least successful leave the country' (p. 3). Ignoring selective outmigration would indicate a steeper wage progression for the cohort
under observation. The problem is aggravated by the fact that many countries carefully register the arrival of new immigrants, but keep no records
of immigrants who leave (p. 4).

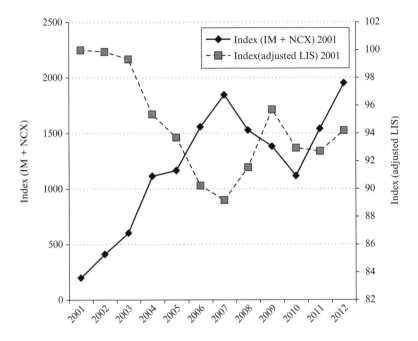

Note: IM = immigration, NCX = net capital exports.

Source: Deutsche Bundesbank and German Federal Bureau of Statistics.

*Figure 7.14   Adjusted labour share in national income for Germany
(2001–12) matched with an immigration plus net capital
exports index*

Based on our earlier analysis of the impact of immigration and net capital
exports on the (adjusted) LIS, we have conducted an empirical investigation
for Germany (1991–2012 and 2001–12). As immigration figures have the
dimension 'thousands of immigrant persons' and net capital exports have
the dimension '€', one cannot simply add the two time series. That would
mean putting together apples and pears. Therefore, we have constructed an
individual index (1991 = 100 and 2001 = 100 respectively) for each variable
and then a compound index that adds up the two individual indices.

In Figure 7.13 it is interesting to register that the compound 'pressure'
of immigration and net capital export flows is strong throughout the
periods under observation, although immigration to Germany was weak
in the second decade of the new millennium and Germany's net capital
exports were weak (in fact they were negative) in the first decade of the
new millennium. In Figure 7.14 one can clearly see that the adjusted LIS

(in both the time periods) comes down – labour loses share of national income – and, inversely, the share of capital in national income increases. Therefore, the empirical findings support our theoretical prediction that both immigration and net capital exports tend to dampen the LIS (see above).

NOTES

1. We will not enter the discussion on how, for example, immigration policies of a host country and education policies of a source country affect the size and quality of labour migration and spending on education. See for an excellent theoretical approach the paper by Djajić and Michael (2014).
2. Notice that the separate and necessarily partial analysis of labour immigration into the North of the world economy and of capital exports out of the North cannot capture general equilibrium effects. If we consider simultaneous or former capital exports in the analysis of labour immigration, the MPL curve of the North should be shifted to the left, that is, inwards, as labour is now less productive. The same effect has to be considered, *mutatis mutandis*, in the South: due to capital imports, the respective MPL curve should be shifted outwards. If, on the other hand, we consider a former or simultaneous import of labour in the analysis of capital exports of the North, the MPC curve of the North should be shifted to the right, that is, outwards, as capital is now more productive. The same effect has to be considered, *mutatis mutandis*, in the South: due to labour emigration, the respective MPC curve should be shifted inwards as capital is now less productive. See, for a similar argument, Facchini and Willmann (2004, p. 3).
3. Notice that it escaped Wildasin (2006, p. 82) that the relevant taxation variable is not taxation as such, but, as we are dealing with a marginal analysis, it is the marginal change in taxation revenue that has to be compared with the marginal cost of providing public services.
4. Bolton and Roland (1986) design a two-country model in order to analyse political equilibria with no mobility and perfect mobility (unification of the two economic areas). In each country, a linear income tax serves to finance, after considering the cost of public funds, a bundle of public goods (pp. 99–100). The equilibrium tax rate is the 'most preferred tax rate of the median voter' (p. 102). They show that 'under perfect mobility, the two countries offer an identical tax and public good package in equilibrium' (p. 102). The same applies to incomes per capita across countries: in equilibrium, they are equal with the consequence that 'the political costs of unification are eliminated' (p. 103).

8. International trade and income distribution

8.1 INTRODUCTION

There can be no doubt that there is no field in the economics of income distribution that has been explored to such an extent and so profoundly as international trade and its implications for the inequality of incomes. This implies that we have to decide in the very beginning of this chapter which aspects we want to choose out of a huge variety of alternatives and which we want address. When doing this, we are fully aware of the fact that each selection of topics and tools has somewhat normative implications.

We have a clear preference for looking at international trade and income distribution from the point of view of globalization. If the latter (see also earlier chapters in this book) can be understood as a process of integration into the world economy, accompanied by an intensified competition on all types of markets and a higher degree of division of work, then we believe the following three approaches seem to fit well:

1. income distribution effects of international trade in a tradeables-non-tradeables framework (Salter, Swan, Meade)
2. income distribution effects of international trade in the neoclassical two-goods setting (Heckscher, Ohlin, Stolper, Samuelson)
3. income distribution effects of international trade in the presence of fragmentation (Deardorff, Jones and Kierzkowski).

8.2 INCOME DISTRIBUTION IN A WORLD OF TRADEABLES AND NON-TRADEABLES

We start (see Sell 2005) our analysis in the vein of the so-called Australian model of international trade that goes back to pioneering works of Salter, Swan and Meade with the following assumptions: the North (South) of the world economy is equipped with a comparative advantage in the production of goods and services in the high-tech sector (low-tech sector). Hence, the North (South) will by tendency import goods and services from

181

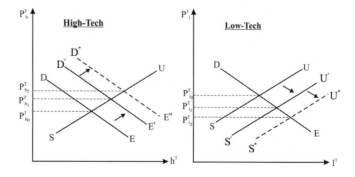

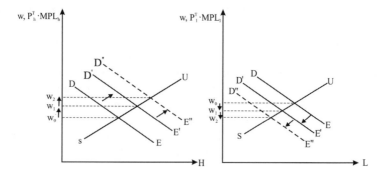

Source: Sell (2005).

*Figure 8.1   The impact of globalization on the (goods, labour) markets for
              tradeable high-tech and low-tech goods*

the low-tech (high-tech) sector, produced with a labour force of medium
to low (medium to high) qualification. In Figure 8.1 we have depicted the
situation in the North of the world economy: in the left part (upper graph),
we see the market for high-tech traded goods and the concomitant labour
market (lower graph); in the right part (upper graph), we recognize respectively (upper graph) the market for low-tech goods and the corresponding
labour market (lower graph).

The impact of globalization will be to induce an additional demand for
tradeable high-tech goods (D′E′) as well as for tradeable services (D″E″)
from the high-tech sector in the North of the world economy. As a consequence, prices, employment and wages will rise in the tradeables producing
high-tech sector of the North. Notice that the price increases on the goods

market will shift the marginal value of labour (P times MPL) outwards and cause higher employment and wages.

In the right part of Figure 8.1 we observe – due to the integration of the South into the world economy – an additional supply of goods (S'U') and of services (S"U") belonging to the tradeables producing low-tech sector. As a consequence, prices, employment and wages will come down in the low-tech sector of the North. Notice that the price decreases on the goods market will shift the marginal value of labour curve inwards and cause lower employment and wages. If there are wage rigidities in the labour market of low qualification, the negative employment effects will be exacerbated. As a result, we observe a sharp rise in the gap between the wages for qualified (or likewise skilled) labour and the wages for unqualified (or likewise unskilled) labour. Inequality of incomes earned via work, hence, is widened.

As the sector of tradeables is intimately connected with the sector of non-tradeables, we also have to consider in our analysis the repercussions of the effects found in the tradeables sector on the sector of non-tradeables. In the subsequent analysis, we depart from the assumption that non-tradeable goods and services are complements to tradeable goods and services.

In Figure 8.2, we have depicted again the situation in the North of the world economy: in the left part (upper graph), we see the market for high-tech non-tradeable goods/services and the concomitant labour market (lower graph); in the right part (upper graph), we recognize respectively (upper graph) the market for low-tech non-tradeable goods/services and the corresponding labour market (lower graph). In analogy to the above analysis, we find that the high-tech sector of non-tradeables will experience a higher demand (D'E'). The latter demand shift will moreover be fostered by the effect of fragmentation (D"E"): as we shall explain in more detail later, fragmentation in production and trade induces an additional demand for (in many cases non-tradeable) services (final assembly, local coordination and communication services). As a consequence, prices, employment and wages will rise in the non-tradeable high-tech sector of the North. Notice that the price increases on the goods/services market will shift the marginal value of labour outwards and cause higher employment and wages.

In the right part of Figure 8.2, we observe – due to the complementarity between tradeable and non-tradeable goods and services – a lower demand for goods (D'E') and of services (D"E") belonging to the low-tech sector of non-tradeables. As a consequence, prices, employment and wages will come down in the low-tech sector of non-tradeables. Notice that the price decreases on the goods and services market will shift the marginal value

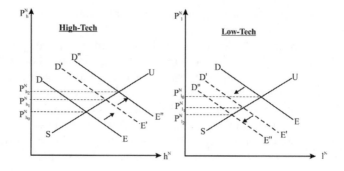

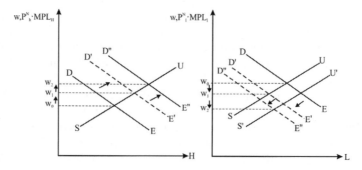

Source: Sell (2005).

Figure 8.2 *The impact of globalization on the (goods, labour) markets for*
non-tradeable high-tech and low-tech goods

of labour curve inwards and cause lower employment and wages. If there
are wage rigidities in the labour market of low qualification, the negative
employment effects will be exacerbated. Notice that immigration into
the low-tech labour market of non-tradeables (S'U') will put additional
pressure on the respective wages. As a result, we observe a rise in the gap
between the wages for qualified (or likewise skilled) labour and the wages
for unqualified (or likewise unskilled) labour also in the sector of non-
tradeables. Inequality of incomes earned via work, hence, is widened too.

In sum, it is again low qualified labour in the North of the world
economy that suffers from the effects of globalization. The gap already
existing with regard to the wages of high qualified labour will be enhanced.
Inequality of incomes earned via work, hence, is widened once more. There

is moreover an additional interesting aspect involved in our above analysis. In Germany (and in many other developed countries), unions are organized by the principle of industry and not by the principle of profession. More precisely, unions of the metal industry bargain over the wages for all of the employees in this sector. This includes the labour force of low and of high qualification, producing either tradeables or non-tradeables. The question that arises is whether such an organization principle of unions makes sense when it comes to the challenges of globalization (see above).

As our above analysis has shown, a high (low) qualified labour force in the high-tech sectors of tradeables and non-tradeables shares a lot of common interests. Therefore, it would make sense to reorganize the structure of unions according to the principle of 'high-tech' vis-à-vis 'low-tech' and not (if it is so) following the principle of industries because the latter principle makes unions bargain simultaneously for the low and for the high qualified labour force. Many intra-union conflicts are then embedded that tend to reduce the bargaining power of the union in question/concerned and that could be avoided following the new principle.

8.3 INCOME DISTRIBUTION IN A HECKSCHER-OHLIN-STOLPER-SAMUELSON (HOS) WORLD

In the following, we present a simple graphical exposition of the so-called HOSS, or simpler, HOS model (see also Hellier 2013, pp. 107–46). We start with these assumptions: there are two factors of production, skilled labour (H) and less skilled labour (L), two goods h (high-tech) and l (low-tech), the production of h being H-intensive and that of l being L-intensive (p. 110). We consider two areas or countries: the North (N) and the South (S). Neither the North nor the South specializes totally in the production of one of these goods. Prices of goods equal costs (no profits due to pure competition, losses imply market exit). There are identical demand functions in both countries, no transport costs and identical technologies (p. 111).

Figure 8.3 reveals that firms choose the input of skilled and unskilled labour according to the relative price of unskilled labour, w/r, where w is the absolute price of unskilled labour and r equals the absolute price of skilled labour. The curve (H/L)h shows the different relative factor inputs in the high-tech-sector, the curve (H/L)l the respective relative factor inputs in the low-tech sector. Each of these curves is a function of the relative factor price, w/r. As can be seen, we have depicted the (H/L)h curve lying strictly above the (H/L)l curve. This means that, at any given factor price ratio (w/r), the production of high-tech goods is more intense in the use of skilled labour than the production of low-tech goods.

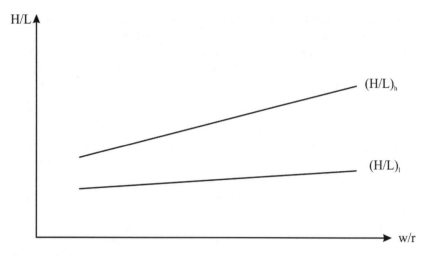

Source: Author.

*Figure 8.3   The neoclassical relationship between relative factor prices and
              factor intensities for high-tech and for low-tech goods*

What is the relationship between factor prices and goods prices? As prices
are equal to production costs under the conditions of competition, they
depend on factor prices. If the costs for unskilled (skilled) labour are high,
then we gauge that the prices of those goods should be high too that use
intensively unskilled (skilled) labour in production.[1]

The stronger this relationship, the more important the input of the
respective factor for production of the final good. As an example, suppose
unions achieve in negotiations with firms a strong increase in the wages for
unskilled (skilled) labour. This will lead to higher costs for this factor of
production, provided that there is no matching rise in the marginal productivity of the respective factor. As a consequence (given that we have a scenario of no losses and no profits), firms will increase especially the prices
of those goods that use intensively unskilled (skilled) labour. By contrast,
prices of goods that use intensively skilled (unskilled) labour will rise to a
lesser extent. Therefore, we can assign to a given relative wage (w/r) a specific ratio of the goods prices. This is the content of the Stolper-Samuelson
curve in Figure 8.4.

Let us continue with our example from above: what are the consequences
for income distribution? Real compensation of the unskilled labour force
has improved relative to both final goods and, inversely, real compensation
of the skilled labour force has deteriorated. A rise in the relative price of
the low-tech good improves the purchasing power of unskilled workers

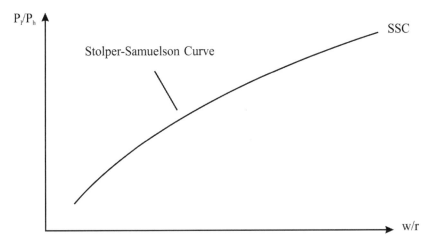

Source: Author.

Figure 8.4   A stylized version of the Stolper-Samuelson curve

and lowers, accordingly, the purchasing power of the skilled workers. Why is this so?

Each factor of production is remunerated in line with its marginal productivity. The latter, as well known, diminishes when the factor input is increased, *ceteris paribus*. If there is now a relative price increase in favour of the low-tech goods and to the detriment of the high-tech goods, input of skilled labour will be increased in both sectors. As a result, we will observe a lower real compensation for skilled labour and a higher real compensation for unskilled labour. Hence, income distribution changes in accordance with relative price and relative wage changes.

Now let us proceed to our third pillar, the Rybczynski line. If we want to derive this function, we first will have to make some assumptions. We take the prices for (and hence the relative price of) final goods as constant. This implies that the rewards to factors of production do not change either. This, in turn, means that the capital intensity with which the two goods (h, l) are produced do not alter. Finally, we take it for granted that full employment prevails for all factors of production. Suppose again that good h (l) uses (un)skilled work relatively intensively, so that

$$H_h/L_h > H_l/L_l \qquad (8.1)$$

In Figure 8.5, we have a traditional Edgeworth box, with the limited amount of L and H on the axes. At the very start of our analysis, we have

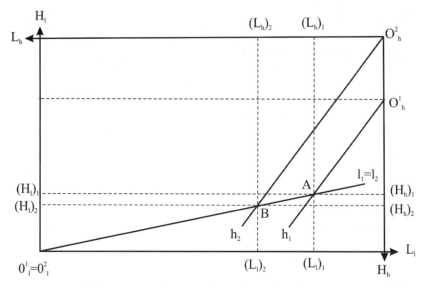

Source: Author.

Figure 8.5   Derivation of the Rybczynski effect within the Edgeworth box

the origins O_1^1, O_h^1. The skilled-unskilled labour intensities for goods h and l determine the allocation of skilled labour and unskilled labour on the contract line. The latter is given by the two paths of expansion h_1, l_1 that intersect at point A. If there is more skilled labour available, the O_h^1 origin is shifted upwards to its new position O_h^2. As goods prices do not change, the H/L intensities do not change either. The equilibrium moves from point A to point B. We can see that less skilled and unskilled labour is allocated to produce good l. The production of l falls, the production of h rises. Notice that the economy's relative endowment H/L has increased and, at the same time, the relative production h/l has gone upwards. So a first specification of the Rybczynski line reads:

$$h/l = f(H/L); f' > 0; f'' < 0 \qquad (8.2)$$

A final, but important question has to be answered: how does a change in the price ratio P_h / P_l affect the position of the Rybczynski line? Hence,

$$h/l = f(H/L; P_h/P_l) \qquad (8.3)$$

The hypothesis introduced here argues that:

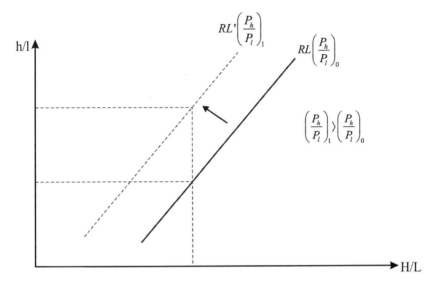

Source: Author.

Figure 8.6 *How is the Rybczynski line affected by relative price changes?*

$$\frac{\partial(h/l)}{\partial(P_h/P_l)} > 0 \qquad (8.4)$$

This hypothesis is always true, as it represents the 'law of demand and supply': if the relative price of the high-tech goods rises, this will expand the relative production of h and reduce the relative production of l. As a result, any positive change in the price ratio of high-tech goods to low-tech goods will shift the original Rybczynski (RL) line to the left (RL'), *ceteris paribus*. This is what we also find in Figure 8.6.

Now that we have 'collected' our three pillars pertaining to the HOS framework, we put them together in a four-graph diagram (Figure 8.7) in order to study the effects of globalization on income distribution of the North (see Landmann and Pflüger 1997): as before, we assume the South (North) to have a comparative advantage in the production of the low-tech (high-tech) good l (h) as it is equipped in relative abundance with unskilled (skilled) labour. Factors of production are compensated with wages w (for unskilled labour) and r (for skilled labour). Initially, there is a relative price P_h / P_l as a consequence of the intersection of 'domestic' relative demand DE and relative supply SU in point A. This situation is depicted in the first quadrant of Figure 8.7. According to the Rybczynski line, there is a

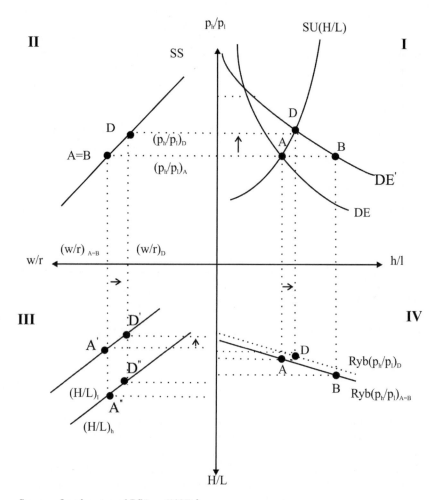

Source: Landmann and Pflüger (1997).[2]

*Figure 8.7   The effects of globalization in the USA as opposed to
Continental Europe*

matching point A in the fourth quadrant. The corresponding intensity of
skilled labour relative to unskilled labour is a sort of average of the skilled
labour intensities for the high-tech good (point A″) and for the low-tech
good (point A′) in the third quadrant. The respective relative wages can
be found on the x axis of quadrant 2; this quadrant contains the Stolper-
Samuelson curve and relates relative wages in equilibrium to relative prices
(in point A of quadrant 2). Drawing a horizontal line from point A in

quadrant 2 to point A in quadrant 1 again gives us the equilibrium on the goods markets with the respective relative production of h/l.

Integration of the South into the world economy has the following effects. The North will experience a higher relative demand towards its high-tech goods (shift from DE to DE′); the North satisfies this higher relative demand by offering a higher relative supply along the SU curve. A new equilibrium is reached in point D. The former relative price $(P_h / P_1)_A$ increases to its new level $(P_h / P_1)_D$. It is obvious that the North has increased (decreased) its relative production of the high-tech (low-tech) good. One important implication of this new equilibrium is that according to the Stolper-Samuelson relationship depicted in quadrant 2, the relative wage for unskilled (skilled) labour must necessarily fall (rise). As a consequence, firms will use in the production of both of the goods less skilled and more unskilled labour. This is what points D′ and D″ tell us in quadrant 3. This is also reflected by point D in quadrant 4, which now, due to the relative price increase from $(P_h / P_1)_A$ to $(P_h / P_1)_D$, lies on an upwards shifted Rybczynski line.

The exposition – as far as the North of the world economy is concerned – applies so far more to the USA than to 'old Continental Europe'. The reason is that in the USA we find a higher degree of wage flexibility (up- and downwards) than in Continental Europe. It would not be unrealistic to design the following scenario for Continental Europe: the relative wage for unskilled labour in relation to skilled labour may become sort of sticky if not fixed downwards. The reasons can be found in minimum wages, but also in further labour market rigidities/regulations and/or the more powerful position of unions in comparison to the Anglo-Saxon world. In terms of Figure 8.7 these facts have the consequence that the relative wage remains where it was before globalization and the integration of the South took place: $(w/r)_{A=B}$.

Following the Stolper-Samuelson theorem depicted in the second quadrant, the relative goods price ratio then stays constant as well: $(P_h / P_1)_{A=B}$ and, moreover, if the North wants to satisfy the relative increased demand of the South at this old (and new) price ratio, it will have to move to point B in the first quadrant. Hence, the North is somewhat forced to increase its relative supply of high-tech goods. According to the old Rybczynski line (quadrant 4) – which is now relevant again – it is more (absolutely and relatively) skilled labour that is needed. In particular, as can be seen from the fourth quadrant, it is now point B that is notable instead of point D. Skilled labour was already fully employed at D and allocated between the high-tech and the low-tech sector. Now, the high-tech sector attracts additionally as many skilled labourers as needed (in line with its own factor intensity of production) to satisfy increased demand.

Conversely, the low-tech sector will now be forced to release a part of its skilled and unskilled labour force. Given the different (but fixed, see below) factor intensities of production, the low-tech sector will release more unskilled labour force than can be used and absorbed efficiently in (by) the high-tech sector. Technically speaking, point B of quadrant 4 on the original and again relevant Rybczynski line is incompatible with A′ and A″ in quadrant 3: these factor intensities sort of 'average' at point A in quadrant 4, while B (located to the right and below A) cannot be the 'average' of factor intensities in A′ and A″!

Hence, at a constant relative price of goods $(P_h / P_l)_{A = B}$ and a concomitant constant factor price ratio $(w/r)_{A = B}$, the high-tech sector expands and the low-tech sector shrinks. The basic reason for the occurrence of unemployment in the labour market for unskilled work is the following. Given the fixed relative wage, there is no room for factor substitution: in principle, at a lower wage for unskilled labour, the high-tech sector could have been willing to employ more of the unskilled labour force!

As a result of our analysis, we find that globalization in the form of a stronger integration of the South into the goods markets of the North definitively has negative effects on the income distribution of wages in the North: either the gap between the wages for skilled and unskilled labour is widened (US scenario) or the rigidity of relative factor prices (Continental Europe scenario) renders part of unskilled labour jobless and hence causes inequality to increase as well.[3] Notice also that the regime of rigid wages in the North reduces inequality in the South (in comparison and opposite to the free trade-flexible wages scenario).

Hellier (2013) objects against this view favoured by authors like Davis (1996) and Landmann and Pflüger (1997) that globalization has other additional and important effects on income distribution that should be taken into account. More precisely, Hellier states that we should differentiate between at least three stages of globalization (2013, pp. 117–24). In the first stage, the South produces only good l, while the North produces l and h. This has a negative effect on income distribution of the North: 'Inequality continuously grows as the South corners an increasing share of the production of l because of its growing size' (p. 119). In the South, inequality remains constant. (p. 120). In the second stage, the South achieves medium size and both areas produce both goods, l and h: here the results of Landmann and Pflüger do apply: 'there is a rising inequality . . . in both the North and the South' (p. 120). In the third stage, however, the South becomes large and produces both l and h, while the North may be left with the production of h only. As a consequence, 'inequality remains constant and high in the North', in the South, the production of h has to be raised and this, in turn, 'raises . . . inequality in the South' (p. 120).

Hence, the evaluation of these three stages in light of the goal of an equitable distribution of incomes is quite negative; throughout the process, income inequality either remains constant or increases.

8.4 INCOME DISTRIBUTION IN A WORLD CHARACTERIZED BY FRAGMENTATION

Situations where some countries can only produce one good can be visualized with the so-called Lerner diagram and its diversification cone (see Hellier 2013, pp. 114–20). The same tool is helpful when it comes to explaining fragmentation in trade. In Figure 8.8, we have depicted two cases (a) and (b) that symbolize the production of one good I with a fixed technology (a) and the production of two goods h, l with a flexible technology (b). In both diagrams, the diversification cone is limited by the two lines k_h, k_l coming from the origin. The area on and between the bordering lines k_h, k_l represents all possible factor intensities that the corresponding country may use for the production of final goods. In the left case (a), the country of concern produces only one final good I (not yet high-tech, but

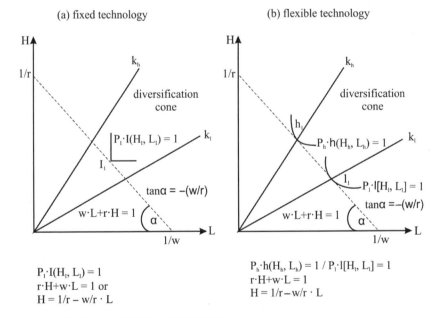

(a) fixed technology   (b) flexible technology

$P_I \cdot I(H_I, L_I) = 1$
$r \cdot H + w \cdot L = 1$ or
$H = 1/r - w/r \cdot L$

$P_h \cdot h(H_h, L_h) = 1 / P_I \cdot l[H_I, L_I] = 1$
$r \cdot H + w \cdot L = 1$
$H = 1/r - w/r \cdot L$

Source: Bartholomae (2011) and Sell (2001b).

Figure 8.8   An introduction to Lerner's diversification cone

more than low-tech) with an intermediate or average factor intensity. The rectangular unit-value curve I_1 stands for all factor combinations that yield a production value of 1 (see first equation below diagram (a)). The falling dotted line, in turn, is a budget constraint for production that assigns unit costs of size 1 to different combinations of L and H (see second and third equations below diagram (a) at given factor prices w and r).

On the right side (b) of Figure 8.8 (see Bartholomae 2011, pp. 73–80), we have depicted the case of a flexible technology, where the bordering lines of the diversification cone k_h, k_l now enable the firm to produce both goods h and l. The convex unit-value curves h_l, l_l stand for all factor combinations that yield a value of 1 (see the first two equations below diagram (a)) in the production of the high-tech good h and the low-tech good l respectively. As we will show subsequently in four distinct graphs, in both cases, (a) and (b), the phenomenon of fragmentation can occur with significant repercussions for income distribution.

In the following, we will abstract from any sort of costs that accrue when products are split into segments or when segments are put together (including the costs of coordination/cooperation). This is far more than an assumption: fragmentation can only be enforced and/or established in the medium to long run, if production of segments plus the compilation of the pieces does not consume more resources than the production of the good at a stretch. Otherwise, we would observe, on a world economy scale, a loss of efficiency.

If each of the single segments now becomes tradeable, specialization in production will a fortiori increase and competition in international trade will rise too. This process will be accompanied by corresponding productivity gains. As a result, the price for the now composite good will be lower than the price of the final good before fragmentation.

This effect can be visualized in Figure 8.9. At the beginning, we have given world prices for the goods 1, 2 and I. Input coefficients are fixed and 'the unit-value isoquants for these three commodities are . . . [as shown in Figure 8.9] with the connecting chords outlining the original Hicksian composite unit-value isoquant' (Jones and Kierzkowski 1998, p. 20). Given the resource endowment point E (E′), the country of concern will produce before fragmentation, for example, good I or 1 (2). The ray from the origin through point I 'would hit the chord connecting the amounts of labour and capital required to produce 1\$ worth of two fragments at the newly established world prices at point I′, lying northeast of I′ (p. 20).

Expecting a fall in the relative price of obtaining a unit of the final (and integrated) commodity, the ratio I I′/OI mirrors the relative price decline of the integrated good: point I′ represents the fact that there is now a need for more skilled labour (H) and for more unskilled labour (L) to sell the good

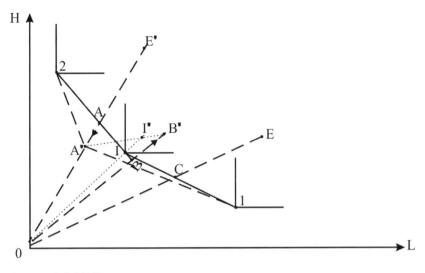

Source: Sell (2001b).

Figure 8.9   Fragmentation in production with linear technology (a)

at a price of $1. Points A and B shows the amounts of capital and labour for each segment that adds up to $1. Over the course of trade, the (previously implicit) prices of the components will change as well; whereas the price of the first component may go up (point A becomes A') in Figure 8.9, the price of the second component will possibly fall (point B becomes B').

Apart from good I, we will now integrate in more detail two further goods (1, 2) into our analysis. Hence, we look at a world of three goods and two components. Given a resource endowment point E, the country in question was able – before fragmentation – to produce good I and good 1. Accordingly, with an alternative endowment point E', a country could produce good I and good 2. In this case, the factor intensities for the production of goods 2 and 1 define and limit the diversification cone of our small open economy. If the quota of its factor endowments is located within the area of factor intensities for the production of good I and good 1 (good 2), the respective economy can produce both good I and good 1 (good 2). The connecting line of the isoquant knots 2, I and 1 represents the so-called composite Hicksian unit-value isoquant. The latter represents alternative usages of the factors of production, skilled labour and unskilled labour. These factors produce goods 1, 2 or I in order to earn efficiently (without a waste of resources) $1 (at alternative factor price ratios).

We recognize the following: after the intensification of trade (with goods, but also with fragments), the new composite Hicksian unit-value isoquant connects – remember that this new composite Hicksian unit-value isoquant is superior to the old one because it has a position closer to the origin – the knots 2, A′ and 1. Now, as it seems, it is no longer worthwhile to produce good I. Also, the production of component B is no longer possible for the domestic economy. This is reflected by the position of the new point B′. The logic of Ricardo, however, implies that there will now be another country in the world economy that is capable (based on a more advanced technology, for example) of producing component B. For the domestic economy, there is the scope – depending on the position of the resource endowment point (E versus E′) – to produce either good 1 or component A or likewise component A and good 2.

We may gauge – in the vein of the Heckscher-Ohlin world – that countries being endowed with relatively abundant skilled labour will specialize before (after) fragmentation in the production of goods 2 and I (component A); meanwhile, countries being endowed with relatively abundant unskilled labour will specialize before (after) fragmentation in the production of goods 1 and I (component B). By tendency, we may formulate: after fragmentation, the North (South) of the world economy will specialize even more than heretofore in the production of goods (and of components) that use intensively skilled (unskilled) labour.

A further interesting aspect of fragmentation is the so-called 'multi-eventer effect' that can be exemplified with the help of Figure 8.10. Before fragmentation, the domestic economy is able to produce goods 2 and I or goods 1 and I. Now, let us assume that in the course of fragmentation, prices of good I and of components A and B decline. As a result, the new (and at the same time, less good) composite Hicksian unit-value isoquant connects the knots 1 and 2: a country that so far had a comparative advantage in the production of good I may find itself confronted in the future with having neither a comparative advantage for the production of component A nor for component B. This effect is quite well known from the Olympic Games: someone who is a good sprinter within the decathlon competition and wins a gold medal in this discipline would have to struggle hard to even reach the final in the individual sprint race.

However, welfare of the domestic economy must not necessarily fall: if domestic consumers have a high preference for good I and if the prices of both components decrease significantly, this positive welfare effect may more than compensate the switch to the less favourable (as it is further away from the origin) composite Hicksian unit-value isoquant.

Alan Deardorff (2001) has modelled fragmentation in a three-goods two-countries HOS graphical approach. In principle, both the North and the South have the possibility to produce[4] two final goods (X, Y) and

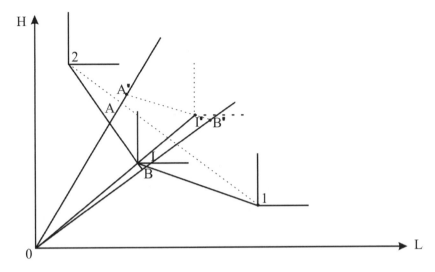

Source: Sell (2001).

Figure 8.10   Fragmentation in production with linear technology (b)

one intermediate input (Z). The latter can be combined with skilled and unskilled labour to produce good X. Hence, good X can either be produced 'from scratch' (then only skilled and unskilled labour are factors of production) or by making use of the component Z.

In Figure 8.11 we have depicted, following Deardorff (2001), another diversification cone of a small open economy that is limited at its borders by the two rays out of the origin, k_X and k_Y. If the endowment point E is outside the diversification cone, as it is in Figure 8.11, only one good will be produced.[5] The country of concern will (before fragmentation) specialize in the production of good X. The optimal solution is given by the boundary point between the iso-cost line with factor prices w_0 and r_0 and the unit-value isoquant X (= 1).[6]

And yet, as Deardorff (2001, p. 131) puts it, 'fragmentation becomes possible everywhere. The technology for producing good X now includes the possibility of producing an intermediate input, Z, one unit of which requires the factors shown by the new unit isoquant Z = 1.' The latter is on the ray k_Z and needs skilled and unskilled labour according to the distance between Z and the origin. 'A unit of good Z can be used together with additional inputs of skilled and unskilled labour to produce a unit of X . . . Assuming that fragmentation is costless, the isoquant for producing a unit of X from Z is simply the factors that are left over out of the original

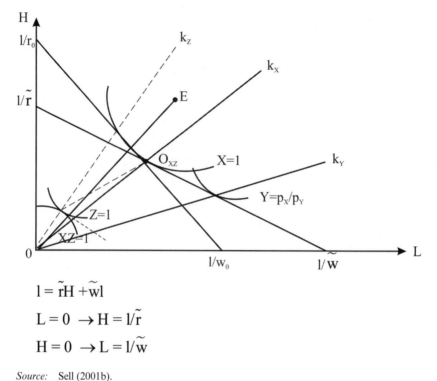

$$1 = \tilde{r}H + \tilde{w}l$$

$$L = 0 \;\rightarrow H = 1/\tilde{r}$$

$$H = 0 \;\rightarrow L = 1/\tilde{w}$$

Source: Sell (2001b).

Figure 8.11   Fragmentation in production with substitutional technology

X = 1 isoquant. That is, the isoquant for producing X from Z can be drawn upside down relative to, say, point O_{XZ} as an origin, and it will then be just tangent to the Z = 1 isoquant' (Deardorff 2001, p. 131).

One can clearly see that the diversification cone is now broader than it was before, the technology for producing Z is more skilled labour intensive than for producing X. The endowment point E is now located between the rays k_Z and k_X. The domestic economy is, hence, capable of producing good X *and* the component Z.

It is important to realize what happens to factor prices (at given prices for the final good and for the intermediate good). 'Evidently from the figure, the wage for unskilled labour has fallen from w_0 to $\tilde{w}$, while the rental on skilled labour has risen from r_0 to $\tilde{r}$. Since prices are fixed, these changes are real as well as nominal' (Deardorff 2001, p. 132). What about gains and losses? The country as a whole tends to gain via fragmentation – given that at constant prices for the goods, the possibilities of production are enhanced – but this result does not apply to each factor of production: '[unskilled] workers here are made worse off as the production process for their product fragments into a (skilled) labour intensive and a (unskilled) labour intensive part, only the former of which necessarily remains viable within their country' (p. 132). Put differently: after fragmentation, the average skilled labour intensity of production is raised (the ray k_z is obviously steeper as the ray from the origin through E). Only the skilled labour-intensive component has a prospect of being produced for some time in the North of the world economy.

If fragmentation does not alter the goods' prices, it will increase production wherever it occurs and, hence, the world's welfare. In the case where fragmentation does indeed affect the goods' prices, one can think of a terms-of-trade deterioration for some of the countries involved.

There exists a widespread view according to which globalization constitutes a big challenge to the factor of production 'unskilled labour', located in the North of the world economy. The quite realistic threat to this factor consists either in a falling real wage rate or – at given wage rigidities – in (higher) unemployment. Regarding this argument from the viewpoint of fragmentation, a more differentiated evaluation is needed. Let us come back for a moment to Figure 8.11. The resource endowment point E stands for an economy that is replete with unskilled labour. After fragmentation has occurred, the production of component B′ seems to be out of reach. As the slope of the knots-connecting line A′1 is less steep than the line I1, it is obvious that the real wage and the wage-rental ratio have fallen. The reason is technical progress in the skilled labour-intensive sector of the economy, a process visualized by the move of point A towards the origin to its new position A′. One should be careful, however, in generalizing such an effect, where the country of concern loses its comparative advantage in the production of an unskilled labour-intensive component to a competitor on the world market. Namely, if we consider a second country with an endowment point E′, here we register an increase in the real wage and the wage-rental ratio (the line 2A′ is steeper than the line 2I). This case demonstrates the possibility that especially those countries that are relatively well endowed with physical capital and with skilled labour have little to fear from losing unskilled labour-intensive produced fragments to competitors on the world market. Conversely, it is not all that clear that only those countries that are abundant with unskilled labour will lose, via fragmentation, unskilled labour-intensive components to the world market and have to face a fall in the real wage.

This effect can be exemplified by means of Figure 8.11. Here, a country well endowed with skilled labour, which produced goods 2 and I before fragmentation, sustains a loss in the real wage rate and exhibits a lower wage-rental ratio after fragmentation. The impact of fragmentation on factor prices and on income distribution is, hence, a rather complex phenomenon. Deardorff (2001) has considered the case (Figure 8.11) of a small country, abundant with skilled labour, which gains via fragmentation the possibility to produce a skilled labour-intensive component. In the aftermath, one can expect the wage for skilled labour to increase and the remuneration of unskilled labour to fall.

Notice that not all the theoretical cases are empirically relevant. Generally speaking, one can say that the effect of 'outsourcing' in the North of the world economy is primarily comparable to the introduction of unskilled labour saving technical progress. As a consequence, the demand for skilled labour is reduced and its price will fall. Opposite to this, the demand for unskilled labour will increase and its price will move upwards. Fragmentation will in particular raise an additional demand for specific services – for instance, capabilities that are necessary for the implementation of final assembly or for the communication and coordination of activities needed when fragments are to be ordered[7] – and thereby cause a direct impact on the splay of wages and salaries in the North of the world economy.

If the majority of components are produced in the South of the world economy, this will induce by itself a higher demand for skilled rather than for unskilled labour in the respective (developing) country. If outsourcing occurs in the South of the world economy, this type of production will – in comparison to further alternatives in such countries of the world economy – tend to use intensively skilled labour.[8] Accordingly, one can expect the wage for unskilled (skilled) labour to fall (to rise) in both regions of the world economy.[9]

8.5 BARGAINING FOR TRADE LIBERALIZATION

As Easterly et al. (2004, p. 51) report, the world has registered 'steadily rising trade GDP ratios from 1950 to 2000', a process that experienced a sharp disruption during the world financial and economic crisis in 2008 and 2009. Since then, the positive development of 50 years of openness has resumed speed and it is a clear sign for an unbroken era of globalization. As a matter of fact, reductions of tariff and non-tariff barriers have contributed to this process too.

A simple approach to model bargaining for tariff reductions between two countries or likewise between two areas of the world economy such as the North and the South is provided by neoclassical theory of trade policy (Ethier 1983, pp. 174–86). Within this framework, trade equilibrium

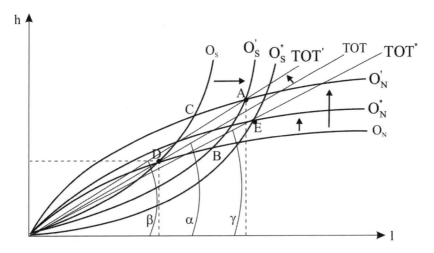

Source: Author.

Figure 8.12 The neoclassical general equilibrium analysis of tariff reductions

is associated with the intersection of the domestic (North) and the foreign (South) 'offer curve'. Before the development of tariff and non-tariff barrier reductions begins, the offer curves of the South, O_s and of the North, O_N intersect at point D (Figure 8.12). This intersection point also represents the equilibrium terms of trade (TOT) under the tariff regime (T):

$$\tan \alpha = \left[\frac{P_1}{P_h}\right]_T = \text{TOT} \qquad (8.5)$$

Now suppose the North and the South enter into negotiations on the reduction of tariffs and non-tariff barriers (F), say under the umbrella of the World Trade Organization. If the North concedes large tariff reductions and the South similarly, but a bit less than the North, the respective offer curves shift to their new positions O'_N and O'_S with the intersection point A. Obviously, trade liberalization now favours the South/is to the disadvantage of the North. The terms of trade change into:

$$\tan \beta = \left[\frac{P_1}{P_h}\right]_F = \text{TOT}' > \text{TOT} = \tan \alpha = \left[\frac{P_1}{P_h}\right]_T \qquad (8.6)$$

In the opposite and more likely case of a higher bargaining power of the North, the South will admit larger tariff reductions than the North. Accordingly, the respective offer curves shift to their new positions O''_N and O''_S with the new intersection point E. Now, by contrast, trade liberalization favours the North/is to the disadvantage of the South. The terms of trade change into:[10]

$$\tan \gamma = \left[\frac{P_l}{P_h}\right]_{F'} = TOT'' < TOT = \tan \alpha = \left[\frac{P_l}{P_h}\right]_T \qquad (8.7)$$

In the following, we concentrate on the effects tariff reductions on products stemming from the South have on factor allocation, production and income distribution in the North. Thereby, we are able to study in more detail the consequences of trade liberalization for the distribution of wage income between skilled and unskilled labour income. In this respect, it is interesting to consider the graph in Figure 8.13: the equilibrium (for the goods h and l) before tariff reduction is characterized by the production point G (to avoid an 'overloading' of the picture, the corresponding consumption point is not drawn) and an international price ratio of AC/AF. Now, a tariff reduction or elimination is implemented that lowers the price

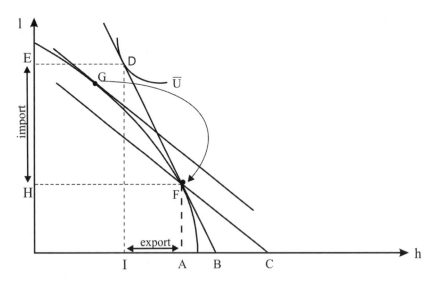

Source: Author.

Figure 8.13   *The effects of trade liberalization (tariff reductions among low-tech goods)*

of l and yields a new international price ratio of AB/AF. The new production point is F and the corresponding consumption point is D. This enables the North to reach a utility level of $\overline{U}$. Accordingly, the North now exports good h in the amount of IA and imports good l in the amount of EH.

What are the consequences for income distribution? First of all, we recognize a terms of trade deterioration for the South and a terms of trade improvement for the North. Secondly, we assume (see above):

$$\left[\frac{H}{L}\right]_h > \left[\frac{H}{L}\right]_l \qquad (8.8)$$

Also, we have seen that due to the tariff reduction for good l, the price ratio P_h, P_l will increase; as a consequence, the remuneration of skilled and of unskilled labour will rise in the h sector and decline in the l sector. Both factors of production will tend to leave the l sector and to move to the h sector. However, given the different factor intensities of production, the l sector will release more unskilled and less skilled labour than convenient for the h sector. As a result, the relative price for skilled labour (in relation to unskilled labour) will increase. Given the substitutability in the production functions of both goods, the production of both goods will become more intensive in the use of unskilled labour. Whether the distribution of wage income will change in the North in favour of skilled labour and to the detriment of unskilled labour depends, as well known, on the degree of homogeneity of the production function. If the latter is 1, the distribution will not be altered. If it is greater (smaller) than 1, a change of the income distribution is to be expected that fosters the weight of unskilled (skilled) labour in income distribution of wages. The aforementioned effects on the factor intensities of production of h and l and on the size of the respective production levels can be visualized with the help of Figure 8.14.

Figure 8.14 includes another Edgeworth box, where the sides of the triangle stand for the amount of skilled (H) and unskilled labour (L) existing in the economy of the North. Initially, the intersection of the two rays in point A shows a moderate production of h and a considerable production of l. A is also a tangential point between the isoquants I_l^A and I_h^A. The tangent of the angle α represents the relative factor price of skilled and unskilled labour. After the reduction of tariffs on good l, the ray of expansion of good h expands, while the ray of expansion of good l shrinks. Now, both rays intersect at point B. At point B, there is also a tangential contact between the isoquants I_l^B and I_h^B. At the same time, both rays are now flatter than before, a clear signal that both productions of good h and l are more intensive in the use of unskilled labour now after the tariff reduction that affects good l. The tangent of the angle β represents the new

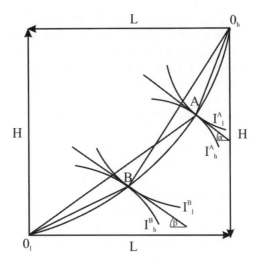

Source: Author.

Figure 8.14   Allocative and price effects of tariff reductions for low-tech goods

relative factor price of skilled and unskilled labour. As tan α > tan β, it is obvious that the relative price for unskilled (skilled) labour has decreased (increased).

When the distributional focus is on labour and (physical) capital, the HOS model predicts that 'tariff reductions in poor-labor-abundant countries are expected to increase the real income of workers and hurt capital owners . . . In developed countries the opposite effect is expected. The empirical evidence remains mixed and somewhat contradictory' (Francois and Rojas-Romagosa 2005, p. 2). As Francois and Rojas-Romagosa allude, one should interconnect the results of Figure 8.12, Figure 8.13 and Figure 8.14: 'for a large country (such as the North in our analysis) . . . positive terms-of-trade gains will slow any rise . . . in capital income shares . . . This in turn means that terms of trade effects will tend to mitigate the inequality effects of [tariff liberalization]' (p. 12). In a structural theoretical and empirical model of heterogeneous firms, Egger et al. (2011) start from the premise that workers have fairness preferences 'relating their effort to the wage they are paid relative to some reference wage, which they consider to be fair' (p. 7). This fair wage mechanism prevents wages from falling to the market clearing level and thereby causes unemployment. Exporting firms are capable of paying an 'exporter wage premium of about 10 percent on average' (p. 26). The authors find that when countries open themselves to trade (via tariff reductions, for example) and the firm structure is heterogeneous (only the very productive firms can afford the fixed and sunk market entry costs when they want to access the market of exports) in the vein of Mélitz (2003), 'trade brings about a greater inequality in firm-level wages everywhere' (Egger et al. 2011, p. 23). The same effect on inequality can be observed among the operating profits across firms in the open trade scenario 'relative to autarky' (p. 26).

In a further paper, Egger and Kreickemeier (2008) find – in a comparable model setting – that 'the impact of economic integration on the distribution of income within countries' (p. 2) is the following: taking for granted that wages on the firm level depend positively on operating profits (p. 11), as 'workers . . . consider profits of the firm they are employed by as a determinant of their fair wage' (p. 10), 'trade liberalization influences the wage profile as it affects firm profits asymmetrically' (p. 6). Already before international economic integration, 'there is income inequality within the group of entrepreneurs and within the group of workers' (p. 16). Conventionally, the 'inequality of entrepreneurial income is more pronounced than the inequality of labour income' (p. 17) and 'an exporter pays higher wages than a non-exporter *ceteris paribus*' (p. 19). The authors show that within their model, opening to international trade – though this goes together with increases of per capita income (gains from trade) – is accompanied by a larger inequality in almost all dimensions: not only does inequality rise between workers and entrepreneurs, but also within the group of entrepreneurs and within the group of workers. The rationale for these three effects is the following:

1. 'There are additional profit gains for the most productive firms, due to exports to the foreign market. As a consequence, average profit income including both exporting and non-exporting firms rises disproportionally, thereby inducing an increase in inter-group [between the group of entrepreneurs, on the one hand, and the group of workers, on the other hand] inequality after the opening up to international trade' (p. 28).

2. 'On the one hand, the exit of the least productive firms reduces all other things equal, intra-group inequality among entrepreneurs. On the other hand, selection of the most productive firms into export status raises these firms' profits and thus intra-group inequality among entrepreneurs. In our setting, it is the second effect that dominates' (p. 28).

3. 'On the one hand, because of the least productive firms pay the lowest wages, exit of these firms lowers inequality of labour income *ceteris paribus*. On the other hand, expansion of the most productive firms

due to exports to the foreign markets raises inequality of labour income, since these firms pay the highest wages' (p. 28). If the latter effect dominates, the distribution of labour income will become more unequal, *ceteris paribus*.

These results may change substantially when embedding a unionized oligopoly model into a general equilibrium framework (Egger and Etzel 2009): under autarky, the existence of unions gives rise to involuntary unemployment (p. 2). When facing international competition/opening to international trade, unions will be disciplined (p. 15) and will lower their wage claims and thereby involuntary unemployment. As a result, given that involuntary unemployment is an important contributor to wage inequality, the latter tends to be reduced (pp. 2, 17). If wages fall and producers continue with market power also in an international environment, the income inequality between profits and wages will move upwards (pp. 3–4, 18). With regard to the distribution of profits, 'there are two counteracting effects at work. On the one hand, there is stronger competition in the open economy, implying that profits at the firm as well as the industry level shrink. For given wages, this effect is counteracted ... by the increase in the number of consumers. On the other hand, unions set lower wages in the open economy [see above], thereby providing an additional source for profit gains. It turns out that the second effect is stronger than the first one if the market power of firms is sufficiently large' (p. 16).

8.6　THE POLITICAL ECONOMY OF TRADE POLICY AND THE CONSEQUENCES FOR THE DISTRIBUTION OF INCOME

An effect known for a long time is that 'groups that lose from trade lobby their governments to restrict trade and protect their incomes' (Krugman and Obstfeld 2009, p. 74). Amelung (1989) has widened this view to the concept or likewise strategy of a 'political economy of import substitution'. Within this framework, which fits more the emerging economies than the traditional developed countries, and which is very close to the infant industry argument, (higher) tariffs induce price increases that enable domestic firms to raise their market share and to crowd out foreign competitors (Amelung 1989, p. 2). There also exists the political economy 'counterpart' of import substitution, namely the so-called 'export promotion strategy'. The corresponding lobby urges politicians to make use of export promotion instruments such as export subsidies, cheap credits for the export sector and so on. Hence, it comes close to what used to be called 'strategic trade policy'. Thirdly, we find a less well-organized (if organized at all, according to the theory of Mancur Olson) group of agents that wants (free) trade to be expanded and pledges against any type of tariffs and non-tariff barriers (Krugman and Obstfeld 2009, p. 75). Basically, this group of agents can be identified as the consumers. Note that the interests of consumers may harmonize with the interests of export producing firms because lower tariffs obviously foster the competitiveness of the domestic export sector as long as (intermediate) import goods are substantial for the production of export goods. This is precisely what the concept of effective protection has told us. In the non-tradeables/tradeables world, it can be shown that the liberalization of imports raises the relative price of exportables (Sell 1988, pp. 638–40) vis-à-vis non-tradeables and hence renders the production of these goods more profitable, *ceteris paribus*.

Hence, to the best of our knowledge, a large part of the relevant literature does not account for the existence of all these three kinds of pressure groups involved: the well-organized lobbies for import substitution and for export promotion, on the one hand, and the less well-organized 'lobby' of consumers (Krugman and Obstfeld 2009, pp. 75, 225), on the other hand. Make no mistake, one should not confound the advocates of free trade with the defenders of export promotion. The latter do not hesitate to handicap foreign competitors when advising the government to implement export subsidies and further explicit or implicit instruments of trade policy. In the following, we will concentrate on the political economy of import substitution and of export promotion. As Figure 8.15 shows, policy makers have in principle – disregarding for a moment any sort of non-tariff barriers or non-subsidy support – four instruments at hand: export subsidies, export taxes, import taxes and import subsidies. For reasons of simplicity, we only consider unit taxes and subsidies (as opposed to *ad valorem* taxes and subsidies).[11]

The following model extends and deepens the approach presented by Francois and Rojas-Romasoga (2005). In their paper, the authors consider both the social welfare effects and the rents generated through import protection. By contrast and at the same time complementing their contribution, we will include the instrument of export subsidies in our own analysis. We assume that there exist two 'policy production functions' – instead of or as an alternative to the more favoured 'policy support or likewise contribution functions' (see Grossman and Helpman 1992; Helpman 1995) and to the so-called 'majority voting models' (Fischer and Serra 1996; Das 1999). The first production function applies to the size of the representative import protection, τ:

$$\tau = \tau(v,\ell); \frac{\partial \tau}{\partial v} = \tau_v > 0; \frac{\partial^2 \tau}{dv^2} = \tau_{vv} < 0; \frac{\partial \tau}{\partial \ell} = \tau_\ell > 0; \frac{\partial^2 \tau}{d\ell^2} = \tau_{\ell\ell} < 0$$

$$(8.9)$$

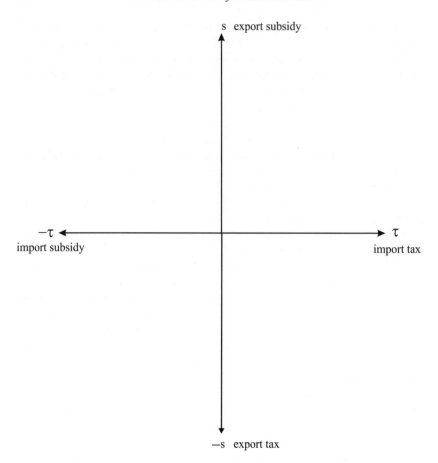

Source: Author.

Figure 8.15   An overview of trade policy instruments

The factor of production, v, is associated with the voters[12] that policy makers of the incumbent government can organize within the representatives of their own political party (say congressmen) and the voters that can be organized among the representatives of other political parties (say coalition partners, as suggested by Hillman 1989, pp. 45–7). The factor of production, ℓ, is associated with the number of lobbying industries that support the government.[13]

The same applies, *mutatis mutandis*, to the production of export promotion and to the size of the representative export subsidy, s:

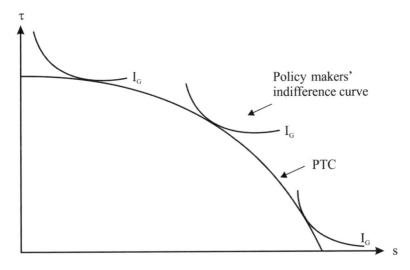

τ

I_G

Policy makers'
indifference curve

I_G

PTC

I_G

s

Source: Author.

Figure 8.16   The political economy equilibrium of trade policy instruments

$$s = s(v,\ell); \frac{\partial s}{\partial v} = s_v > 0; \frac{\partial^2 s}{dv^2} = s_{vv} < 0; \frac{\partial s}{\partial \ell} = s_\ell > 0; \frac{\partial^2 s}{d\ell^2} = s_{\ell\ell} < 0 \quad (8.10)$$

Taking total derivatives of both production functions enables us to calculate the marginal rate of substitution between the unit tariff rate τ and the unit export subsidy s (see Siebert 2000b, pp. 40–41):

$$\frac{d\tau}{ds} = -\frac{\dfrac{\partial \tau}{\partial v}dv + \dfrac{\partial \tau}{\partial \ell}d\ell}{\dfrac{\partial s}{\partial v}dv + \dfrac{\partial s}{\partial \ell}d\ell} \quad (8.11)$$

In Figure 8.16, we have depicted the resulting political production possibilities or likewise political transformation curve (PTC). Given the above sketched properties of the respective production functions, we can expect a concave curvature of the PTC. Trade policy may, hence, either fully 'specialize' in the production of import tariffs or, alternatively, fully 'specialize' in the production of export subsidies. If none of these extreme alternatives prove to be ideal, trade policy may choose in principle any point on the PTC. However, we need to know the utility thoughts of the politicians associated with different protection regimes if the intention is to find a political economy optimum. Here, we expand the policy makers' utility function U(τ) proposed by

Francois and Rojas-Romasoga (2005, pp. 14–16) and the set of policy instruments (p. 14) by including (see above) a representative export subsidy, s:

$$U(\tau, s) = \lambda_1 SW(\tau, s) + \lambda_2 \rho(\tau, s); \text{ with SW = social welfare function and}$$
$$\rho = \text{rents} \qquad (8.12)$$

The (explicit) social welfare function SW captures the original idea of Sen (1997) according to which both a higher real per capita mean income and a more equal income distribution generate social welfare (p. 10):

$$SW = \left[\left(\frac{\bar{y}}{p_c} \right)(1 - G) \right] \qquad (8.13)$$

By contrast, ρ 'represents (lobbying) rents generated for government through protection' (p. 14) and export promotion. Total differentiation of the policy makers' utility function yields:

$$dU = \frac{\partial U}{\partial \tau} d\tau + \frac{\partial U}{\partial s} ds \qquad (8.14)$$

The partial derivatives with regard to τ and ρ are given by:

$$\frac{\partial U}{\partial \tau} = \lambda_1 \frac{\partial SW}{\partial \tau} + \lambda_2 \frac{\partial \rho}{\partial \tau}; \frac{\partial U}{\partial s} = \lambda_1 \frac{\partial SW}{\partial s} + \lambda_2 \frac{\partial \rho}{\partial s} \qquad (8.15)$$

Hence, we can calculate the marginal rate of substitution between τ and s or the slope of a government's indifference curve:

$$\frac{d\tau}{ds} = -\frac{\lambda_1 \dfrac{\partial SW}{\partial s} + \lambda_2 \dfrac{\partial \rho}{\partial s}}{\lambda_1 \dfrac{\partial SW}{\partial \tau} + \lambda_2 \dfrac{\partial \rho}{\partial \tau}} \qquad (8.16)$$

The discussion of the partial derivatives of the determinants of the utility function on the right side of the above equation is far from being trivial and will be done step by step. The comparatively easiest consideration is about the impact on ρ:

$$\frac{\partial \rho}{\partial \tau}, \frac{\partial \rho}{\partial s} > 0 \qquad (8.17)$$

It is plausible to assume that the rents that accrue to the government through tariffs and export subsidies 'granted' to lobbying industries increase with the size of these policy instruments before an optimum is reached (p. 15). It is, however, much less clear which signs can be expected vis-à-vis the impact of the above-mentioned policy instruments on social welfare (SW):

$$\frac{\partial SW}{\partial \tau}; \frac{\partial SW}{\partial s} \overset{?}{=} \tag{8.18}$$

When assessing the effect of a tariff on social welfare (SW), one has to distinguish between the effect on real average per capita income and the effect on inequality (see above).

As far as the first effect is concerned, Francois and Rojas-Romasoga (2005, p. 10) distinguish between the terms of trade effect and the allocation or economic efficiency effect. As was shown in Figure 8.12, the terms of trade effect is ambiguous *ex ante*. It depends on the elasticity of the offer curves involved and on the reaction power of the foreign country whose producers are being taxed by the domestic government. Let us assume it is positive. The total effect on social welfare is then positive as well, if the terms of trade effect outweighs the presumably negative allocation effect. As the small country will not be able to generate positive terms of trade effects via tariffs, the negative allocation effects will dominate, so that 'the impact of the tariff on mean income is strictly negative' (p. 10). The likelihood for a positive net effect on mean income for the large country, in turn, will be higher, the more inelastic the foreign offer curve (Ethier 1983, p. 175), *ceteris paribus*, and the weaker the capability of foreign countries to get revenge for the imposition of tariffs by the domestic government.

But what can we say about the effects of tariffs on income inequality and thereby on social welfare? If only tariff reduction or maintenance of protection is put to the vote, and if the country of concern exports skill-intensive goods (and, hence, is skill abundant) and imports labour-intensive goods (and, hence, is labour scarce), one may expect that 'voters with high skill levels will favor low tariff rates, but voters with low skills will be better off if the country imposes a high tariff' (Krugman and Obstfeld 2009, p. 222). This political economy argument is undisputed. But in our context, we have a social welfare function – as a part of the government's utility function – which invariably will punish any increase of the Gini coefficient. In the above Krugman and Obstfeld example of a skill-abundant country, the imposition of a (higher) import tariff on labour-intensive goods will reduce the Gini coefficient and hence the inequality of wages for skilled and unskilled labour, *ceteris paribus*.

In the opposite case of an (unskilled) labour-abundant country, the imposition of import tariffs on skill-intensive goods will raise the Gini coefficient and hence the inequality of wages for skilled and unskilled labour, *ceteris paribus* (Francois and Rojas-Romasoga 2005, p.15). In the following, we assume the inequality reducing factors to dominate and therefore that $\partial SW/\partial \tau > 0$. It remains to be discussed whether $\partial SW/\partial s > 0$. If so, the marginal rate of substitution (see above) between τ and s is negative and the government's indifference curves have a convex nature as depicted in Figure 8.16. In principle, the government's indifference curves, J_G, can determine a protection regime inclined more towards taxes (export subsidies) or one that gives both instruments a comparable weight.

What about the role of export subsidies? In the political economy equilibrium model of Grossman and Helpman (1992), it is shown under quite general conditions that 'joint welfare is higher under an output-subsidy regime than under a trade-policy-only-regime [which only allows for import taxation]. It follows that each lobby prefers an institutional setting where output subsidies are allowed' (p. 33). The main reason for this conclusion rests on the affinity of lobbies to direct income transfers. But, as in any other case of government expenditures, export subsidies have to be financed either by taxes (Kohler and Felbermayr 2002a, p.719) or by new debt.[14] Let us assume that the export subsidy is financed by a lump sum tax (Kohler and Felbermayr 2002a), T_a. The short-run impact should be positive as long as the additional export revenues induced by a unit subsidy payment create a net positive income effect:

$$\frac{dY}{dEX} + \frac{dY}{dT_a} > 0 \qquad (8.19)$$

Written in this form, the export multiplier, as the first term on the left side, conveys the impression that exports are autonomous. If we take into account the impact of the unit export subsidy, we achieve:

$$EX = EX(s); \ dEX = \frac{\partial EX}{\partial s} ds \qquad (8.20)$$

This effect can be visualized with the help of Figure 8.17.

Before the payment of a unit export subsidy, export demand (ED) and export supply (ES) intersect at point A. After the introduction of the export subsidy, the ES schedule is shifted rightwards to its new position ES' and point B symbolizes the new equilibrium. As the diagram shows, export subsidies have the effect of not only increasing the export value of the small economy (by ΔEX), but also raising the domestic price of

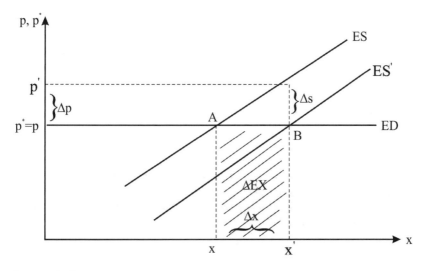

Source: Author.

Figure 8.17 The effects of export subsidies on prices and output in the export market

producers (in Figure 8.17, from p to p′), which again demonstrates the protectionist nature of this trade policy instrument.

But can we be confident that $\partial SW/\partial s > 0$? Here again, we have to consider the medium to long-run effects and to distinguish between the effect of export subsidies on real average per capita income (allocation/efficiency versus terms of trade effects) and the likely effect on the inequality of incomes (Kohler and Felbermayr 2002b, p. 845). The allocation/efficiency effects of export subsidies are usually assessed to be negative on balance. But this judgement hinges strongly upon the assumption of perfectly competitive markets. In the case of oligopolies, for example, the theory of strategic trade policy has shown that the imposition of export subsidies can be a powerful instrument to achieve higher market shares for the domestic firm.[15] The latter, in turn, enhance the possibilities of greater market experience and of a higher endogenous growth of the firm. As far as the terms of trade effects are concerned, the small open economy, by definition, is unable to influence its own terms of trade. For a large economy, the higher the likelihood of a terms of trade deterioration, the less elastic foreign demand for domestic exports, *ceteris paribus*. In net terms, hence, the total effect on real average per capita income is ambiguous or slightly negative. With regard to the likely effect on the inequality of incomes, it is undisputed that export subsidies raise the incomes of the protected sector (Kohler and Felbermayr 2002a, p. 720) to the detriment of the unprotected sector.[16] If the protected sector uses intensively (un)skilled labour, the difference in the remuneration vis-à-vis unskilled labour will increase (decrease), *ceteris paribus*. As a consequence, $\partial SW/\partial s$ may become rather small or slightly negative. The marginal rate of substitution between τ and s or the slope of a government's indifference curve, J_G, considering both numerator and denominator, will most likely remain negative on balance, just as we have assumed from the very beginning above.

Other contributions to the political economy of trade policy embed median voter models (Fischer and Serra 1996; Das 1999) of the choice between trade and autarky within intra-industry trade settings in the vein of Krugman (Fischer and Serra 1996). A special emphasis is put here on the reactions of the median voter to real income effects, to changes in the availability of varieties and to unfavourable changes in the income distribution due to free trade (as opposed to the alternative of autarky): 'opening trade has two main effects. First, it increases the number of varieties available, and second, it increases the *mean* real wage of the relatively abundant factor while reducing the *mean* real wage of the relative scarce factor' (pp. 42–3, emphases added). At the same time, 'prospects for free trade are dimmer when increased inequality reduces the skilled labour stock of the median voter' (p. 60). More precisely: if the distribution of skilled labour is skewed to the right (steep to the left), then the median of skilled labour is below the average (Sell and Stratmann 2013, p. 79). The gains from trade – proportional to the amount of skilled labour one owns – will hence be lower for the median voter than for the 'average voter' and the 'possibility of trade rejection cannot be eliminated' (Fischer and Serra 1996, p. 55).

Das (1999) makes use of the median voter approach with the purpose to endogenize both trade protection and the distribution of wealth in a small economy framework. With production factors labour and land, the domestic economy imports the labour-intensive produced good and exports the land-intensive produced good. Not surprisingly, 'as the international price of the labor-intensive good rises . . . wealth income inequality falls' (p. 1). In more detail: the higher price for the import good '(a) increases real wage, (b) lowers land rent, (c) improves wealth of the median household, (d) reduces inequality and (e) leads to less trade protection' (p. 11).

Papers by Grossman and Helpman (1992) and Helpman (1995) belong to the 'classical' contributions to the political economy of trade policy. These papers have a lot in common with our own approach in that they also want to identify 'optimal trade policies' when interest groups are around and 'lobbies are protected by import tariffs or[17] export subsidies in the political equilibrium' (Grossman and Helpman 1992, p. 21).

8.7 EMPIRICAL FACTS AND FIGURES

There exist a confusingly high number of empirical papers on the impact of trade liberalization/globalization on the distribution of incomes (see for a brief survey Chusseau and Dumont 2013, pp. 29–32). Many of them doubt – especially in the case of the US economy – the 'naive applicability of the HOS model' (see above). There is not enough space in this section to take into account all of the approaches/findings. We concentrate instead on a few remarkable contributions. One of them is the paper presented by Felbermayr et al. (2013): when analysing the rising wage inequality in Germany – with a substantial acceleration since 1993 – they find that 'observable worker characteristics, as stressed in traditional trade theories, do not help in explaining the rise in inequality' (p. 28).[18] In their empirical analysis, they assess 'the relative importance of international trade, labour and product market regulation for the evolution of German wage inequality' (p. 35): 'higher competition in the product market . . . has a strong effect on inequality, potentially accounting for the whole increase in German wage dispersion' (p. 45). Over the course of competition, 'large firms fill their vacancies at a higher rate by making them more attractive, that is, by offering higher wages. Hence wage dispersion can be understood as a by-product of firms' growth process' (p. 35). Certainly, the authors cannot rule out the possibility that it was globalization together with the European common market which intensified and fostered that competition. It comes naturally that increased competition (in export markets) causes intensified market exit for the less productive and yet a reduction of profit margins/lower wages for the more productive firms. In principle, the more productive firms should pay higher wages, but 'the exporter wage premium becomes negative . . . for plants two standard deviations above the mean' (Felbermayr et al. 2012, p. 6). One reason for this outcome is that 'intensified competition . . . reduces the bargaining position of the union, which has a negative effect on wages' (p. 7).

The most far-reaching statement with regard to the impact of free trade on personal income distribution was put forward by Egger and Kreickemeier (2008). They show within their model that opening to international trade is accompanied by a larger inequality in almost all dimensions: not only does inequality rise between workers and entrepreneurs, but also within the group of entrepreneurs and within the group of workers (pp. 16–19, 28). In such a case, the Gini coefficient is the appropriate measure of inequality despite the objections of Thomas Piketty (2014, see Chapter 1). Further empirical papers confirm the findings of Egger and Kreickemeier (2008): 'Trade liberalization and economic globalization increase income inequality' (Bergh and Nilsson

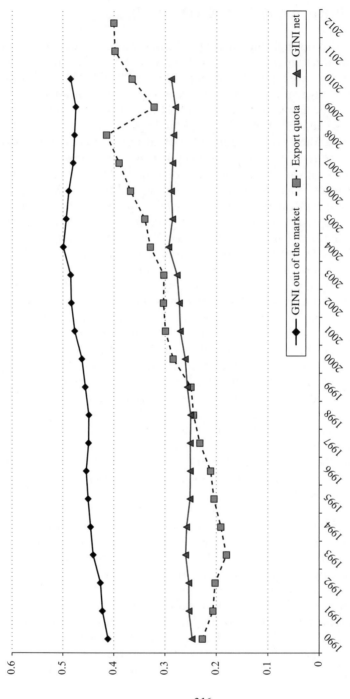

Source: German Federal Bureau of Statistics, courtesy of Markus Grabka (DIW).

Figure 8.18 Export quotas and personal income distribution for Germany (1990–2012)

2010, p. 489). This result holds in the first place for middle and high income countries.

An interesting 'add on' is provided by Lee (2006): his panel estimation results cover 14 European countries over the period 1951–92. Lee, as others, wants to inquire whether globalization tends to increase inequality. He finds that with regard to FDI, 'i.e. it leads to a rising inequality in the host countries' (p. 792). 'FDI may have been rewarding skilled labors if we are in the dualistic framework of skilled and unskilled labors' (p. 795). By contrast, the estimated coefficients for trade – as a contributing factor to more inequality of incomes – 'are insignificant' (p. 795).

Figure 8.18 presents a simple, but straightforward test for the above hypothesis: if the export quota (here for Germany in the past two decades) rises, this development should go together with a concomitant increase in the Gini coefficient. As Figure 8.18 reveals, this is truly the case. Both for the Gini coefficient 'out of the market' (before the government redistributes) and for the 'net' Gini coefficient (after redistribution of the government) there is a high correlation with the German export quota. However, the correlation is higher between the Gini coefficient 'out of the market', on the one hand, and the export quota, on the other hand. This is what theory makes us expect.

NOTES

1. The inverse reasoning that considers the impact of goods prices on factor prices leads to the following result. In the first place, higher prices for a final good will incentivize firms to increase the supply of the respective good (say, good 1) and to reduce the supply of the other good (say, good 2). Accordingly, the demand will increase for the factor of production that is intensively used in the production of good 1. Its marginal value will be raised by the increment of the good's price (good 1). See for more details Max Albert (1994, pp. 103–9).
2. See Muysken and Nekkers (1999, p. 6) for a somewhat similar graphical approach.
3. Notice that efficiency wages in the North have quite similar effects as rigid relative wages: 'In the North, openness results in a decrease in the full employment wage of unskilled workers that falls below the efficiency wage. As firms enforce the latter, openness comes with the unemployment of unskilled workers in the North' (Hellier 2013, p. 124).
4. 'Fragmentation becomes possible everywhere' (Deardorff 1998, p. 16).
5. See Dixit and Norman (1982, p. 58).
6. By analogy, $Y = p_x / p_y = 1 / p_y$ represents the isoquant that stands for the output level Y and which equals the production value of one unit of money (say US dollar). If $p_y = 2$, then the isoquant represents half a unit of Y.
7. See Burda and Dluhosch (2000, pp. 11ff.).
8. Following Kohler (2000, p. 11), the coordination task that comes up in the presence of outsourcing implies (both in the case of foreign private investment and in the case without foreign private investment) at least two elements of costs: 'In either case, maintaining a transport and communications network which facilitates fragmentation is likely to entail a significant fixed cost element ... In addition, international

fragmentation will typically involve a variable cost which may be conveniently modeled as a "surcharge-equivalent" ζ on the foreign wage rate. The interpretation is straightforward. Due to differences relating to language, standards, and jurisdiction, firms must hire $1 + \zeta$ units of foreign labor, in order to obtain one unit of effective labor input in foreign production of fragment 2.'

9. See Feenstra (1998, p. 42).
10. Notice that in Figure 8.12 we refrain from depicting indifference curves for the South and the North, something that is indispensable if one wants to identify optimal tariffs. In addition, in Figure 8.12, we do not consider inelastic offer curves nor the case of the small country (which leaves the terms of trade unaffected by tariff changes).
11. Note that Grossman and Helpman are among the very few contributions that consider all of these four trade policy instruments (1992, p. 21).
12. More precisely, the incumbent government calculates with a high number of voters beyond a necessary quorum (say, 50 per cent) in the parliament. The idea is that the policy instrument intensity will be higher, the larger the support the government receives in the congress.
13. More precisely, the incumbent government calculates with a high share of lobbying industries out of a total of relevant industries. The idea is here again that the policy instrument intensity will be higher, the larger the support the government from lobbying industries. Hence, voting parliamentarians and lobbying industries are (though limited) substitutes in the production of subsidies/tariffs.
14. See Weisskoff's (1976) case study on Puerto Rico for an applied, empirical analysis of export subsidies.
15. Peter Neary has shown theoretically that 'subsidies are unambiguously desirable in a simple Cournot duopoly model although this result is highly sensitive to changes in underlying assumptions' (Neary 1988, p. 1). Wang (2004) has supplemented this insight by looking at the strategic interrelationship between the imposition of subsidies, on the one hand, and the likelihood for countervailing duties, on the other hand (p. 158). Wang (2009) also discusses the simultaneous elimination of export subsidies under oligopoly in the vein of Brander and Spencer (1985): 'It is shown that the incentive for subsidizing exports to occur will exist when all subsidizing countries are forced to withdraw their subsidies on exports simultaneously' (Wang 2009, p. 629).
16. In agriculture, export subsidies have a redistributive role too. They tend to transfer a surplus from consumers and taxpayers to farmers. This result, however, does not hold in the 'small-export equilibrium' (Holloway 2002, p. 243).
17. This 'or' is obviously equivalent to a logical 'and'.
18. However, the authors do admit that 'increased trade may have played a role in shaping the German wage distribution' (Felbermayr et al. 2013, p. 34).

9. Final remarks

9.1 REDISTRIBUTION POLICIES

Today, 'the rich world is rich, but the governments of the rich world are poor' (Piketty 2014, p. 540). This correct evaluation may be supplemented by the observation that it has primarily been globalization that has contributed so much to the demise of the welfare state. 'Between 1920 and 1980, the share of national income that the wealthy countries chose to devote to social spending, increased considerably' (p. 475). As Rodrik (2000) argues, this trend was reinforced in the 1980s and (at least partially) in the 1990s as OECD governments intended to insure their economies against the growing external risks of an increasing openness/globalization (pp. 66–85). A good measure for this effect is the share of expenditures for social security in GDP (p. 68).

In fact, 'social expenditure in OECD countries, with the exception of Norway, has increased up to the mid-1990s' (Chen et al. 2014, p. 1). This picture has changed dramatically since the beginning of the new millennium (see Sell and Stratmann 2012, p. 19): 'globalisation imposes new constraints on governments' ability to redistribute income or protect their citizens through the welfare state' (Vannoorenberghe and Janeba 2013, p. 2). At the same time, globalization has made it all the more difficult to tax the (highly mobile) factor of production capital and, as a consequence, a higher tax burden strikes the (rather immobile) factor of production labour (Rodrik 2000, p. 81). Add to this the many times evoked observation of the explosion in the remuneration of the high and the top management. Progression in the income tax system has been unable to cope with these developments. Therefore, it is only seemingly convincing to present empirical evidence arguing for complementarity between the welfare state and openness (see Chen et al. 2014) when the time series used begins in 1995 and ends in 2009 (the year in which most governments fought the world economic crisis with huge stabilization programmes; see for such a procedure, for example, Chen et al. 2014, p. 5) and when a country's competitiveness is measured by the rather unspecific total factor productivity (TFP) growth (p. 7).[1] Make no mistake, even if it was true that governments in some countries have maintained or even increased social insurance programmes, this does not change the picture: the effectiveness of those policies is more than doubtful if they cannot contribute to stabilize the distribution of incomes. As a result and this is supposed to be a main conclusion of the analysis in this book, governments have increasingly lost since the beginning of the new millennium their capacity to correct the skewness of personal income distribution according to the preferences of the society.

An important strand of literature discusses whether the extent of redistribution policies 'is larger in [small] open than in closed economies' (p. 5), given redistributive policies tend to be more distortive (measured as discrepancy to the first best sectorial allocation solution (p. 20)) in an open economy than in closed economies and whether cross-sectorial redistributive policies (which compress the whole distribution of net wages across sectors) (p. 12) may reduce the well-known inefficiency consequences of redistributive policies (pp. 3–7). Though intellectually appealing and interesting, this sort of reasoning will not be discussed further in this section. If redistribution policy is (no longer) effective, it is a rather academic and hence irrelevant debate for our purpose. A much more challenging question has to do with the redistributive instruments chosen and their relative adequacy: governments may, for example, 'impose a sector-specific sales tax or subsidy' or 'use a proportional income tax imposed on workers' (p. 10). This field of discussion is, however, primarily reserved to the discipline of public finance and not to the discipline of distributional economics.

Before we proceed to a sort of econometric proof of our hypothesis, we should steer our attention for a moment to the usage of different Gini coefficients: it is important, if not essential, to distinguish accurately between the Gini coefficient out of the market and the Gini coefficient net of government interventions. It is astonishing to realize how many contributions to the literature do not even recognize the significance of this difference: only the first one reflects the dynamics of income distribution as an (much more than) accompanying by-product of the market forces. If the Gini net coefficient does not deviate significantly from the Gini coefficient out of the market, this can, in principle, be attributed to either of the two following mechanisms: the government, and so society, are satisfied with the (increasing) degree of inequality that emerges from the market processes (see above) or income distribution policy is no longer capable of altering the effects as represented by the Gini coefficient out of the market. But, and this is a most accepted view in the literature, a significant shift in the preferences towards 'less state' and 'more market' has not occurred at the beginning of the new millennium. Therefore, we can be strongly confident in the relevance of the second mechanism described above. Following the philosophy of this book, this implies the cognizance that former equilibria in the distribution of incomes have been lost.

Table 9.1   On the ineffectiveness of redistribution policies: the case of Germany (1991–2011)

VARIABLES	(1)	(2)	(3)
	Gini net	Gini net	Gini net
Gini o.o.m.	0.562***	0.0706	0.740***
	(0.0677)	(0.0912)	(0.201)
Constant	0.00776	0.222***	−0.0767
	(0.0314)	(0.0402)	(0.0971)
Observations	21	10	11
R-squared	0.783	0.070	0.601

Note: Standard errors in parentheses; *** $p < 0.01$, ** $p < 0.05$, * $p < 0.1$; (1) 1991–2011, (2) 1991–2000, (3) 2001–11.

Source: Author's estimations using data from the German Federal Bureau of Statistics, courtesy of Markus Grabka (DIW).

In Table 9.1[2] we have tested the recent (in)effectiveness of redistribution policies in the case of Germany (which may well represent the situation in many other OECD countries). For that purpose, we analyse the correlation between the two key Gini coefficients (out of the market, o.o.m.) and net (after government intervention) in different phases and by means of a simple regression experiment. This is quite in line with the methodological condition formulated by the IMF: 'evaluating the redistributive impact of fiscal policies requires a comparison of incomes after taxes and transfers with those that would exist without them' (IMF 2014, p. 14).

What are the results? If we look at the total time span between 1991 and 2011 (1), but especially at the most recent period (3), the correlation between the two distinct Gini coefficients turns out to be quite significant. This is a clear sign that the government was unable to implement effective redistribution policies.

As opposed to that, the period between 1991 and 2000 (2) reveals no significant correlation between the two distinct concepts of the Gini coefficient, a result that we take as a strong indicator for some sort of policy effectiveness in the field of redistribution. By contrast, the constant in the linear regression equation, which serves here as the second independent variable, now shows a high degree of significance that points to the likelihood of omitted variables.

What are the reasons for this totally different evaluation of policy effectiveness? In Germany, for example, we can observe since 2003 a precipitous fall of social expenditure as a percentage of GDP (Sell and Stratmann

2012, p. 20). This is remarkable: as the IMF diagnoses, most of the reduction in income inequality is due to and has been achieved 'on the expenditure side through transfers' (p. 15). In advanced economies, the average Gini for disposable income (net, see above) was 14 percentage points below that of the average market income Gini (o.o.m., see above) in 2005. 'The redistributive impact of transfers accounts for about two-thirds of the decrease in the Gini' (p. 15).

These findings are somewhat surprising though: as the IMF (2014, p. 9) reports, between the late 1990s and the late 2000s, public support for redistribution policies 'increased substantially in Finland, Germany and Sweden and also in China and India' (p. 9). At the same time, the IMF – following the OECD (2011) – finds that 'the decrease in the redistributive power of fiscal policy has been attributed to fiscal reforms in many economies since the mid-1990s that have reduced the generosity of unemployment and social assistance benefits as well as income tax rates, especially at higher income levels' (IMF 2014, p. 17). The latter is demonstrated impressively by the IMF with the help of a chart (figure 12, p. 37) that collects information about the development of the top personal income tax (PIT) between 1980 and 2012 for almost all relevant areas of the world economy: 'The median top PIT rate ... dropped from 59 percent in 1980 to 30 percent today' (p. 37). As well known, this period of time is also characterized by the fact that globalization has gathered speed. Has fiscal policy resigned against the fierce power of technological change, high mobility and economic integration? It seems as if – in the words of H.-W. Sinn (2004) – the welfare state has lost in part its orientation. The 'new systems competition', organized as locational competition between entire countries or economic regions, is misguided already for logical reasons: governments are elected to correct for market failures and unwarranted market outcomes, but surely not for fostering market competition and/or for participating in a race to the bottom with regard to tax rates.

Against this background, it appears, on the one hand, strange to see the IMF (2014, pp. 21–43) discuss extensively the 'design of efficient redistributive fiscal policy' in a situation where its mere effectiveness is at stake. On the other hand, shaping redistributive policy more efficiently may contribute to make it more effective as well. The IMF discusses a bulk of specific policy recommendations that will not be replicated here. It should suffice to emphasize some major proposals, such as:

- improving the targeting and reducing the adverse labour market effects of social spending (p. 25)
- increasing the effective retirement age (p. 25)

- incorporating pension incomes into a progressive income tax system (p. 26)
- making (family, unemployment) benefit cuts progressive (p. 27)
- strengthen incentives to take up employment (p. 33)
- supporting education reforms that focus on improving access by low income groups (p. 34)
- make personal income taxation (more) progressive (pp. 23, 36)
- tax capital even in light of its mobility, but beware of substantial efficiency costs (p. 39)
- don't forget to tax wealth (Piketty!), but take into account the possibilities of tax evasion!

Even if this menu card can serve as a helpful device for present and future redistribution policies: is there enough room to manoeuvre? Is redistributive fiscal policy perhaps no longer consistent with fiscal sustainability (p. 21)? What about the large fiscal consolidations underway in a large number of countries? Do they have a potential negative impact on inequality (p. 43)? As the IMF correctly reports, 'fiscal consolidation typically leads to a short-run reduction in output and employment, which is often associated with a decline in the wage share . . . Increasing unemployment also tends to widen inequality, since unskilled wages fall relative to skilled wages as employers hoard skilled labour' (p. 44).

What about the medium to long-term effects of redistribution policies on growth and inequality? This question is all the more important in light of our political economy modelling in Chapter 6. Make no mistake, redistribution policies are meant to be policy interventions with the aim to reduce inequality. In their empirical studies, Ostry et al. (2014, pp. 17–26) find that 'the average redistribution, and the associated reduction in inequality, is . . . associated with higher and more durable growth' (p. 26). Such outcomes do not in principle contradict a non-linear relationship between inequality (measured by the Gini index), on the one hand, and per capita economic growth, on the other hand. Once inequality has gone too far, any redistributive policy that intends to counteract such development is capable of increasing economic growth. Interestingly, the authors also find that 'when redistribution is already high, . . . there is evidence that further redistribution is indeed harmful to growth, as the Okun "big trade-off" hypothesis would suggest' (p. 23). No empirical statement could better reinforce the view of the above-mentioned non-linearity. Put differently: obviously, there is some degree of inequality needed for high economic growth.

Last, but not least, one has to realize that wealth is even more unequally distributed than income, 'as indicated by the higher Gini coefficients'

(Lipton 2014, p. 3). The future challenge for redistribution policies, hence, is here particularly high, but it goes beyond the scope of this book to address the wealth distribution subject. It may be deferred to a future monograph.

9.2   THE SCOPE FOR FUTURE RESEARCH

It is an obvious phenomenon that neither the economics of distribution nor the economics of redistribution have incorporated significantly behavioural economics into their own intellectual edifice. This applies to fairness theory (Fehr and Schmidt 1999; Bolton and Ockenfels 2000), which has boosted the concept of inequity aversion, but also the much less known notion of 'equity aversion' (Sell and Stratmann 2009). Given the fact that inequity aversion is widespread over the relevant literature, we want to concentrate in the following on 'equity aversion' and demonstrate at the end of this section with the help of three examples how this type of social preference can inspire the economics of distribution and of redistribution. Notice that the following three examples reflect the three traditional methods to calculate the GDP: application (or spending) of income, generation of income and distribution of income (see Sell and Engelkamp 2013, pp. 195–208).

The first example stems from the political economy literature and provides the case of both income generation and income spending. Alesina and Angeletos (2005) have given a simple, but robust definition of fairness: [With] 'fairness . . . we capture a social preference for reducing the degree of inequality induced by luck and unworthy activities' (p. 961). An almost synonymous notion for this sort of social preference is 'inequity aversion' (Fehr and Schmidt 1999). By contrast, those inequalities in income and wealth, which can be traced back to distinct 'efforts' and 'talents', are judged to be fair. But what if the existing inequality of incomes – even without adverse social circumstances – does not fully reflect those actually present differences in talents and efforts? To capture this effect, one may well define another social preference that should be labelled consequently 'equity aversion'. This makes a difference not only to Anthony Downs (1968), but also to the mainstream fairness literature (see Fehr and Schmidt 1999; Bolton and Ockenfels 2000) that only concedes a social preference of inequity aversion. But let us go step by step. The modified function of individual preferences set up by Alesina and Angeletos (2005) reads:

$$U_i = u_i - \gamma(1 - \Omega) \tag{9.1}$$

where U_i stands for the private utility that is generated by consumption, investment and 'effort choices'. The parameter $\gamma \geq 0$ represents the size of demand for fairness and $(1 - \Omega)$ symbolizes the loss of utility associated with unjustified social circumstances such as luck of being born into a rich family and unworthy activities such as corruption, cronyism, rent seeking and so on. When $\Omega = 1$, there is full fairness present in the society, so that demand for (additional) fairness collapses to zero. If $\Omega < 1$, this situation helps some individuals to take the lead and to reap recusant advantages over other individuals and there remains an additional demand for fairness. If we now want to take account of the preference of equity aversion, we have to split the variable Ω into two components ω und π:

$$\Omega = \omega + \pi \tag{9.2}$$

Notice that the small ω is equivalent as regards the substance to the large Ω from above, whereas $(1 - \pi)$ constitutes the loss of utility that occurs even if there are no unjustified social circumstances, but when the compensation system is not well suited to the different productivities and performances of the employees. This can happen if we are confronted with highly aggregated collective negotiations, systematic deviations from the marginal productivity of labour principle, inadequate bonuses and so on. If $\pi = 1$, there is no institutional bias against equity aversion in the society. Now, we augment our above utility function by a widened notion of fairness and we achieve:

$$U_i = u_i - \gamma(1 - \omega)(1 - \pi) \tag{9.3}$$

It is noteworthy to mention that Alesina and Angelos (2005) seem to have thought of such an enlarged concept of fairness: 'Endogenizing the concept of fairness, and understanding why societies consider some sources of inequality justifiable and others unfair, is an exciting direction of research, but it is beyond the scope of our paper' (Alesina und Angeletos 2005, p. 971).

The existence of such a second type of social preferences can be established not only on the grounds of institutional and/or functional deficiencies in the system of payments but also (see Chapter 5) with interdependencies in consumer behaviour first detected by Harry G. Johnson (1971). When consumers follow both the 'keep ahead of the Smiths' attitude – which tends to signal equity aversion – and also a 'keep up with the Joneses' pattern of behaviour – which tends to demonstrate inequity aversion – we may rewrite our utility function as follows:

$$U_i = \ln x_i - \gamma(1 - \omega)(1 - \pi) \qquad (9.4)$$

Total utility U_i depends (with the usual characteristics) positively on the endowment with the bundle of private goods, x_i. Given the weighting parameter γ, the expression $(1 - \gamma)$ symbolizes the loss of utility associated with a too high degree of inequity (the consumption pattern of family Jones appears to be too far away to be reachable), whereas the term $(1 - \pi)$ stands for losses of utility in the context of a too high degree of equity (the consumption pattern of family Smith appears to be too close/too little distant to our own).

Bjornskov et al. (2010) have provided an analytical framework that belongs to the economics of happiness and can serve for our second example. This makes the case of income generation. Now, utility (U_i) is directly associated with income (y_i) that is generated by effort (e_i). This effort invested to earn income has a negative and quadratic direct effect on utility.[3] Hence,

$$U_i = y_i(e_i) - 0.5e_i^2 \qquad (9.5)$$

and

$$y_i(e_i) = g(e_i)[1 - (1 - \pi)(1 - \omega_i)] \qquad (9.6)$$

'Income increases with effort according to the strictly concave function g.' The parameter $\pi[0,1]$ is a lack of institutional bias parameter. 'The closer its value is to one, the more reliable is the impact of individual effort on individual income. The value of this parameter is identical for all individuals. We assume that the true value of π is unknown to the individual decision-makers' (Bjornskov et al. 2010, p. 11).

On the other hand, $\omega_i[0,1]$ is an idiosyncratic parameter reflecting, for example, the family background or the place of birth of an individual. In general, ω_i captures anything in the personal background of an individual that may make it more difficult for her to earn an income based upon her own effort. Bjornskov et al. (2010) identify fairness with the parameter π. This is wrong according to Alesina and Angeletos (2005) and Sell and Stratmann (2009): π symbolizes rather an institutional setting that rewards different talents and capabilities with different wages and hence satisfies the demand for inequity (equity aversion). By contrast, it is ω that has been characterized by Alesina and Angelos (2005) correctly as a proxy for fairness in the society (see above).

Individuals can observe the institutional framework of their society, but the mix of formal and informal institutions in any modern society is generally too complex to make any exact *ex ante* knowledge of the true value of π very likely. Therefore, the authors assume that every individual bases her decisions on her own individual estimate $\tilde{\pi}_i$. Our parameter ω_i from above is thought of by the authors as being determined randomly. It is drawn from an individual-specific distribution. The distribution itself is characterized by a continuous and unimodal density $f_i(\omega_i)$ in the range (0, 1). The expected value of the idiosyncratic parameter for individual i is defined as $\hat{\omega}_i$. The authors assume that the distribution of $\hat{\omega}_i$ over the population is skewed to the right (steep to the left), and also unimodal. Further, they assume that their own $\hat{\omega}_i$ is known to all individuals. Individuals cannot, however, observe the value of ω_i that is eventually drawn. They can only observe income and effort, but have no definitive knowledge about how much of the result is due to bad (good) institutions, or an (un-)lucky draw of the idiosyncratic parameter. Furthermore, the authors assume that $\hat{\omega}_i$ is inherited: individuals from poorer families or worse neighbourhoods are characterized by lower values of $\hat{\omega}_i$. However, even individuals from unfavourable backgrounds have a chance to draw a favourable high ω_i from the distribution (p. 11). In order to maximize individual expected utility, the following function has to be differentiated with regard to effort, e:

$$\max_{e \geq 0} \int_0^1 f_i(\omega_i) \left\{ g(e_i) \left[1 - (1 - \tilde{\pi}_i)(1 - \omega_i) - \frac{1}{2} e_i^2 \right] \right\} d\omega_i \qquad (9.7)$$

The first order condition reads:

$$g'(e_i) [1 - (1 - \tilde{\pi}_i)(1 - \hat{\omega}_i)] = e_i \qquad (9.8)$$

Hence, the higher individual effort, the larger the marginal productivity of effort, $g'(e_i)$, the lower the expected bias in the institutional settings of the society, $(1 - \tilde{\pi}_i)$ and the higher the expected degree of fairness, ω_i. Furthermore, we can infer from the two equations above (Bjornskov et al. 2010, p. 12) that optimal effort, e_i^*, is a function of:

$$e_i^* = e_i^* (\tilde{\pi}_i, \hat{\omega}_i) \text{ with } e_i^* > 0 \text{ and } e_{i\hat{\omega}}^* > 0 \qquad (9.9)$$

Here redistribution policy comes into play. The authors assume the existence of two instruments: 'a proportional income tax with rate t levied on labour income, and of a guaranteed transfer income $y_T(t)$ paid to those individuals who do not earn a market income' (p. 13). This makes it easy to calculate a stringent *ex ante* condition for labour market participation of individuals:

$$(1 - t)\left\{ g(e_i^*)[1 - (1 - \tilde{\pi}_i)(1 - \hat{\omega}_i)] - \frac{1}{2}e_i^{*2} \right\} > y_T(t)^4 \quad (9.10)$$

This implies that there must exist – for any given expected tax and transfer system $\{t, y_T(t), \tilde{\pi}_i\}$ – a threshold value of ω_i^T 'where for any $\hat{\omega}_i > \omega_i^T$' the individual decides in favour of labour market participation' (p. 14). Hence, there is need for a minimum of expected equity to incentizeve individuals to work. Although not considered by the authors, we believe the same should hold for $\tilde{\pi}_i$: there must exist – for any given tax and transfer system $\{t, y_T(t), \hat{\omega}_i\}$ – a threshold value of π_i^T 'where for any $\tilde{\pi}_i > \pi_i^T$' the individual decides in favour of labour market participation. Hence, there is a need for a minimum of expected inequity to incentivize individuals to work. Altogether, and translated into the language of the Gini coefficient, a minimum of equity defines a ceiling value for G; *mutatis mutandis*, a minimum of inequity defines a floor value for G.

What is the scope of action for redistribution policy? The role played by guaranteed income transfers is already addressed by means of the above inequality. For any set of a given expected transfer system, equity and inequity expectations $\{y_T(t), \hat{\omega}_i, \tilde{\pi}_i\}$, there exists a threshold value of (expected) income tax rate t^T levied on labour income, 'where for any $t > t^T$', the individual decides against labour market participation: if higher taxes and higher guaranteed income transfers are the instruments of redistribution, it follows that 'redistribution is *ex ante* only in the interest of individuals who plan not to participate in the labour market' (p. 14).

What about the situation *ex post*? First of all, we look at the *ex post* market income:

$$y_i^* = g\{e_i^*(\tilde{\pi}_i, \hat{\omega}_i)\}[1 - (1 - \pi)(1 - \omega_i)] \quad (9.11)$$

As in any ex-post situation, now the realizations of the variates decide: 'the larger the variance of ω_i in the population, the larger the inequality of incomes, ceteris paribus' (p. 15). *Mutatis mutandis*, it must hold that the lower π, the larger the (unjustified) equity of incomes, *ceteris paribus*. In the case of unexpected high tax increases, this is a disutility to all individuals who decided *ex ante* to participate in the labour market while it is favourable to individuals who decided *ex ante* to receive guaranteed income transfers. High unexpected taxes, in turn, are the more likely, the higher the probability for increases in income inequality. The latter, again, is the more likely, the greater the revealed variance of ω_i (see above). But the most important insight is the following: 'perceiving the income generation process as fair lowers the demand for income redistribution' (p. 22). In light of our enlarged concept of fairness, this outcome means that there exists a personal income distribution characterized by a specific Gini coefficient. This coefficient, in turn, will be located between a floor and a ceiling value of G, as explained above. Whenever it does so, the associated society has achieved 'equilibrium' in personal income distribution.

Our third example makes the case of income distribution and extensively draws on the contribution of Sell and Stratmann (2013). The basic idea is to attempt to utilize the model of prospect theory (Kahnemann and Tversky 1979) to establish equilibrium of personal income distribution. As well known, this approach assumes bounded rationality in the decision-making process of individuals. The selfsame persons tend to give a too high weight to small probabilities, whereas the opposite holds for very large probabilities: the latter receive a too small importance. If, for example, a formerly certain incident loses its status of certainty but is still a very likely event, one can observe that individuals will attach a subjective probability weight to this occurrence much lower than the 'objective' likelihood of such an incident. By contrast, the opposite will happen in the case of low 'objective' probabilities of occurrence: an incident, formerly excluded as a possible occurrence, may now become an event with a tiny probability of occurrence. According to Kahnemann and Tversky (1979), individuals will tend to give to this event a 'probability premium': the subjective likelihood weight attached to this incident will be significantly higher than the 'objective' probability this occurrence would actually justify. This distorted view makes the individuals buy lottery tickets even if the expected value of inpayments is negative. The same persons will react based on the most insignificant doubt they have towards their partner/lover with distrust if not with a cessation of their liaison.

A quite popular application example for prospect theory is the phenomenon of 'perceived inflation'. In this case, the agents' perception of price increases (decreases) deviate substantially from the actually measured price movements. As a sort of rule, individuals will overestimate (underestimate) the effect of higher (lower) prices. Brachinger (2005a) alludes the following three reasons for this behaviour. (1) Individuals observe much more often the mostly prolonged price increases of goods and services of daily needs than price changes of other (important) items that belong to and have a considerable weight in the consumer basket. Such items are, for example, expenditures for rent, insurance premia and so on. If there is a price decline among these services/goods, it will have a significant impact on the measured inflation rate, but this outcome is much less reflected in the subjective appreciation of the economic agents.

By contrast, goods and services of daily needs may become more expensive, but this will not lead to a significant loss of purchasing power for the consumers given the minor weight of these items in the consumer basket. In the opposite case of a price decline, the same applies, *mutatis mutandis*. However, this is quite different in the case of price reductions for items with a high weight in the consumer basket. 'Objectively', consumers gain purchasing power, but this effect is not registered accordingly by the affected individuals.

A second reason (2) alleged by Brachinger (2005) has to do with the fact that prices are evaluated by agents always with reference to a benchmark: 'when visiting a restaurant, an agent may perhaps expect a price for the menu of 60 Euros. The latter would serve as a benchmark or point of reference: if the individual finds that the actual price for the menu is only 45 Euros, he will perceive a (slight) subjective gain. Things are different, however, when he expects 30 Euros as the price for the menu, but realizes the actual price for the menu to be 45 Euros: now he perceives a (considerable) subjective loss' (Brachinger 2005, p. 1003). This leads us to Brachinger's third (3) and most decisive point: consumers have an explicit loss aversion, they attach a much more negative value to price increases in comparison to the positive value they associate with price declines. In other words, their 'appraisal function' will be concave in the case of gains, but convex in the case of losses (Brachinger 2005b, p. 641).

The graphical analysis in Figure 9.1 makes an attempt to integrate the notions of 'inequity aversion' and 'equity aversion' into the concept of prospect theory. In order to make things comprehensive and comparatively easy to understand, we distinguish between the actual dispersion of incomes (measured by a Gini coefficient, G), the perceived skewness of income distribution ($\hat{G}$) and the equilibrium distribution of personal incomes ($\tilde{G}$). We have discussed above some of the pros and cons when using the Gini coefficient to measure inequality of incomes, so that we are aware of its advantages and disadvantages. We believe it is a useful tool to measure the concentration of incomes and it is closely linked to the standard deviation of the logarithm of incomes (see, for example, Blümle 1975, pp. 45–50) that we have used to proxy the distribution of wages in Chapter 3. It remains to say that the data basis for different Gini coefficients is comparatively large and robust. We may now have a look at Figure 9.1 where the major ingredients of our hypothesis are depicted.

Assume we have in the beginning and as a starting point equilibrium in personal income distribution located at the centre of the diagram (origin of ordinates). If now, for whatever reason, the Gini coefficient moves upwards, this will have the following effects in the vein of prospect theory: agents will perceive costs (PC) that are higher than those associated with the 45 degree line. In other words: the slope of the convex function that symbolizes the 'feelings of inequity aversion' (thin line) is steeper than 1. At the same time, perceived utility from the viewpoint of 'equity aversion'

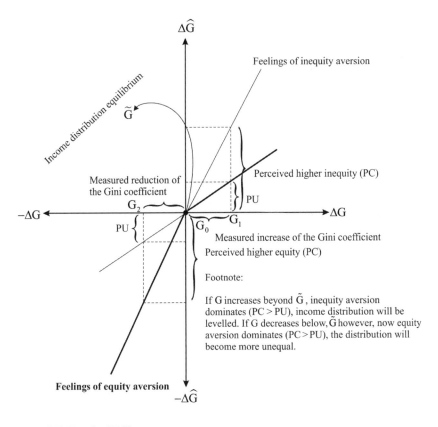

PU ~Perceived Utility
PC ~Perceived Costs

Source: Sell and Stratmann (2013).

Figure 9.1 *Inequity and equity aversion within the framework of prospect theory*

(PU) is lower than PC. The function that stands for the 'feelings of equity aversion' (thick line) has a concave curvature in the first quadrant and it is considerably flatter than the 45 degree line. As a result, we find that the perceived costs associated with inequity aversion dominate the perceived utility associated with equity aversion: PC > PU. If societies experience a loss of their equilibrium in the distribution of incomes, the question arises whether this effect is only transitory or permanent. If it is permanent, it would imply that the society is willing to adapt to the new situation and/or reluctant to take contradictory policy action. We believe that it should be transitory rather than permanent; otherwise the concept of equilibrium does not make much sense. Accordingly, redistribution policy will make use of its instruments to restore the original – which implies a levelling of income distribution – or to smooth the path to a new equilibrium.

In the opposite case of a reduction in the Gini coefficient, we have symmetric results: now we find a convex curve in the third quadrant that represents perceived costs associated with equity aversion. These perceived costs (PC) are much higher as the slope of the 45 degree line would predict. The slope of the 'feelings of equity aversion curve' (thick line) is larger than 1 and also larger than the slope of the perceived utility from the viewpoint of 'inequity aversion' (PU). This is obvious, given the flat and concave nature of the 'feelings of inequity aversion curve' (thin line). As a result, we find that the perceived costs associated with equity aversion dominate the perceived utility associated with inequity aversion: PC > PU. Fiscal policy will now either actively choose instruments to increase G or let the market forces alone contribute to this effect. Once again, the idea is to either restore the initial equilibrium or to search for a new equilibrium, provided the social preferences allow for such a switch.

As we have demonstrated with the help of three examples, the political economy approach, the economics of happiness and also prospect theory can contribute to further development of the theory of social preferences – which now integrate both inequity and equity aversion – and to the design of a new concept of 'optimal taxation' and 'optimal transfer policy' within the discipline of public economics. We hope that the ideas put forward in this book will incentivize young researchers to steer their attention and interest in this direction.

9.3   SUMMARY OF FINDINGS

The Introduction serves primarily to make the reader, slowly but surely, familiar with the concept of equilibrium in the area of income distribution: we depart from the premise that societies can only live in peace and prosperity in the medium to long run if there is some sort of equilibrium realized in the economy. Therefore, we discuss income distribution on all three levels of equilibrium concepts in economics: market equilibrium, bargaining equilibrium and political economy equilibrium.

Before introducing our own ideas, however, we comment extensively on the important contribution of Thomas Piketty (2014): besides the discussion of 'technical aspects' of his thoughtful analysis, we question the existence of an equilibrium concept in his approach. Now as it stands, the impression from the first (and second) reading is rather ambiguous.

We, instead, believe that some degree of inequality is accepted, if not warranted, by society. Whenever the modus is lower than the median and the arithmetic average of personal incomes, one can expect a majority of the population to be satisfied by and large with their own status, given their group of reference. However, German society – to give a significant example – has changed its evaluation of the distribution of personal incomes since 1995 dramatically: while in 2000, the last (!) year of the old millennium, the approval rate was 35 per cent and the rate of rejection stood at 47 per cent, the same sample of interviewed persons accepted the concentration of incomes in 2010 with a rate of only 21 per cent, while 58 per cent denied the fairness of such income distribution. This outcome shows that earlier equilibria may be destroyed and that societies are challenged to search – in their own interest – for new equilibria. In our view, which is founded both theoretically and empirically, the forces of globalization have contributed substantially to the erosion of income distribution equilibria.

A first view on the empirical facts impressively shows that on a world scale level, there seems to be a process of convergence underway in the figures of income concentration for different income groups. This sort of 'mobility' in income distribution is well documented and reflected in upward trends for the Gini coefficients (both out of the market and net of taxation/ transfers) as well as in downward trends for the wage share in developed countries such as Germany between 1990 and the present.

In a decentralized economy, plans of the involved agents can be coordinated either by the market process – that is, by adjustable prices and the flexible response of demand and supply – or by the contract seeking forces driven by bargaining agents or, last but not least, by the voting power of the electorate. In 'Various concepts of equilibrium in economics', we put forward the idea that market, contractual and political economy outcomes are rather a by-product of the distributional contest that is in the background of all economic actions. This view disagrees with the traditional conviction that income distribution is a sort of by-product of market processes, bargaining situations or elections. The chapter illustrates all three channels for the income distribution contest by taking the example of bandwagon and snob effects in the goods market equilibrium, the efficient exchange of goods between households in the bargaining framework and, last but not least, the rational partisan business cycle that can explain equilibrium values for unemployment and the inflation (rate).

The chapter on 'Income distribution and the labour market' first sheds light on the wage gap for skilled and unskilled labour and the factors that may widen or reduce this gap, both in the short and in the long run. After a short view on the role of market imperfections, we address the issue of minimum wages and of efficiency wages. We are able to show that minimum wages induce unemployment among unskilled workers. This result is widespread and quite robust. Moreover, we demonstrate that minimum wages for unskilled labour are an inappropriate policy instrument to change income distribution in favour of unskilled workers. We call this result the 'irrelevance theorem of minimum wages'. As far as efficiency wages are concerned, their distributional impacts are at least twofold: on the one hand, there exist both theoretical arguments and empirical evidence that they tend to increase the inequality between the employed and the unemployed part of the labour force. On the other hand, efficiency wages are capable of diminishing the gap between wage earners and capital income earners. It is not yet clear whether there exists a stable trade-off between unemployment and overall inequality: from first glance, the impression is that the USA (Europe) can pay the price for higher inequality of incomes (unemployment) with lower unemployment (inequality of incomes). The theory of efficient contracts deserves, in this respect, a special interest because it allows us to discuss a 'pure' distributional conflict between wages and profits at a given employment.

In the political economy part of the chapter, we explicitly model the heterogeneity problem in wage negotiations: very frequently, workers with different skill levels are represented by the same union; unions, however, when seeking a higher level of union membership, have a tendency to reduce the spread of wages during the negotiations with the employers in comparison to a situation where each employee is paid according to their marginal productivity. It is shown that it is important to have a considerable skewness in the distribution of wages if the goals pursued by the unions consist in raising the average wage rate and the total wage sum. If unions want to limit, at the same time, the size of wage dispersion, a classical 'trade-off' appears. In optimum, hence, unions offer their members an attractive mix of wage size and wage skewness. This result is founded both theoretically and empirically. Our empirical investigations for Germany confirm the findings of other authors with regard to larger samples of countries that skilled (unskilled) labour has gained (lost) importance in the last 20 years. At the same time, remuneration for skilled (unskilled) work has become more (less) attractive.

The chapter on 'Income distribution and the capital market' starts with a traditional rent/welfare analysis of the capital market. We are able to replicate a long-standing insight that says that (economic) growth in conjunction with stable or even lower prices tends to reduce the distributional conflict between savers and investors. With the help of the New Austrian

Business Cycle Theory (ABCT), we can show how the Target2 mechanism made it possible to shift purchasing power during the years 2008–12 from the GLNF countries to the so-called GIIPS countries (Greece, Ireland, Italy, Portugal, Spain), financed by a money-printing process and substituting regular capital flows. In a comprehensive static welfare evaluation of Target2, we find overall net welfare gains for the GIIPS countries. In contrast, the GLNF countries (Germany, Luxembourg, Netherlands, Finland) suffer from net welfare losses due to the Target2 mechanism. That is, what we find is a zero-sum game with the GLNF countries losing and the GIIPS countries winning in this distributional contest. This result matches the earlier finding that the aggregated effects of the Target2 balances on the monetary base add up to nil at the ECB level.

The analysis of bargaining in the capital market makes use of the Edgeworth box framework and of a simultaneous matrix game. There exist two Nash equilibria: one when both agents exploit (E) each other and another one when both agents defect (D). However, mutual cooperation is not worse in terms of payoffs than the expected value of exploitation/being exploited. But as mutual cooperation is not a Nash equilibrium, only banking supervision is capable of enforcing fair contracts in the credit market.

In the political economy or likewise partisan section of the chapter, we formalize the existing trade-off for firms – which is significant under realistic assumptions – and go beyond the irrelevance theorem of Modigliani-Miller: firms quoted at the stock exchange have to face the alternatives of payout policies vis-à-vis retention policies. There are good reasons to assume that small (large) share-holders have a preference for payout over retention policies. As reported in the literature, firms in Germany tend to offer rather stable payout levels/dividend payments. That is, when the size of profits falls (rises), the payout ratio is adjusted upwards (downwards). This is a strong hint that backs the hypothesis that the associated firms act as partisans for (this time in favour of) the group of small stockholders: stabilizing dividend payments to become a foreseeable stream of income helps the small stockholders to smooth their consumption expenditures. Our own empirical analysis for Germany (1991–2010) supports the view that stock market quoted firms tend to plan payouts so that retentions – given the pitfalls of the business cycle – are to a large extent a mere residual.

In 'Income distribution and the business cycle', we start with the empirically still robust premise that during the phases of upswing and boom, the overall income distribution tends to change in favour of profits, while during the phases of downswing and recession the opposite is true, that is, income distribution tends to change in favour of labour income. When modelling income distribution during the business cycle, two-class models in the vein of Nicholas Kaldor serve to establish some benchmark results, but reality often looks pretty much more like a three person or likewise three class society. In such an environment, the middle class plays an essential role. In this setting, and contrary to some conventional wisdom, it can be shown that a decrease in inequality might even increase the average propensity to save. In a three class society, income redistribution during the cycle will affect more the lower and the upper incomes than the middle income class. Since it is a stylized fact that income distribution changes in favour of lower (upper) income groups during the downswing (upswing) phases of the cycle, the behaviour of the middle class will be dominated by a 'keeping ahead of the Smiths' attitude in the case of a downswing and by a 'keeping up with the Joneses' attitude in the case of an upswing. The latter pattern in consumption behaviour, in turn, is a signal for the existence of equity aversion as a social preference. For the economic research on the business cycle it could be a remarkable result that the social preference of equity aversion tends to dampen the effects of both downturns and upswings, thus smoothing the cycle.

After modelling bargaining between unions and firms in a game-theoretic setting, we present a political economy model of the currency union. This seems to be quite appropriate in times of EMU. In our approach, which comes in the vein of the Nordhaus model, there exists a trade-off between unemployment and the concentration of incomes. For governments in a currency union, an optimal strategy is to reduce unemployment to a lower level by election day and to accept a more unequal distribution of incomes that will be associated with this policy. As soon as there are expectations of a more equal distribution, the short-run trade-off curve shifts outwards and the government loses its majority. During the election period, the government will endeavour to dampen expectations of a more even income distribution. This is only possible by means of a policy of fiscal contraction (such as heavy taxation of leading consumers) that will be associated with rising levels of unemployment. Immediately before the election the government distributes its 'presents' to leading consumers and thus succeeds in pushing demand and reaching an optimal point for re-election again. Note that different from our modelling, the EMU is still characterized by sovereign national governments.

What about the empirical facts? Again we stick to figures from Germany. It seems to be a stylized fact that during the years of observation (1992–2007), comparatively high values of the Business Climate Index – provided, for example, by the Munich IFO Institute – (during upswing and boom) is accompanied by relatively high rates of income concentration. Conversely, comparatively low values of the Business Climate Index (during downswing and recession) seem to go with lower rates of income concentration. When confronting the development of the IFO Business Climate Index with the evolution of the corporate profit quota in Germany (1991–2010), one can see that in this case, the corporate profit quota matches on average quite well the course in the value of the IFO Business Climate Index.

In 'Income distribution and economic growth', we primarily address the relationship between the concentration of incomes (measured by the Gini coefficient), or likewise specific income forms such as profits, on the one hand, and the real rate of per capita (or likewise absolute) economic growth, on the other hand. This fits into the well-known debate about the trade-off between equity and efficiency. The competitive process is described (following Blümle 1989b) within a closed national economy as an interaction between innovators (advancing prey) and pursuing imitators (pursuing hunters). Both groups of market players make investments, but the imitators are given the role of ensuring that the (new) technological knowledge created by the innovators is being diffused. Innovators see to it that their own production methods are more cost-effective, thus causing a profit disparity among vendors (the famous curve provided by Enrico Barone). This attracts imitators onto the market whose investments cause the new knowledge to be diffused while also triggering an erosion of the profit disparity that existed before. However, with the disappearance of 'difference profits', real investment decreases too, and financial investment becomes more attractive. If difference profits increase again due to the occurrence of autonomous technological progress, profit dispersion will, as a result, increase again. The system moves in the direction of a point where a minimum is reached in the real investment quota. From there on, the investment quota will increase again as a result of high pioneer profits and increases in profit dispersion.

Making use of an analogy to the theory of efficient wages, we demonstrate possible bargaining equilibria – all of them efficient contracts – between unions and firms that have contradictory views on benefits and costs of a high rate of wage increases/a high dispersion of wage increases.

In the final section of the chapter, we present our own social optimization model that, as we believe, can help to understand how income distribution and economic growth are jointly determined in political equilibrium. It seems to be quite obvious that both a quite equal as well as an extremely unequal distribution of personal incomes are of disadvantage to economic growth. A main function of economic growth, namely, is – as has been stressed quite often – that it tends to work as a 'social damper'. During economic development, necessary redistributions of income are more easily implemented in the social environment if this process is not a zero-sum game: in this case, only additional incomes are redistributed. Only if the (re)distribution of incomes continues to become more uneven during economic growth, then social instability may emerge. The empirical test for our approach stands somehow in contrast to conventional 'growth-equity-empiricism'. Instead of estimating or likewise plotting a bunch of Gini coefficients against a huge and undifferentiated sample of per capita economic growth rates stemming from a large sample of developed and developing countries, we prefer to go by pieces: we first identify the empirical relevance of the Kuznets curve, considering both 'poor' and 'rich' countries. Thereafter, we look for conditional convergence among 'rich countries' and conditional divergence for 'poor countries'. As each of these pieces confirms the underlying theory (see above), we suggest that the empirical findings do not contradict the hypothesis of a non-linear relationship between the Gini coefficient, on the one hand, and the per capita real growth rate of income, on the other hand.

In 'Factor mobility and income distribution', we initially discuss extensively the impact of labour and of capital mobility in the famous two-countries marginal productivity specific factor diagrams. The graphical analysis suggests that capital owners will improve (deteriorate) their relative and absolute position in the North (South) in the aftermath of free labour migration. Moreover, the gains of capital owners in the North outweigh the losses of capital owners in the South. In contrast, owners of low and medium working qualifications will deteriorate (improve) their absolute and relative position in the North (South) following a liberalization of labour flows. However, the losses for the factor of production labour in the North fall short of the gains achieved by labour in the South. When differentiating between the immigration of unskilled and skilled work, there is an indication of increasing inequality in the case of unskilled immigration and a strong rationale for the conjecture that skilled immigration reduces inequality. We are able to show that globalization tends to equalize factor prices. Distributional effects are contradictory: on the one hand, domestic capital owners win more than foreign capital owners lose; on the other hand, the domestic losses for labour are more pronounced than the gains for labour in the foreign country. Therefore, it seems to be that the comparatively immobile factor of production, labour, loses during globalization, while the more mobile factor of production, capital, is on the winning side. Results change quite a bit when the economy of concern has to face rigid real wages: in the case of rigid wages, the North will clearly lose welfare, whereas the South still profits from the new division of labour in the world economy. The interesting implication reads that rigid wages in the North make autarky more profitable than free trade/free flow of capital goods. Quite opposed to this, the South profits from rigid wages in the North and prefers globalization in comparison to autarky.

It is a fairly rational assumption that firms are interested both in international competitiveness as well as in social peace. We put forward a bargaining solution where firms compensate unions' members for wage decreases (in conjunction with higher real interest rates) induced by the forces of globalization with better working conditions.

For policy makers, there exists a political economy trade-off: while the free movement of factors of production serves to maximize income and the international competitiveness of the domestic economy, the lack of regulation for labour and capital flows puts into danger a socially acceptable share for labour in national income. In contrast, the regulation of factors' mobility (capital export controls, immigration laws) can help to better achieve the distributional goal, but have to be paid by losses in allocative efficiency and hence in output units. Furthermore, we were able to detect the following mechanism: as social welfare programmes belong to the major expenditure categories of public spending, one may expect that the Gini coefficient out of net incomes is lowered in the political economy equilibrium in comparison to the social planner equilibrium.

In order to investigate empirically the impact of both labour immigration and capital exports on income distribution, we have constructed – again for the case of Germany – an individual index (1991 = 100 and 2001 = 100, respectively) for each variable and then a compound index that adds up the two individual indices. Our empirical findings support the earlier theoretical prediction that both immigration and net capital exports tend to dampen the overall labour income share.

In 'International trade and income distribution', we start with an in-depth analysis of globalization within the tradeables/non-tradeables – high-tech/low-tech framework. Both rising demand for high-tech goods and increasing supply of low-tech goods tend to widen the gap between the wages of the skilled and unskilled labour force. It seems that high (low) qualified labour force in the high-tech sectors of tradeables and of non-tradeables share a lot of common interests. Therefore, it would make sense to reorganize the structure of unions according to the principle of 'high-tech' vis-à-vis 'low-tech' and not (if it is so) following the principle of industries. After reviewing briefly the Heckscher-Ohlin, the Stolper-Samuelson and the Rybczynski theorems, we find that globalization in the form of a stronger integration of the South into the goods markets of the North has definitively negative effects on the income distribution of wages in the North: either the gap between the wages for skilled and for unskilled labour is widened (US scenario) or the rigidity of relative factor prices (Continental Europe scenario) renders part of unskilled labour jobless and hence causes inequality to increase as well. Notice also that the regime of rigid wages in the North reduces inequality in the South (in comparison to the free trade – flexible wages scenario).

Globalization goes together with fragmentation in production and trade. Once fragmentation is significant, the North (South) of the world economy will specialize even more than heretofore in the production of goods (and of components) that use intensively skilled (unskilled) labour. If fragmentation does not alter the goods prices, it will increase production wherever it occurs and, hence, the world's welfare. In the case where fragmentation does indeed affect the goods prices, one can think of a terms of trade deterioration for some of the countries involved.

The terms of trade will also be affected, when countries bargain over tariff reductions: assuming the North has more bargaining power than the South, tariff reductions will concern in the first place low-tech goods. As a result, the relative price for skilled labour (in relation to unskilled labour) will increase. Given the substitutability in the production functions of both goods, the production of both goods will become more intensive in the use of unskilled labour. Whether the distribution of wage income will change in the North in favour of skilled labour and to the detriment of unskilled labour depends on the degree of homogeneity of the production function. Further differentiations can be made, once the model structure is altered. For example, for a large country (such as the North in our analysis) positive terms of trade gains will slow any rise in capital income shares. This in turn means that terms of trade effects will tend to mitigate the inequality effects of tariff liberalization.

In the remainder of the chapter we model a political economy/rent seeking model for the usage of different tax policy instruments such as tariffs and export subsidies. The effects of these instruments on income distribution/social welfare are ambiguous though: the imposition of a (higher) import tariff on labour-intensive goods will reduce the Gini coefficient and hence the inequality of wages for skilled and unskilled labour, *ceteris paribus*. In the opposite case of an (unskilled) labour-abundant country, the imposition of import tariffs on skill-intensive goods will raise the Gini coefficient and hence the inequality of wages for skilled and unskilled labour, *ceteris paribus*. It is undisputed that export subsidies raise the incomes of the protected sector to the detriment of the unprotected sector. If the protected sector uses intensively (un)skilled labour, the difference in the remuneration vis-à-vis unskilled labour will increase (decrease), *ceteris paribus*.

Testing empirically the impact of globalization on income distribution, we find that there is a high positive correlation between the upward development of Germany's export quota, on the one hand, and the two concepts for the Gini coefficient (in the time span between 1990 and 2012), on the other hand.

In 'Final remarks', we first test for the (in)effectiveness of redistribution policies taking the case of Germany. One result for the period 2001 and 2011 is that the correlation between the two distinct Gini coefficients turns out to be quite significant. This is a clear sign that the government was unable to implement effective redistribution policies. Opposed to this insight, the period 1991–2000 reveals no significant correlation between the two distinct concepts of the Gini coefficient, a result that we take as a strong indicator for some sort of policy effectiveness in the field of redistribution. In the remainder of the chapter, we concentrate on the concept of 'equity aversion' and demonstrate with the help of three examples how this type of social preference can inspire the economics of distribution and of redistribution.

NOTES

1. It is astonishing to realize that these authors just 'assume' without discussion that TFP is a good proxy for a country's competitiveness. Already in the 1990s, one can find a rich literature that analyses in depth the pros and cons of different concepts of competiveness like the real exchange rate, nominal labour unit costs or even Tobin's Q. See for an overview Maass and Sell (1998).
2. See for a comparable correlation analysis Ostry et al. (2014, p. 14). The authors find a comparatively low correlation of the Gini net income, on the one hand, and the Gini of gross income, on the other hand, for the OECD countries (1960–2010).
3. This corresponds to the classical theory of 'pain of working' (see Sell and Engelkamp 2013, pp. 446–8).
4. It is assumed that the 'tax rate will be adjusted to balance the budget' (Bjornskov et al. 2010, p. 15).

Bibliography

Adler, M. and K.-D. Schmid (2012), 'Factor shares and income inequality. Empirical evidence from Germany 2002–2008', *SOEP Papers on Multidisciplinary Panel Data Research*, No. 460.

Albert, M. (1994), *Factor Price Equalization (Faktorpreisausgleichtheorem)*, Tübingen: J.C.B. Mohr Siebeck.

Alesina, A. (1987), 'Macroeconomic policy in a two-party system as a repeated game', *Quarterly Journal of Economics*, **102**, 651–78.

Alesina, A. and G.-M. Angeletos (2005), 'Fairness and redistribution', *American Economic Review*, **95** (4), 960–80.

Alesina, A. and R. Perotti (1994), 'The political economy of growth: a critical survey of the recent literature', *World Bank Economic Review*, **8** (3), 351–71.

Alesina, A. and R. Perotti (1996), 'Income distribution, political instability and investment', *European Economic Review*, **40** (6), 1203–28.

Alesina, A. and D. Rodrik (1994), 'Distributive politics and economic growth', *Quarterly Journal of Economics*, **109** (2), 465–90.

Alonso Neira, M.A., J. Rallo and J.R.P. Bagus (2011), 'La crisis subprime a la luz de la teoría Austriaca del ciclo económico: expansion crediticia, errores de decision y riesgo moral', *Revista de Economía Mundial*, **28**, 145–74.

Amelung, T. (1989), *The Political Economy of Import Substitution and Trade Liberalization. The Example of Turkey (Die politische Ökonomie der Importsubstitution und der Handelsliberalisierung. Das Beispiel Türkei)*, Kieler Studien No. 227, Tübingen: J.C.B. Mohr.

Anwar, S. (2008), '(International) factor mobility, wage inequality and welfare', *International Review of Economics & Finance*, **17**, 495–506.

Anwar, S. (2010), 'Wage inequality, increased competition, and trade liberalization: short run vs long run', *Review of International Economics*, **18** (3), 574–81.

Arnold, L. (2006), *Macroeconomics (Makroökonomik)*, 2nd edn, Tübingen: J.C.B Mohr Siebeck.

Atkinson, A.B. (1997), 'Bringing income distribution in from the cold', *Economic Journal*, **107** (441), March, 297–321.

Bagus, P. and D. Howden (2011), *Deep Freeze. Iceland's Economic Collapse*, Auburn, AL: Ludwig von Mises Institute.

Balaglou, C.P. and H. Peukert (1996), *About the Ancient Economic Thought (800–31 b.o.t.). A Commented Bibliography (Zum antiken ökonomischen Denken der Griechen (800–31 b.o.t.). Eine kommentierte Bibliographie)*, Marburg: Metropolis Verlag.

Banerjee, A.V. and E. Duflo (2003), 'Inequality and growth: what can the data say?', *Journal of Economic Growth*, **8** (3), 267–99.

Banerjee, A.V. and E. Duflo (2008), 'Inequality and growth: what can the data say?', in C.B. Barrett (ed.), *Development Economics*, Vol. 4: *Development Macroeconomics*, London: Routledge, pp. 168–203.

Barr, T. (2005), *Advanced Intermediate Microeconomics. A Human Centered Approach*, available at http://www.tavisbarr.com/index. php?page=textbook (accessed 16 February 2015).

Barro, R.J. (1996), 'Determinants of economic growth. A cross-country empirical study', NBER Working Paper, No. 5698. Cambridge, MA.

Barro, R.J. and D. Gordon (1983a), 'Rules, discretion, and reputation in a model of monetary policy', *Journal of Monetary Economics*, **12**, 101–21.

Barro, R.J. and D.B. Gordon (1983b), 'A positive theory of monetary policy in a natural rate model', *Journal of Political Economy*, **91** (4), 589–610.

Barro, R.J. and V. Grilli (1994), *European Macroeconomics*, Houndsmill, Basingstoke: Macmillan.

Barro, R.J. and X. Sala-i-Martin (2004), *Economic Growth*, 2nd edn, Cambridge, MA: MIT Press.

Bartholomae, F. (2011), The *Heterogeneity of Consumption and the Structure of International Trade. An Analysis Within the Context of the Theory of Intra-industry Trade (Konsumentenheterogenität und Struktur des Außenhandels. Eine Analyse im Kontext der Theorie des intra-industriellen Handels)*, Wiesbaden: Gabler.

Bastagli, F., D. Coady and S. Gupta (2012), 'Income inequality and fiscal policy', IMF Discussion Note, 28 June.

Beichelt, F.E. and D.C. Montgomery (2003), *Teubner-Paperback of Stochastics: Probability Theory, Stochastic Processes, Mathematical Statistics (Teubner-Taschenbuch der Stochastik: Wahrscheinlichkeitstheorie, Stochastische Prozesse, Mathematische Statistik)*, 1st edn, Wiesbaden: Teubner-Verlag.

Benabou, R. (1996a), 'Inequality and growth', NBER Working Paper, No. 5658, Cambridge, MA.

Benabou, R. (1996b), 'Unequal societies', NBER Working Paper, No. 5583, Cambridge, MA.

Benhabib, J. (2003), 'The tradeoff between inequality and growth', *Annals of Economics and Finance*, **4**, 491–507.

Benhabib, J. and A. Rustichini (1991), 'Social conflict, growth and inequality', Economic Research Reports, Working Papers 91–46, C.V. Starr Center for Applied Economics, New York University, Faculty of Arts and Science, Department of Economics, New York.

Bergh, A. and T. Nilsson (2010), 'Do liberalization and globalization increase income inequality?', *European Journal of Political Economy*, **26**, 488–505.

Berlemann, M. and G. Markwardt (2006), 'Variable rational partisan cycles and electoral uncertainty', *European Journal of Political Economy*, **22**, 874–86.

Berthold, N. and A. Brunner (2010), 'How unequal is the world?' ('Wie ungleich ist die Welt?'), *Wirtschaftswissenschaftliche Beiträge des Lehrstuhls für Volkswirtschaftslehre, insb. Wirtschaftsordnung und Sozialpolitik*, No. 111, Würzburg.

Bhattacharjee, A. and S. Holly (2010), 'Rational partisan theory, uncertainty and spatial voting: evidence for the Bank of England's MPC', Cambridge Working Paper in Economics, No. 1002, Department of Applied Economics, Faculty of Economics, University of Cambridge.

Bjornskov, C. et al. (2010), 'Inequality and happiness: when perceived social mobility and economic reality do not match', CESifo Working Paper, No. 3216, Munich.

Blanchard, O. (1998), 'Revisiting European unemployment: unemployment, capital accumulation and factor prices', NBER Working Paper, No. 6566, May, Cambridge, MA.

Blanchard, O. (2000), 'The economics of unemployment – shocks, institutions, and interactions', Lionel Robbins Lectures, London School of Economics.

Blanchard, O. and G. Illing (2003), *Microeconomics* (*Mikroökonomie*), 5th edn, München and Boston, MA: Pearson Education.

Blau, F.D. and L.M. Kahn (2013), 'Immigration and the distribution of incomes', CESifo Working Paper, No. 4561.

Blümle, G. (1972), 'The distribution of wealth, personal income distribution and economic growth' ('Vermögensverteilung, personelle Einkommensverteilung und Wirtschaftswachstum'), *Kyklos*, **25**, 457–80.

Blümle, G. (1975), *Theory of Income Distribution. An Introduction* (*Theorie der Einkommensverteilung. Eine Einführung*), Berlin, Heidelberg and New York: Springer Verlag.

Blümle, G. (1988), 'Personal income distribution and consumption demand – a microeconomic analysis' ('Personelle Einkommensverteilung und Konsumnachfrage – Eine mikroökonomische Partialbetrachtung'), in J. Klaus and P. Klemmer (eds), *Wirtschaftliche Strukturprobleme und soziale Fragen. Analyse und Gestaltungsaufgaben*, Berlin: Duncker & Humblot, pp. 145–56.

Blümle, G. (1989a), 'Income distribution theory, income distribution policy' ('Verteilungstheorie, Verteilungspolitik'), in Görres-Gesellschaft (ed.), *Staatslexikon*, 7th edn, Vol. 5, Freiburg, Berlin and Wien: Herder, pp. 719–23.

Blümle, G. (1989b), 'Economic growth and the business cycle in the presence of difference profits – a Schumpeterian model of economic development' ('Wachstum und Konjunktur bei Differenzgewinnen – Ein Schumpeter-Modell der wirtschaftlichen Entwicklung'), in H.J. Ramser and H. Riese (eds), *Contributions to Applied Economics* (*Beiträge zur angewandten Wirtschaftsforschung*), Berlin, Heidelberg and New York: Springer Verlag, pp. 13–37.

Blümle, G. (1990), 'On the "blessing" of economic inequality' ('Vom "Segen" ökonomischer Ungleichheit'), in T. Dams (ed.), *Beiträge zur Gesellschafts- und Wirtschaftspolitik. Grundlagen-Empirie-Umsetzung*, Berlin: Duncker & Humblot, pp. 139–54.

Blümle, G. (1992), 'Personal income distribution as a mode of expression for equilibrium in income distribution. A comment on the relativization of a goal for personal income distribution' ('Personelle Einkommensverteilung als Ausdruck eines Verteilungsgleichgewichts. Anmerkungen zur Relativierung des Ziels der personellen Einkommensverteilung'), in H. Mäding, F.L. Sell and W. Zohlnhöfer (eds), *Economics by Order of Political Consulting – Basic Questions and Scopes. Commemorative Publication for Theodor Dams* (*Die Wirtschaftswissenschaft im Dienste der Politikberatung – Grundsatzfragen und Anwendungsbereiche. Festschrift für Theodor Dams*), Berlin: Duncker & Humblot, pp. 209–25.

Blümle, G. (2005), 'Theory and policy of income distribution' ('Verteilungstheorie und Verteilungspolitik'), Mimeo, Freiburg i. Br.

Blümle, G. and F.L. Sell (1998), 'A positive theory of optimal personal income distribution and growth', *Atlantic Economic Journal*, **26** (4), 331–51.

Bolton, G.E. and A. Ockenfels (2000), 'ERC: a theory of equity, reciprocity, and competition', *American Economic Review*, **90** (1), 166–93.

Bolton, P. and G. Roland (1986), 'Distributional conflicts, factor mobility, and political integration', *American Economic Review*, **86** (2), 99–104.

Borjas, G.J. (2005), *Labor Economics*, Boston, MA, New York and London: McGraw-Hill Irwin.

Bosch, M. and M. Manacorda (2010), 'Minimum wages and earnings inequality in urban Mexico', CEPR Discussion Paper, No. 7882, June, London.

Boulding, K.E. (1981), 'Equity and distribution – on the interdependency of markets and transfers' ('Gerechtigkeit und Verteilung – Die Wechselwirkung von Märkten und Transfers'), in F. Klanberg and

H.-J. Krupp (eds), *Einkommensverteilung*, Königstein and Taunus: Verl.-Gruppe Athenäum-Hain-Scriptor-Hanstein, pp. 207–23.

Brachinger, H.W. (2005a), 'The Euro as Teuro? Perceived inflation in Germany' ('Der Euro als Teuro? Die wahrgenommene Inflation in Deutschland'), *Wirtschaft und Statistik*, **9**, 999–1013.

Brachinger, H.W. (2005b), 'An index of consumer prices and the phenomenon of perceived inflation' ('Verbraucherpreisindex und wahrgenommene Inflation'), *WISU*, **34** (5), 640–42.

Braeuer, W. (1981), *Ancestors of Economics. About Economics of the Ancient World and of the Middle Ages* (*Urahnen der Ökonomie. Von der Volkswirtschaftslehre des Altertums und des Mittelalters*), Ölschläger-Verlag: München.

Brakman, S., H. Garretsen, C. van Marrewijk and A. van Witteloostuijn (2006), *Nations and Firms in the Global Economy. An Introduction to International Economics and Business*, Cambridge and New York: Cambridge University Press.

Brander, J.A. and B.J. Spencer (1985), 'Export subsidies and international market share rivalry', *Journal of International Economics*, **18**, 83–100.

Brennan, M. (1962), 'A note on dividend irrelevance and the Gordon valuation model', *Journal of Finance*, **44** (1), 1115–21.

Bronfenbrenner, M. (1971), *Income Distribution Theory*, Chicago, IL and New York: Aldine.

Buch, C.M. (2013), 'Has labor income become more volatile? Evidence from international industry-level Data', *German Economic Review*, **14** (4), November, 399–431.

Bullock, J.G., A.S. Gerber and S.J. Hill (2013), 'Partisan bias in factual beliefs about politics', Mimeo, Department of Political Science, Yale University.

Burda, M.C. and B. Dluhosch (2000), 'Fragmentation, globalization and labor markets', CESifo Working Paper, No. 352, München.

Cachanosky, N. (2012), 'The Mises-Hayek business cycle theory, fiat currencies and open economies', *Review of Austrian Economics*, **25**, doi: 10.1007 and s11138-012-0188-2.

Cahuc, P. and A. Zylberberg (2004), *Labor Economics*, Cambridge, MA and London: MIT Press.

Card, D. and A.B. Krueger (1997), *Myth and Measurement: The New Economics of the Minimum Wage*, Princeton, NJ: Princeton University Press.

Chang, R. (1994), 'Income inequality and economic growth: evidence and recent theories', *Economic Review*, **79** (4), 1–10.

Chen, Y.-F. et al. (2014), 'Globalisation and the future of the welfare state', *Kiel Policy Brief*, No. 76, June, Kiel Institute of the World Economy.

Chiang, A.C. (1984), *Fundamental Methods of Mathematical Economics*, 3rd edn, Singapore: McGraw-Hill International Editions.

Chusseau, N. and M. Dumont (2013), 'Growing income inequalities in advanced countries', in J. Hellier and N. Chusseau (eds), *Growing Income Inequalities. Economic Analyses*, Houndsmill, Basingstoke: Palgrave Macmillan, pp. 13–47.

Clark, W.R. and V. Arel-Bundock (2012), 'Independent but not indifferent: partisan bias in monetary policy at the Fed', Mimeo. Also published in *Economics and Politics*, 2013, **25** (1), 1–26.

Daniel, C. and C. Sofer (1998), 'Bargaining, compensating wage differentials, and dualism of the labor market: theory and evidence for France', *Journal of Labour Economics*, **16** (3), 546–75.

Das, S.P. (1999), 'Endogenous distribution and the political economy of trade policy', Mimeo, Indian Statistical Institute, New Dehli.

Davis, D.R. (1996), 'Trade liberalization and income distribution'. NBER Working Paper, No. 5693, Cambridge, MA.

De Angelo, H. et al. (2006), 'The irrelevance of the MM dividend irrelevance theorem', *Journal of Financial Economics*, **79**, 293–315.

De Grauwe, P. (1992), *The Economics of Monetary Integration*, Oxford: Oxford University Press.

De Soto, J.H. (2009), *The Theory of Dynamic Efficiency*, London and New York: Routledge.

Deardorff, A. (1998), 'Fragmentation across cones', Research Seminar in International Economics, School of Public Policy, University of Michigan, Working Paper, No. 427.

Deardorff, A.V. (2001), 'Fragmentation in simple trade models', *North American Journal of Economics and Finance*, **12**, 121–37.

Delogu, M., F. Docquier and J. Machado (2013), 'The dynamic implications of liberalizing global migration', CESifo Working Paper, No. 4596, Munich.

Dixit, A.K. and V. Norman (1982), *The Theory of International Trade (Außenhandelstheorie)*, München: Oldenbourg.

Djajić, S. and M.S. Michael (2014), 'International migration of skilled workers with endogenous policies', CESifo Working Paper, No. 4748, Munich.

Downs, A. (1968), *An Economic Theory of Democracy (Ökonomische Theorie der Demokratie)*, Tübingen: J.C.B. Mohr.

Duesenberry, J.S. (1967), *Income, Saving and the Theory of Consumer Behavior*, 5th edn, Cambridge, MA: Harvard University Press.

Dumont, M. (2013), 'Is there a trade-off between wage inequality and unemployment?', in J. Hellier and N. Chusseau (eds), *Growing Income Inequalities. Economic Analyses*, Houndsmill, Basingstoke: Palgrave Macmillan, pp. 147–71.

Dustmann, C. and J.-S. Görlach (2014), 'Selective outmigration and the estimation of immigrants' earnings profiles', CESifo Working Paper, No. 4617, Munich.

Easterly, W., J. Williamson and A.V. Banerjee (2004), 'Channels from globalization to inequality: productivity world versus factor world (with comments and discussion', *Brookings Trade Forum*, Globalization, Poverty and Inequality, Washington, DC: Brookings Institution Press, pp. 39–81.

Egger, H. and D. Etzel (2009), 'The impact of trade on employment, welfare, and income distribution in unionized general oligopolistic equilibrium', CESifo Working Paper, No. 2895, Munich.

Egger, H. and U. Kreickemeier (2008), 'Fairness, trade and inequality', CESifo Working Paper, No. 2344, Munich.

Egger, H., P. Egger and U. Kreickemeier (2011), 'Trade, wages, and profits', University of Tübingen Working Papers in Economics and Finance, No. 23, Tübingen.

Ellis, L. and K. Smith (2007), 'The global upward trend in the profit share', BIS Working Papers, No. 231, Bank for International Settlements, Basel.

Engelkamp, P. and F.L. Sell (2013), *Introduction to Economics* (*Einführung in die Volkswirtschaftslehre*), 6th edn, Berlin, Heidelberg and New York: Springer.

Ethier, W.J. (1983), *Modern International Economics*, New York and London: W.W. Norton & Company.

Fabozzi, F.J. and F. Modigliani (2009), *Capital Markets. Institutions and Instruments*, 4th edn, Upper Saddle River, NJ: Pearson International Edition.

Facchini, G. and G. Willmann (2004), 'The political economy of international factor mobility', Mimeo, Department of Economics, University of Illinois, Illinois and Department of Economics, Universität zu Kiel, Kiel.

Faigle, P. (2011), 'A lot for a few' ('Viel für wenige'), *Die Zeit*, available at http://www.zeit.de/wirtschaft/2011-04/gerechtigkeit-reichtum (accessed 16 February 2015).

Feenstra, R.C. (1998), 'Integration of trade and disintegration of production in the global economy', *Journal of Economic Perspectives*, **12** (4), 3–50.

Fehr, E. and K.M. Schmidt (1999), 'A theory of fairness, competition, and cooperation', *Quarterly Journal of Economics*, **114** (3), 817–68.

Felbermayr, G. et al. (2012), 'International trade and collective bargaining outcomes: evidence from German employer-employee data', IAB Discussion Paper, No. 7 and 2010, Nürnberg.

Felbermayr, G. et al. (2013), 'Firm dynamics and residual inequality in open economies', CESifo Working Paper, No. 4666, Munich.

Fichtner, F. et al. (2012), 'The distribution of income: an important item for economic forecasting' ('Die Einkommensverteilung: Eine wichtige Größe für die Konjunkturprognose'), *DIW – Wochenbericht*, **79** (22), 3–10.

Fischer, R. and P. Serra (1993), 'Does income inequality reduce growth?', *Revista de Análisis Económico*, **8** (1), 99–111.

Fischer, R. and P. Serra (1996), 'Income inequality and choice of free trade in a model of intra-industry trade', *Quarterly Journal of Economics*, **111** (1), 41–64.

Forbes, K.J. (2000), 'A reassessment of the relationship between inequality and growth', *American Economic Review*, **90** (4), 869–87.

Forster, E. and H. Steinmüller (1976), 'Income distribution and the business cycle' ('Einkommensverteilung und Konjunktur'), *Jahrbücher für Nationalökonomie und Statistik*, **191** (3), 212–28.

Francois, J.F. and H. Rojas-Romagosa (2005), 'Equity welfare, and the setting of trade policy in general equilibrium', World Bank Policy Research Working Paper, No. 3731, October.

Friedman, M. (1953), 'Choice, chance and the personal distribution of income', *Journal of Political Economy*, **61** (4), 277–90.

García-Montalvo, J. (2013), 'Spanish myths' ('Spanische Mythen'), *Handelsblatt*, **28**, 1 February, p. 15.

García-Penalosa, C. and S.J. Turnovsky (2013), 'Income inequality, mobility and the accumulation of capital', CESifo Working Paper, No. 4559, Munich.

Garrison, R.W. (2001), *Time and Money. The Macroeconomics of Capital Structure*, London and New York: Routledge.

Goerke, L. and M.J. Holler (1997), *Models of the Labour Market* (Arbeitsmarktmodelle), Berlin, Heidelberg and New York: Springer.

Gordon, R.J. and I. Dew-Becker (2008), 'Controversies about the rise of American inequality: a survey', NBER Working Paper, No. 13982, Cambridge, MA.

Green, F. (2013), *Skills and Skilled Work. An Economic and Social Analysis*, Oxford: Oxford University Press.

Grossman, G.M. and E. Helpman (1992), 'Protection for sale', NBER Working Paper, No. 4149, Cambridge, MA.

Grund, C. and N. Westergaard-Nielsen (2008), 'The dispersion of employees' wage increases and firm performance', *Industrial and Labour Relations Review*, **61** (4), 485–501.

Harrod, R.F. (1938), 'Scope and method of economics', *Economic Journal*, **48**, 383–412.

Heckelman, J.C. (2006), 'Another look at the evidence for rational partisan cycles', *Public Choice*, **126**, 257–74.

Helland, L. (2011), 'Partisan conflicts and parliamentary dominance: the Norwegian political business cycle', *Public Choice*, **147** (1–2), 139–54.

Hellier, J. (2013), 'The north-south HOS model, inequality and globalization', in J. Hellier and N. Chusseau (eds), *Growing Income Inequalities. Economic Analyses*, Palgrave Macmillan, pp. 107–46.

Hellier, J. and N. Chusseau (2013), *Growing Income Inequalities. Economic Analyses*, Houndsmill, Basingstoke and New York: Palgrave Macmillan.

Helpman, E. (1995), 'Politics and trade policy', NBER Working Paper, No. 5309, Cambridge, MA.

Hibbs, D. (1977), 'Political parties and macroeconomic policy', *American Political Science Review*, **71** (1), 1467–87.

Hicks, J. (1939), 'The foundation of welfare economics', *Economic Journal*, **49**, 696–712.

Hillman, A.L. (1989), *The Political Economy of Protection*, London, Paris, New York and Melbourne: Harwood Academic Publishers.

Hirschmann, A.O. (1989), *Economic Development, the Market and Ethics – Divergent Considerations (Entwicklung, Markt, Moral – Abweichende Betrachtungen)*, Hanser: München and Wien.

Holloway, G. (2002), 'When do export subsidies have a redistributional role', *American Journal of Agricultural Economics*, **81**, 234–44.

Howells, P. and K. Bain (2007), *Financial Markets and Institutions*, Harlow and New York: FT Prentice Hall.

Howells, P. and K. Bain (2008), *The Economics of Money, Banking and Finance. A European Text*, 4th edn, Harlow and New York: FT Prentice Hall.

IMF (International Monetary Fund) (2014), 'Fiscal policy and income inequality', IMF Policy Paper, 23 January, Washington, DC.

Irmen, A. (2008), 'Cross-country income differences and technology diffusion in a competitive world', University of Heidelberg, Department of Economics, Discussion Paper Series, No. 480.

Johnson, H.G. (1951), 'A note on the effect of income redistribution on aggregate consumption with interdependent consumer preferences', *Economica*, **18**, 295–7.

Johnson, H.G. (1952a), 'The effects of income-redistribution on aggregate consumption with interdependence of consumer preferences', *Economica*, **19**, 131–47.

Johnson, H.G. (1952b), 'The matrix multiplier and an ambiguity in the Keynesian concept of saving', *Economic Journal*, **52**, 197–200.

Johnson, H.G. (1971), 'Macroeconomics of income-redistribution' ('Makroökonomie der Einkommensumverteilung'), in B. Külp and W. Schreiber (eds), *Soziale Sicherheit*, Köln and Berlin: Kiepenheuer & Witsch, pp. 161–78.

Jones, R.W. and H. Kierzkowski (1998), 'A framework for fragmentation', in S.W. Arndt and Henry Kierzkowski (eds), *Fragmentation. New Production Patterns in the World Economy*. Oxford: Oxford University Press, pp. 17–34.

Kahanec, M. and K.F. Zimmermann (2008), 'International migration, ethnicity and economic inequality', IZA Discussion Paper, No. 3450, Bonn.

Kahnemann, D. and A. Tversky (1979), 'Prospect theory. An analysis of decision under risk', *Econometrica*, **47**, 263–91.

Kaldor, N. (1939), 'Welfare propositions of economics and interpersonal comparisons of utility', *Economic Journal*, **49**, 549–52.

Kaldor, N. (1955), 'Alternative theories of distribution', *Review of Economic Studies*, **23**, 83–100.

Kermer, S. (2007), *Urbanisation, Migration and Economic Progress* (*Verstädterung, Migration und wirtschaftliche Entwicklung*), Berlin, Hamburg, London and Münster: LIT-Verlag.

Kibet, B. et al. (2010), 'The level of corporate dividend payout to stockholders: does optimal dividend policy exist for firms quoted at the Nairobi stock exchange?', *International Business & Economics Research Journal*, **9** (3), 71–84.

Kirzner, I.M. (1973), *Competition and Entrepreneurship*, Chicago, IL: University of Chicago Press.

Kohler, W. (2000), 'A specific-factors view on outsourcing', *Arbeitspapier* No. 0020, Institut für Volkswirtschaftslehre, Sozial- und Wirtschaftswissenschaftliche Fakultät, Johannes Kepler Universität Linz.

Kohler, W. and G. Felbermayr (2002a), 'Efficiency and the distributional effects of globalisation' ('Effizienz- und Verteilungswirkungen der Globalisierung'), *WISU*, **31** (5), 715–22.

Kohler, W. and G. Felbermayr (2002b), 'Efficiency and the distributional effects of globalisation (II)' ('Effizienz- und Verteilungswirkungen der Globalisierung (II)'), *WISU*, **31** (6), 843–51.

Köksal, B. and A. Caliskan (2012), 'Political business cycles and partisan politics: evidence from a developing economy', *Economics and Politics*, **24** (2), 182–99.

Krugman, P. and M. Obstfeld (2009), *International Economics. Theory and Policy*, 8th edn, Boston, MA, San Francisco, CA and New York: Pearson Addison Wesley.

Külp, B. (1974), *Theory of Income Distribution* (*Verteilungstheorie*), Stuttgart: Gustav Fischer, UTB No. 308.

Külp, B. (1975), *Welfare Economics I. The Welfare Criteria* (*Wohlfahrtsökonomik I. Die Wohlfahrtskriterien*), Tübingen: J.C.B. Mohr.

Kuznets, S. (1955), 'Economic growth and income inequality', *American Economic Review*, **45** (1), March, 1–28.

Landmann, O. and M. Pflüger (1997), 'Income distribution and foreign trade: distributional effects of globalisation' ('Verteilung und Außenwirtschaft: Verteilungswirkungen der Globalisierung'), in H. Hesse and M. Stadler (eds), *Verteilungsprobleme der Gegenwart: Diagnose und Therapie*, Tübingen: J.C.B. Mohr Siebeck, pp. 127–57.

Lane, J. (2011), 'Inequality and the labor market', in W. Salverda, B. Nolan and T.M. Smeeding (eds), *The Oxford Handbook of Economic Inequality*, Oxford: Oxford University Press, pp. 204–29.

Lange, O. (1968), *An Introduction to Econometrics* (*Einführung in die Ökonometrie*), Tübingen: J.C.B. Mohr Siebeck.

Lee, J.-E. (2006), 'Inequality and globalization in Europe', *Journal of Policy Modeling*, **28**, 791–6.

Lewitt, S.D. and S.J. Dubner (2006), *Freakonomics: Surprising Answers to Quotidian Questions of Life* (*Freakonomics: überraschende Antworten auf alltägliche Lebensfragen*, trans. Gisela Kretzschmar (from English to German), München: Riemann.

Lipton, D. (2014), 'Fiscal policy and income inequality', IMF Mimeo, presented at the Peterson Institute for International Economics, Washington, DC, 13 March.

Lydall, H. (1968), *The Structure of Earnings*, London: Oxford University Press.

Maass, H. and F.L. Sell (1998), 'Wage moderation, the exchange rate and employment – an analysis with particular emphasis on capital markets and the trade structure' ('Lohnzurückhaltung, Wechselkurs und Beschäftigung – unter besonderer Berücksichtigung des Kapitalmarkts und der Handelsstruktur'), *Zeitschrift für Wirtschaftspolitik*, **47** (1), 78–108.

Machin, S. (2011), 'Changing wage structures: trends and explanations', in D. Marsden (ed.), *Employment in the Lean Years. Policy and Prospects for the Next Decade*, Oxford: Oxford University Press, pp. 134–50.

Mandeville, B. (1980), *The Fable of the Bees*, 3rd edn, English translation of *Die Bienenfabel*, Frankfurt a.M.: Suhrkamp Verlag, Suhrkamp Taschenbuch Wissenschaft 300.

Manning, A. (2003), *Monopsony in Motion*, Princeton, NL: Princeton University Press.

Manning, A. (2011), 'Minimum wages and wage inequality', in D. Marsden (ed.), *Employment in the Lean Years. Policy and Prospects for the Next Decade*, Oxford: Oxford University Press, pp. 134–50.

Maurice, S.C. (1974), 'Monopsony and the externally imposed minimum wage', *Southern Economic Journal*, **41** (2), 283–7.

McGowan Jr, C.B. (2005), 'A simplified approach demonstrating the irrelevance of dividend policy to the value of the firm', *Applied Financial Economics Letters*, **1–2**, 121–4.

Meeusen, W. and V. Stavrevska (2013), 'Efficiency wages and inequality', in J. Hellier and N. Chusseau (eds), *Growing Income Inequalities. Economic Analyses*, Houndsmill, Basingstoke: Palgrave Macmillan, pp. 201–23.

Mélitz, M.J. (2003), 'The impact of trade on intra-industry reallocations and aggregate industry productivity', *Econometrica*, **71** (6), 1695–725.

Mishkin, F.S. and S.G. Eakins (2009), *Financial Markets and Institutions*, 5th edn, Boston, MA, San Francisco, CA and New York: Pearson International Edition.

Modigliani, F. and M.H. Miller (1958), 'The cost of capital, corporation finance, and the theory of investment', *American Economic Review*, **47** (3), 377–413.

Murphy, K.M., A. Shleifer and R. Vishny (1989), 'Income distribution, market size, and industrialization', *Quarterly Journal of Economics*, **104** (3), August, 537–643.

Muysken, J. and G. Nekkers (1999), 'Skilled-unskilled wage differentials, unemployment and hours of work: the case of America and Europe', Paper presented at the Path to Full Employment Conference, 2–3 December, CofFEE, University of Castel, Australia.

Neary, J.P. (1988), 'Export subsidies and national welfare', Working Paper No. WP88 and 9, UCD Centre for Economic Research, School of Economics, University College Dublin.

Neumark, D. and W.L. Wascher (2008), *Minimum Wages*, Cambridge, MA and London: MIT Press.

Nicholson, W. (1992), *Microeconomic Theory. Basic Principles and Extensions*, 5th edn, Fort Worth, TX and Philadelphia, PA: The Dryden Press.

Nordhaus, W.D. (1975), 'The political business cycle', *Review of Economic Studies*, **42** (2), 169–90.

OECD (2011), *Divided We Stand: Why Inequality Keeps Rising*, Paris: OECD.

Offe, C. (1991), 'The dilemma of simultaneity – democratisation and the market economy in Eastern Europe' ('Das Dilemma der Gleichzeitigkeit – Demokratisierung und Marktwirtschaft in Osteuropa'), *Merkur, Deutsche Zeitschrift für europäisches Denken*, **45** (4), 279–92.

Ostry, J.D. et al. (2014), 'Redistribution, inequality and growth', IMF Discussion Note, SDN/14/02, February, Washington, DC.

Palokangas, T. (2002), 'The political economy of collective bargaining', CESifo Working Paper, No. 719, May. Also published in *Labour Economics*, **10** (2), 2003, 253–64.

Palokangas, T. (2004), 'Union-firm bargaining, productivity improvement and endogenous growth', *Labour*, **18** (2), 191–205.

Pareto, V. (1895), 'La Courbe de la Répartition de la Richesse', *Giornale degli Economiste*, January.

Pen, J. (1973), *Income Distribution*, London: Penguin Books.

Persson, T. and G. Tabellini (1994), 'Is inequality harmful for growth? Theory and evidence', *American Economic Review*, **84** (3), 600–621.

Piketty, T. (2014), *Capital in the Twenty-first Century*, trans. Arthur Goldhammer, Cambridge, MA and London: Harvard University Press.

Pritchett, L. (2000), 'Understanding patterns of economic growth: searching for hills among plateaus, mountains, and plains', *World Bank Economic Review*, **14** (3), 221–50.

Rama, M. (1997), 'Organized labor and the political economy of product market distortions', *World Bank Economic Review*, **11** (2), 327–55.

Ramser, H.J. (1987), *Theory of Income Distribution* (*Verteilungstheorie*), Berlin, Heidelberg and New York: Springer Verlag.

Ravier, A.O. (2001), 'Rethinking capital-based macroeconomics', *Quarterly Journal of Austrian Economics*, **14** (3), 347–75.

Rayp, G. (2013), 'Growing inequalities, globalization and trade unions', in J. Hellier and N. Chusseau (eds), *Growing Income Inequalities. Economic Analyses*, Houndsmill, Basingstoke: Palgrave Macmillan, pp. 175–200.

Rios-Avila, F. and B.T. Hirsch (2012), 'Unions, wage gaps, and wage dispersion: new evidence from the Americas', IZA Discussion Paper 6757, July, Bonn.

Rodrik, D. (1999), 'Where did all the growth go? External shocks, social conflict, and growth collapses', *Journal of Economic Growth*, **4**, 385–412.

Rodrik, D. (2000), *The Boundaries of Globalisation* (*Grenzen der Globalisierung*), Frankfurt a.M. and New York: Campus.

Roine, J. and D. Waldenström (2011), 'On the role of capital gains in Swedish income inequality', Uppsala Center for Fiscal Studies, Department of Economics Working Paper 2011:4, Uppsala Universitet.

Sachs, J.D. (1989), 'Social conflict and populist policies in Latin America', NBER Working Paper, No. 2897, Cambridge, MA.

Saint-Paul, G. (1993), 'On the political economy of labor market flexibility', *NBER Macroeconomics Annual*, Chicago, IL: University of Chicago Press, Working Paper, pp. 151–87.

Salerno, J.T. (2011), 'A reformulation of Austrian business cycle theory in light of the financial crisis', *Quarterly Journal of Austrian Economics*, **15** (1), 3–44.

Schoeck, H. (1987), *Envy and the Society* (*Der Neid und die Gesellschaft*), 5th edn, Frankfurt a.M: Ullstein Verlag.

Scully, G.W. (2002), 'Economic freedom, government policy and the trade-off between equity and economic growth', *Public Choice*, **113**, 77–96.

Seidel, T. (2005), 'Welfare effects of capital mobility with rigid wages', *Applied Economics Quarterly*, **56**, 61–75.

Sell, F.L. (1982), *The Consumptive Character of Income Generation. On the Interdependence of Consumption Theory and Multiplier Theory* (*Der Konsumcharakter der Einkommensentstehung. Zur Interdependenz von Konsum- und Multiplikatortheorie*), Institut für Allgemeine Wirtschaftsforschung, Freiburg: Rudolf Haufe Verlag.

Sell, F.L. (1988), 'True exposure: the analysis of trade liberalization in a general equilibrium framework', *Review of World Economics*, **124** (4), 635–52.

Sell, F.L. (1993), *The Economics of Developing Countries* (*Ökonomik der Entwicklungsländer*), Frankfurt a.M., Berlin, Bern, New York, Paris and Wien: Lang Verlag.

Sell, F.L. (1995), 'The currency conversion controversy', *MOCT-MOST*, **5** (4), 27–53.

Sell, F.L. (1997), 'Political business cycles within a (European) Monetary Union', *International Review of Economics and Statistics*, **44** (1), 1–22.

Sell, F.L. (1999), 'Requirements for immobile factors of production on the background of globalisation' ('Anforderungen an immobile Produktionsfaktoren vor dem Hintergrund der Globalisierung'), in H. Berg (ed.), *Globalisierung der Wirtschaft: Ursachen, Formen, Konsequenzen*, Berlin: Schriften des Vereins für Socialpolitik, N.F., Band 263, pp. 69–102.

Sell, F.L. (2001a), 'What does the globalisation promise to low-income countries? A comment on the paper of Matthias Lutz' ('Was verspricht die Globalisierung für die Niedrigeinkommensländer? Korreferat zum Beitrag von Matthias Lutz'), in R. Schubert (ed.), *Entwicklungsperspektiven von Niedrigeinkommensländern – Zur Bedeutung von Wissen und Institutionen*, Berlin: Duncker & Humblot, pp. 71–86.

Sell, F.L. (2001b), 'Fragmentation – international trade under the conditions of vertical globalisation: an overview' ('Fragmentierung – Außenhandel unter den Bedingungen vertikaler Globalisierung: Ein Überblick'), *Außenwirtschaft*, **56** (4), 517–46.

Sell, F.L. (2005), 'Globalisation, labour markets and qualification' ('Globalisierung, Arbeitsmärkte und Qualifikation'), in A. Freytag (ed.), *Weltwirtschaftlicher Strukturwandel, nationale Wirtschaftspolitik und politische Rationalität. Festschrift für Jürgen B. Donges zum 65. Geburtstag*, Köln: Kölner Universitätsverlag, pp. 173–88.

Sell, F.L. (2007), *Current Problems of European Economic Policy* (*Aktuelle Probleme der Europäischen Wirtschaftspolitik*), 2nd edn, Stuttgart: Lucius & Lucius.

Sell, F.L. (2012), 'The turnaround in energy policy takes the scope' ('Die Energiewende raubt den Spielraum'), *Handelsblatt*, **53**, March, p. 8.

Sell, F.L. (2014), 'How much inequality do we need' ('Wieviel Ungleichheit ist nötig?'), *Wirtschaftswoche*, **33**, August, p. 34.

Sell, F.L. and P. Engelkamp (2013), *Introduction to Economics* (*Einführung in die Volkswirtschaftslehre*), 6th edn, Berlin, Heidelberg and New York: Springer.

Sell, F.L. and S. Kermer (2013), *Problems and Solutions in Economics. An Exercise Book* (*Aufgaben und Lösungen in der Volkswirtschaftslehre. Arbeitsbuch zu Engelkamp and Sell*), 3rd edn, Berlin, Heidelberg and New York: Springer.

Sell, F.L. and D.C. Reinisch (2013), 'How do the Eurozone's Beveridge and Phillips curves perform in the face of global economic crisis?', *International Labor Review*, **152** (2), 191–204.

Sell, F.L. and F. Stratmann (2009), 'Equity aversion, inequity aversion and economic welfare: on the macroeconomic substantiation of microeconomic utility functions', Universität der Bundeswehr München, Fachgruppe für Volkswirtschaftslehre, Discussion Paper, No. 2, Neubiberg.

Sell, F.L. and F. Stratmann (2012), 'Is there an equilibrium in Germany's income distribution? Two and a half theoretical concepts and five empirical proofs' ('Verteilungs(un)gleichgewicht in Deutschland: Zweieinhalb theoretische Konzepte und fünf empirische Belege'), Working Papers in Economics, Universität der Bundeswehr München, Economic Research Group, No. 1, Neubiberg.

Sell, F.L. and F. Stratmann (2013), 'Is there an equilibrium in Germany's income distribution? Theoretical foundation and some empirical facts' ('Verteilungsgleichgewicht in Deutschland? Theoretische Fundierung und einige empirische Fakten'), *WiSt*, **42** (2), 77–83.

Sen, A.K. (1974), 'Information bases of alternative welfare approaches: aggregation and income distribution', *Journal of Public Economics*, **3** (4), 387–403.

Sen, A. (1997), 'From income inequality to economic equality', *Southern Economic Journal*, **64** (2), 383–401.

Shelton, C.A. (2007), 'The information content of elections and varieties of the partisan political business cycle', Wesleyan Economic Working Paper 2007-003.

Shelton, C.A. (2012), 'The information content of elections and varieties of the partisan political business cycle', *Public Choice*, **150** (1/2), 209–40.

Siebert, H. (2000a), 'Economic perspectives for ageing societies. Challenges for Europe in the next forty years' ('Wirtschaftliche Perspektiven für alternde Gesellschaften. Welche Herausforderungen auf Europa in den nächsten vierzig Jahren zukommen'). *Neue Zürcher Zeitung*, No. 198, p. 103.

Siebert, H. (2000b), *International Trade (Außenwirtschaft)*, 7th edn, Stuttgart: Lucius & Lucius.

Sieg, G. (1997), 'A model of partisan central banks and opportunistic political business cycles', *European Journal of Political Economy*, **13**, 503–16.

Sinn, H.-W. (2004), 'The new systems competition', *Perspektiven der Wirtschaftspolitik*, **5** (1), 23–38.

Sinn, H.-W. (2005), 'Migration, social standards and replacement incomes. How to protect low-income workers in the industrialized countries against the forces of globalization and market integration', *International Tax and Public Finance*, **12**, 375–93.

Sinn, H.-W. (2010), *Rescuing Europe*, CESifo Forum Special Issue, August, Munich, pp. 1–22.

Sinn, H.-W. and T. Wollmershäuser (2011), 'Target loans, current account balances and capital flows: the ECB's rescue facility', NBER Working Paper, No. 17626, November, Cambridge, MA.

Standard & Poor's Capital IQ (2014), *How Increasing Income Inequality is Dampening U. S. Economic Growth, and Possible Ways to Change the Tide*, Global Credit Portal, Economic Research, pp. 1–20, available at http://www.globalcreditportal.com/ratingsdirect/renderArticle (accessed 16 February 2015).

Tinbergen, J. (1956), 'On the theory of income distribution', *Weltwirtschaftliches Archiv*, **77**, 155–75.

Tinbergen, J. (1963), *On the Theory of Economic Policy*, 2nd edn, Amsterdam: North Holland.

Tinbergen, J. (1964), *Economic Policy: Principles and Design*, Amsterdam: North Holland.

Vannoorenberghe, G. and E. Janeba (2013), 'Trade and the political economy of redistribution', CESifo Working Paper: Trade Policy, No. 4062, Munich.

Vaubel, R. (2005), 'Consequences of globalisation for social policy – theory and empirical evidence' ('Sozialpolitische Konsequenzen der Globalisierung – Theorie und Empirie'), in A. Freytag (ed.), *Weltwirtschaftlicher Strukturwandel, nationale Wirtschaftspolitik und politische Rationalität*, Köln: Kölner Universitätsverlag, pp. 143–58.

Vaubel, R. (2008), 'The political economy of labor market regulation by the European Union', *Review of International Organizations*, **3** (4), 435–65.

Von Bechtolsheim, C. (2014), 'Too narrowly considered' ('Deutlich zu kurz gegriffen'), *Handelsblatt*, **102**, p. 48.

Von Burkhausen, R. et al. (1999), 'Testing the significance of income distribution changes over the 1980s business cycle. A cross-national comparison', *Journal of Applied Econometrics*, **14** (3), 253–72.

Von Burkhausen, R. et al. (2006), 'How the distribution of after-tax income changed over the 1990s business cycle: a comparison of the United States, Great Britain, Germany and Japan', Michigan Retirement Research Center Working Paper, No. 2006-145.

Von Hayek, F.A. (1929), *Monetary and Business Cycle Theory* (*Geldtheorie und Konjunkturtheorie*), Beiträge zur Konjunkturforschung, Österreichisches Institut für Konjunkturforschung (ed.), Wien and Leipzig: Hölder-Pichler-Tempsky a.G.

Von Hayek, F.A. (1931), *Prices and Production*, London: Routledge.

Von Hayek, F.A (1977), *Three Lectures in Democracy, Equity and Socialism* (*Drei Vorlesungen über Demokratie, Gerechtigkeit und Sozialismus*), Tübingen: Mohr Siebeck.

Wang, Y.-T. (2004), 'Countervailing duties, foreign export subsidies and import tariffs', *Japanese Economic Review*, **55** (2), 153–61.

Wang, Y.-T. (2009), 'On the simultaneous elimination of export subsidies under oligopoly', *Applied Economics*, **41**, 629–31.

Weisskoff, R. (1976), 'Income distribution and export promotion in Puerto Rico', Yale University Economic Growth Center Paper, No. 245, New Haven, CT.

Wellisch, D. and U. Walz (1998), 'Why do rich countries prefer free trade over free migration? The role of the modern welfare state', *European Economic Review*, **42** (8), 1595–612.

Werner, T., F.L. Sell and D. Reinisch (2013), 'Price effects of minimum wages: evidence from the construction sector in East and West Germany', Universität der Bundeswehr München, Fachgruppe für Volkswirtschaftslehre, Discussion Paper, No. 4, Neubiberg.

Wildasin, D.E. (2006), 'Global competition for mobile resources: implications for equity, efficiency and political economy', *CESifo Economic Studies*, **52** (1), 61–110.

World Bank (1978–96), *World Development Report*, Washington, DC: World Bank.

World Bank (2013), *Jobs*, World Development Report, Washington, DC: World Bank.

World Bank (2014), *Risk and Opportunity. Managing Risk for Development*, World Development Report, Washington, DC: World Bank.

Yun, H.-M. (1992), *On the Correlation between Economic Growth and Income Distribution in the Context of Political Economy* (*Zum Zusammenhang zwischen Wirtschaftswachstum und Einkommensverteilung im Rahmen der Politischen Ökonomie*), Pfaffenweiler: Centaurus Verlag.

Index